High Technology Europe

High Technology Europe
Strategic Issues for Global Competitiveness

Philippe de Woot

Basil Blackwell

A report from the FAST Programme (Forecasting and Assessment in Science and Technology) of the Commission of the European Communities.

Copyright © ECSC – EEC – EAEC, Brussels – Luxembourg, 1990

Publication No. EUR 11691 EN of the Commission of the European Communities, Directorate-General Telecommunications, Information Industries and Innovation, Scientific and Technical Communication Unit, Luxembourg

First published 1990

Basil Blackwell Ltd
108 Cowley Road, Oxford OX4 1JF, UK

Basil Blackwell, Inc.
3 Cambridge Center
Cambridge, Massachusetts 02142, USA

All rights reserved. Except for the quotation of short passages for the purposes of criticism and review, no part of this publication may be reproduced, stored in a retrieval system, or transmitted, in any form or by any means, electronic, mechanical, photocopying, recording or otherwise, without the prior permission of the publisher.

Except in the United States of America, this book is sold subject to the condition that it shall not, by way of trade or otherwise, be lent, re-sold, hired out, or otherwise circulated without the publisher's prior consent in any form of binding or cover other than that in which it is published and without a similar condition including this condition being imposed on the subsequent purchaser.

Neither the Commission of the European Communities nor any person acting on behalf of the Commission is responsible for the use which might be made of the following information.

British Library Cataloguing in Publication Data

A CIP catalogue record for this book is available
from the British Library.

Library of Congress Cataloging in Publication Data

High technology Europe: strategic issues for global competitiveness
  [edited by] Philippe de Woot.
    p.   cm.
  Bibliography: p.
  Includes index.
  1. High technology industries—Europe. 2. Competition,
International. I. Woot, Philippe de.
HC240.9.H53H54 1989
338.4′762′00094–dc20   89–14851 CIP

ISBN 0–631–17104–5

Typeset by Footnote Graphics, Warminster, Wilts
Printed in Great Britain by
Billing and Son Ltd, Worcester

Contents

Preamble		ix
List of Participants in the Penelope Project		x
Acknowledgements		xii
Introduction and Executive Summary		1
Notes		7
1	**Competition and Strategic Capability: Some Basic Concepts**	**8**
1.1	Industrial competitiveness	8
1.2	New forms of competition	9
	1.2.1 Competition by innovation and technical progress	9
	1.2.2 Global competition	11
1.3	Competitive advantages	13
1.4	Strategic capability	15
	1.4.1 A sound base or the importance of 'turnaround'	15
	1.4.2 Development and management of key resources	16
	1.4.3 Quality of strategic choice	17
	1.4.4 Capacity for innovation and change	17
1.5	The value chain and industrial cooperation	18
1.6	Importance of the environment	19
1.7	Corporate and societal responsibilities	20
1.8	Competition: a destructive or creative process?	22
	1.8.1	22
	1.8.2	24
Notes		**26**

2 Some Thoughts on the Competitiveness of European Enterprises — 28
- 2.1 Unequal competitiveness — 28
  - 2.1.1 World leaderships — 28
  - 2.1.2 Disturbing lags — 32
- 2.2 A process destroying or enhancing competitiveness? — 35
  - 2.2.1 The American model — 35
  - 2.2.2 The Japanese model — 39
  - 2.2.3 The European model — 47
- 2.3 Example of the electronics industry — 53
  - 2.3.1 Europe lags overall but has some successes — 54
  - 2.3.2 Computers — 57
  - 2.3.3 Components — 60
  - 2.3.4 Telecommunications — 64

Notes — 77

3 International Cooperation — 80
- 3.1 Direct investment abroad — 80
- 3.2 Cooperation as a competitive strategy — 88
  - 3.2.1 Different forms — 88
  - 3.2.2 An external strategic weapon which can lead to dominance — 90
- 3.3 Management of cooperation — 95
  - 3.3.1 Day-to-day management — 96
  - 3.3.2 Strategic management — 98
- 3.4 Cooperation and competitive models — 99
  - 3.4.1 The Japanese model — 100
  - 3.4.2 The American model — 102
  - 3.4.3 The European model — 103
- 3.5 The case of the aviation industry — 106
  - 3.5.1 Vital need for cooperation — 107
  - 3.5.2 Airbus: an example of successful cooperation — 110
  - 3.5.3 The importance of management models: the case of military aircraft — 115
- 3.6 Brief description of other cases — 118
  - 3.6.1 Importance of strategic cooperation management: the case of the computer — 118

3.7	SME cooperation	121
3.8	The case of engineering	122
Notes		**124**

4 Research and Innovation — 127
4.1 Much European R&D but little exploitation — 128
4.2 The reason lies more with the corporate strategy than the R&D — 131
    4.2.1 — 131
    4.2.2 — 133
4.3 External incentives to competitive innovation — 135
    4.3.1 The market or demand — 135
    4.3.2 Technological opportunities or supply — 138
    4.3.3 The industrial structure — 140
4.4 R&D cooperation — 143
    4.4.1 Motivation for R&D cooperation — 144
    4.4.2 Forms of R&D cooperation — 148
    4.4.3 Radial cooperation — 151
    4.4.4 Unequal cooperation — 152
4.5 Management of R&D and innovation — 153
    4.5.1 Exploiting the technological environment — 153
    4.5.2 Close relation between R&D and marketing — 155
    4.5.3 Management of research staff — 155
    4.5.4 R&D decentralisation and integration — 157
    4.5.5 Innovation as an entrepreneurial process — 158
    4.5.6 Management of technological resources — 158
    4.5.7 Role of top management — 160
Notes — **160**

Final Comments — **163**
Sense of urgency — 163
Priority mechanisms of a global approach — 164
Concluding thoughts — 169
Notes — **170**

Appendices — **171**
Notes — **218**
References — **219**
Index — **226**

Preamble

This initial report represents a beginning rather than an end. Circumstances demanded speedy preparation on the basis of existing knowledge and research. However, although it is not the outcome of a long-term project, the report could well prove the catalyst for a project of that kind.

Following an initiative by FAST[1] and the Catholic University of Louvain, it was felt that it would be useful to carry out a more detailed study of the competitive strategies employed by undertakings in the high-technology sectors, in order to clarify European policy in the field of science and technology. Thus was born the **PENELOPE** Project.

We selected a network of business schools which agreed to cooperate with this in view; the participants are listed on the next page. The topics were defined at two meetings in Brussels and because of the time-scale it was decided to use only existing material. Again because of time constraints, the contributions were somewhat fragmentary and some arrived late. None the less there was sufficient convergence of ideas to justify the author's venturing to advance certain views which may not only be useful to FAST but could also serve as a framework for a large-scale European research project.

---

[1] FAST: Forecasting and Assessing Science and Technology.

Participants in the Penelope Project

Promoter

- Prof. Philippe de Woot and Eduardo Arenas
  University of Louvain
  IAG (Institute of Administration and Management)

Members

- Prof. Maurice Saias
  University of Aix-Marseilles
  Institute of Business Administration

- Profs Gianfranco Piantoni and Alessandro Sinatra
  Bocconi University
  School of Business Management

- Prof. Gianni Lorenzoni
  Bologna University

- Prof. Horst Albach
  Bonn University

- Prof. Pierre Goetschin
  IMEDE: Lausanne

- Prof. Yves Doz
  INSEAD: Fontainebleau

Participants in the Penelope Project

- Prof. John Stopford
  London Business School

- Profs Miguel Gallo and J. Carlos Jarillo
  University of Navarre
  IESE (Institute of Advanced Business Studies)

- Prof. Gunnar Hedlund
  Stockholm School of Economics

Europe is made up of countries which are 'too small for what is great in their make-up and too great for what is small'.

(Raymond Aron)

Acknowledgements

The author and publisher wish to thank the following who have kindly given permission for the use of copyright material: Airbus Industrie (figs 3.4 and 3.5); Centre D'Études Prospectives et D'Informations Internationales with Organisation for Economic Co-operation and Development, Paris, from *Issues in Science and Technology*, 1986 (fig. 2.1); Y. Doz, et al. 'Strategic Partnership: Success or Surrender?' Working Paper, Insead, 1986 (fig. 3.3); Economica for fig. A7.1 from P. de Woot and X. Desclee, 'Le management stratégique des groupes industriels', *Economica*, Paris, 1984; and for figs A1.1, A1.2 and A1.3 from Institut Français de Relations Internationales, Rapport Ramsès 86–7, Compétitions et affrontements, *Economica*, Paris, 1986; *The Economist* for figs 2.6, A9.1, A12.1 and A15.1 from the following issues of *The Economist*: 23rd Nov. 1985, 4th Feb. 1989, 26th April 1986 and 23rd Nov. 1985; European Round Table of Industrialists, 'Clearing the Lines', Nov. 1986 (fig. A18.1); *Financial Times*, 31st Dec. 1986 (table A19.1); Macmillan Publishing Company for fig. A8.1 from Kenichi Ohmae, *Triad Power: The Coming Shape of Global Competition*, The Free Press, Exhibit 11-1. Copyright © 1985 by Kenichi Ohmae and McKinsey & Company, Inc.; and for fig. A5.1 adapted from Michael E. Porter, *Competitive Strategy: Techniques for Analysing Industries and Competitors*, The Free Press, fig. 2–1. Copyright © 1980 by The Free Press; *Le Nouvel Economiste*, No. 555, 29th Aug. 1986 (tables 3.8 and A4.1); Organisation for Economic Co-operation and Development for fig. A1.0, tables 2.5, A1.1 and A1.2 from *Issues in Science and Technology*, 1986; SRI International for figs A9.2, A9.3, A9.4 and A23.1 from M. Gorbis and K. Yorke, 'Strategic Partnerships: A New Corporate Response', Report No. 730, SRI Business Intelligence Program (1985–6); Time Inc. Magazines for table A3.1 for material from *Fortune*, Aug. 1986. Copyright © 1986 by Time Inc.

Introduction and Executive Summary

To a large extent the European future of the EEC countries depends on the long-term strategies of their enterprises.

Since several FAST research projects have highlighted the decisive role of multi-national companies, an analysis of the conditions of their strategic performance seems essential. Only by better understanding the mechanisms of competitive strategy can we demonstrate the relevance of a European policy for science and technology.

Despite the important role of European multi-nationals, the contribution of innovative SMEs (Small- and Medium-size Enterprises) to economic progress must not be overlooked. Clearly a whole industrial and technological fabric is involved and whatever the emphasis on large enterprises, individual entrepreneurs have their own importance.

Consequently, this report is deliberately written from the viewpoint of the enterprise and its ability to win in the face of competition; it looks at the conditions of strategic success in a world in which competition is becoming global. Particular attention has been paid to the questions of industrial cooperation and innovation.

The report is only a pilot study and is not based on exhaustive research into the enterprises or sectors mentioned. It takes certain global or sectorial facts and attempts to apply to them the concepts and analytical methods of disciplines having a bearing on the strategic management of enterprises.

Whilst the use of conceptual models can lead to what may sometimes be regarded as an over-simplified or unduly systematic

2 Introduction and Executive Summary

view of the facts, its value lies in its presentation of some of the processes and base constraints which our enterprises must adopt as an essential part of their strategy or pay the price, even though many enterprises manage to circumvent them.

The main theses of the book are the following:

- Competition in high-tech sectors is marked by two main characteristics:

  - The struggle is on a world scale and demands a strategic planning capability on an international scale.
  The areas of technology become more and more interdependent and cross-fertilisation creates new generations of technology which are broader and more complex.

- Efficient enterprises in these sectors have created competitive advantages for themselves at international level by developing a strategic capability of a quality and dimensions equal to the task. The components of such a capability are:

  - A strong and sound financial basis which can mobilise the resources needed to take the risks inherent in progress at world level.
  - Key strategic resources: management skills, marketing networks, R&D and technological dominance, relations, alliances, etc.
  - Organisational skill: a balanced value chain, mastery of complexities, potential for change and innovation, staff motivation, etc.
  - Methods of control and anticipation: MIS (Management Information Systems) – internal and external: analytical and decision-making tools for future choices, dynamic management of products portfolio, markets and alliances in the face of competitors' strategies.

  Whether enterprises will maintain their dominant position in the major future generations of technology depends on the strength of their strategic capability.

- European enterprises have scored some successes in high-tech sectors but are losing ground overall to their American and Japanese competitors. The lag may be explained as follows: European enterprises are tied to a model of development which destroys competitiveness whereas their competitors benefit from a model which creates competitiveness. Lack of a homogeneous home market and the absence of large-scale joint projects hold our enterprises back from developing a strategic capability as powerful as that of their world competitors. They thus risk being trapped in a vicious circle:

- Few large-scale opportunities and overly narrow horizon at home.
- Inadequate strategic capability.
- Disadvantages in international competition.
- Low profitability.
- Inability to lift themselves to the level of their world competitors.

This is not the whole story, since European success stories exist. The model seems to hold good, however, for a number of advanced-technology sectors and major future developments.

There are many reasons why our enterprises use this model which destroys competitiveness: compartmentalised markets, dearth of major European projects, nationalistic industrial policies, etc. Viewed from the angle of business competitiveness, the 'national champion' policy has been a disaster.

- The globalisation of competition and the advance of technology are going ahead far faster than the construction of Europe. Our external competitors are not waiting for the unification of Europe before they launch their attack on our enterprises and markets. Thanks to a strategic capability which is already on a world scale they often outclass our scattered 'national' enterprises, forcing them to react by becoming international in turn. Generally speaking, however, Europe does not provide a sufficiently large base for them to do so in the high-tech sectors and instead of setting up solid European bases our enterprises are tending to internationalise outside Europe, particularly in the USA. This is the case with capital investment and company takeovers, with alliances and cooperative ventures.

- Our enterprises pay the price for this situation: they are forced to become international, global, with no comparable domestic base to that enjoyed by American or Japanese enterprises. Lacking a very large continental market in which to develop a proper strategic capability, they are in danger of facing world competition as second raters with inadequate capability. A number of consequences may follow:
  - Independent international development (no alliances or cooperative ventures) may be more difficult, even impossible. Our enterprises would then be forced to turn to the 'second choice' – development by alliances, or joint or cooperative ventures.
  - Risk of cooperation with far more powerful foreign partners who would then retain the initiative in any progress, our enterprises being retained on a dependent or subcontracting basis.
  - Our enterprises may be forced to occupy a purely peripheral position in major alliances set up with an eye to new generations of technology.

- International cooperation is rapidly becoming a feature of every sector where the cost and complexity of technical progress exceed the capacity of the individual enterprise. This is happening even with the largest firms such as IBM, Boeing, Philips, Matsushita, Siemens, ATT, etc. Cooperation in Europe has yielded spectacular successes like the Airbus and Ariane. Given this kind of project, enterprises react fast attaining a degree of cooperation which renders them competitive on the world scale. However, a number of points have to be made in this respect:
  - Whilst cooperation can serve as an effective strategic tool towards competitiveness, it is also a means whereby one partner might acquire dominance over another. A balance of strength plus sensitive management are thus essential features of an alliance.
  - Various cooperative models exist, particularly in the field of large publicly financed projects. Those which place political

logic (the protection of national interests) before economic sense (efficiency relative to the competition) yield mediocre results in terms of competitiveness and it is therefore important to select the most effective cooperative models for major European projects and not to penalise our enterprises with excessive nationalistic constraints.

- It is important for our enterprises to hold key positions in major future developments. If American or Japanese firms are in the driving seat there is a danger that our enterprises will occupy purely marginal or peripheral positions. Thus if Europe wants to retain mastery of such developments it must launch joint projects in which our enterprises can play a central role, notably in the forefront of progress.
- As has been well illustrated by the Airbus, a strong European base born of cooperation permits a far more effective global strategy: having established a minimum base in Europe, the aircraft is winning more and more orders in the USA and elsewhere with an effect on MacDonnell-Douglas throughout the world.

● Europe has strong R&D potential but makes poor use of it. This is not primarily because our enterprises are scientifically or technically inferior but because their strategic capability falls short. Lacking sufficiently ambitious or forward-looking strategies they fail to turn their R&D and innovations to competitive international advantage.

Increased European demand for technology (market pull) will encourage firms to raise their strategic sights and will at the same time promote a more European technological supply (technology push) not merely in the field of fundamental and applied research but also with regard to training and cooperation between industry and universities and between one enterprise and another.

More is required if R&D and innovation are to be turned to international competitive advantage: what is needed is a more vigorous development of the European industrial framework and promotion of the processes of 'creative destruction'.[1] This demands increased competition at European level plus gradual elimination of the 'national champion' mentality. If 'creation' is to outweigh 'destruction' decisively, cooperative strategies must be developed in a framework of major European projects.

The success of European technological cooperation projects such as Esprit or Eureka shows that enterprises are willing to cooperate and respond readily to incentives.

However, certain important facts should be borne in mind:

- Technological cooperation is only part of a greater whole; whilst it can contribute to creating a common market or major collective projects, it cannot replace them.
- Most existing technological cooperation involves non-European partners; the most worthwhile technological cooperation projects for future developments are of the 'radial' type because the parties can derive benefit from the combined nature of the new techniques; this is particularly true of information technology, biotechnology and bionics.
- Quality of R&D/innovation management is of decisive importance to cooperation; second-rate management can jeopardise the effectiveness of an alliance or the requisite balance of strength. The key factors of good management here, which are becoming well understood, relate particularly to management style; structural flexibility and speed of reaction; openness on the environment; the ability of an enterprise to combine its marketing, production and R&D skills.

• From the strategy angle two factors must be emphasised, namely the urgent need for change and the need for a global approach. International competition is developing faster than European integration and our enterprises are paying the price. Promotional measures exist which could improve the situation:

- Large-scale European projects
- More and greater cooperation
- The opening of public procurements
- Unified standards
- Improved supply of technology
- Development of the social and strategic capability of enterprises

A global approach requires action on all these fronts simultaneously to achieve convergent and cumulative results. Only such a policy can help our enterprises to achieve the size, complexity and longevity which mark the only way to international competitiveness.

NOTES

1 Schumpeter (1949).

1

Competition and Strategic Capability: Some Basic Concepts

This chapter sets out some of the basic concepts used in the project and tries to illustrate them with concrete examples of the competitive situations facing European multi-nationals. The conceptual part of the chapter rests on the state-of-the-art understanding of strategy as found in the business schools listed in the introduction.

1.1 INDUSTRIAL COMPETITIVENESS

Competitiveness is:

- the capacity of a firm
- under free and fair market conditions
- to produce goods and services that meet the test of international markets
- while, at the same time, maintaining or expanding its real income.[1]

Starting from this definition, the firm's strategic objectives can be defined as follows:

- Achieving efficiency in current operations: profitability of capital employed.
- Managing risk: optimising the risk-return position of the firm.

- Innovating, learning, adapting: developing the adequate resources and structures to remain competitive in the long run.[2]

If, for internal or external reasons, an enterprise cannot attain these objectives, it will go into a decline which will jeopardise its survival.

1.2 NEW FORMS OF COMPETITION

1.2.1 Competition by innovation and technical progress

- This is no new thing but the explosive progress of science and technology renders it more important than hitherto. Schumpeter's concept of creative destruction applies increasingly and to more and more sectors:

> The competition which really counts is competition of new goods, new methods, new supply sources, new types of organisation (e.g. control of larger units), in other words, competition which commands a decisive cost or quality advantage and which affects not existing firms' profit margins and size of output but their very foundations and existence. Just as bombardment is far more effective than battering down a gate, so this form of competition is much more effective than the other. So much greater is its significance that the speed at which competition in the normal sense operates becomes relatively unimportant because the powerful mechanism for raising production and cutting prices long-term is quite different.[3]

The effect of creative destruction on competitiveness is well understood. What is new is its acceleration and sectorial and geographical generalisation. From this it follows that an enterprise in control of technical progress holds a decisive competitive weapon. The range and number of inventions, total expenditure on R&D and the increasing interdependence between disciplines and technologies all make this type of competition by innovation

10 Competition and Strategic Capability

increasingly important. Numerous studies of the R&D effort make it clear that technology is an offensive weapon which enterprises must be able to use if they are to conquer new markets (see appendix 1).

- R&D creates new sectors, the so-called high-tech industries. These are the industries of the future which constitute highways to economic expansion and their growing markets are the stake for which the world is engaged in competitive strife.

  Of course, the definition of high-tech sectors depends on the criteria chosen. Three types are generally applied:
  - Employment of scientific and technical staff
  - Expenditure on R&D
  - The nature of the sector's products

  The breadth of the definition depends on which criterion is taken, the most rigorous being ratio of R&D spending to sales. If we adopt a minimum of twice the ratio applying in industry in general we find six high-tech sectors:
  - Pharmaceuticals
  - Office and EDP (Electronic Data Processing) equipment
  - Telecommunications
  - Electronics
  - Aircraft and aircraft parts
  - Rockets and spacecraft

- Behind the high-tech sectors loom the great technologies of the future or 'metatechnologies' as they are sometimes called, to denote the vast range of sectors and products which they command. Applications are countless and not entirely foreseeable; many interact with each other and inter-connections are multiplying. An important feature is the frequency with which they give rise to new technological 'families' or 'clusters' of products.

  We see their importance to the great international competitive battles and the size of the stakes for which Europe and European enterprises are contending. Here again classifications vary but there are generally agreed to be four major areas:

Competition and Strategic Capability

- Information technology
- Biotechnology
- Optical electronics
- Advanced materials

Technical progress has also reached most existing industrial and service sectors. CAM–CAD (Computer Assisted Manufacturing–Computer Assisted Design) processes, for example, have made major gains in the productivity and creativity of traditional industries and are thus giving new impetus to the conquest of cost or differentiation advantages which are the key to competitive leadership. In the service industries, advances in computers and telecommunications have literally changed the ground rules of competition and this is true of banking, insurance, transport, information and so on. Technical progress is thus throwing out a challenge to more and more enterprises irrespective of size and sector.[4]

Finally, technical progress is striding across the boundaries of economic activity and upsetting the established balance of sectors. Computer technology provides a very significant example: there is a two-way relationship between computer technology and office/EDP equipment and both have their effect on telecommunications. All three areas of activity employ robotics and none of them can do without components or software. The result is the emergence of genuine new industrial families and new clusters of inter-dependent activities which are sending the notions of sectors or of enterprise product-market strategies back to the drawingboard. We shall see the same thing in the near future with 'bionics', involving control over biotechnology, computers and advanced materials (see appendices 3 and 4).

1.2.2 Global competition

Today there is world competition in a whole range of activities: high-tech equipment (aviation, telecommunications, computers, etc.), a number of worldwide durable and non-durable consumer goods (hi-fi, video, soft drinks, jeans, hamburgers, etc.) and a number of important services (banking, insurance, tourism, consultancy, data banks, executive search, etc.)[5]

The Triad is now a well known phenomenon.[6] For many enterprises the geographical market of reference is no longer a country or a continent but all the major industrialised countries, particularly Europe, North America and Japan; this more or less homogeneous grouping of 700 million consumers is their natural market. All future competitive capability will have to be at this level for it is no longer enough to be effective at home; unless an enterprise is also highly competitive outside its own country and holds a satisfactory share of the Triad market it can be beaten on its own ground by Japanese or American competitors with the comparative advantages of world leaders. Some reasons for this globalisation are:

- The spread of technical progress is now so fast that any innovation must be introduced on all three Triad markets *simultaneously*; a delay in any one of them exposes the enterprise to defeat by a competitor able to launch a similar development and take over the market before the enterprise has time to react.
- The 700 million consumers are shaping into a more homogeneous market as the gap in incomes, consumer structures and education narrows.[7]
- The development cost of some capital items is so high that it can be amortised only on a world basis ($3 billion for a new commercial aircraft, $1 billion for a new central telephone exchange).
- The industrial fabric is also becoming more homogeneous as the Triad accounts for 70–80% of consumption and output of many goods and services. In fact, the declining share of wages and salaries in costs makes it less worthwhile moving activities to low-wage countries; furthermore, the Triad countries offer immense benefits in terms of outlets, subcontracting, finance, R&D, etc.; and many (particularly Japanese) enterprises are being led by fluctuating exchange rates to invest abroad and they turn to the most advanced countries.
- Deregulation also helps to exacerbate international competi-

tion; the fact that it started in a country as powerful and advanced as the USA heightens its aura of commercial aggressiveness which is already being felt by markets affected.

Appendix 4 shows the Triad concentration and the investment flows which strengthen the trend. It is worth noting in passing that only Japanese enterprises are already truly 'triadic', the USA and Europe still being largely 'Atlantic'. The head start taken by some enterprises in world-scale development can make them dominant in their particular sector and whilst such dominance is never absolute or totally secure, it confers very powerful competitive advantages and contributes to creating unequal situations. Certain companies, e.g. IBM and Boeing, are already to some extent in this position (see appendices 3 and 4). The main objective of globalisation is world leadership and the resulting competitive advantages. This affects first and foremost certain European enterprises threatened by large American and Japanese competitors and is discussed in chapter 2.

Two important tools are emerging to deal with the globalisation of competition: first, mastery of technical progress and innovation and second, international cooperation. Later stages of the chapter cover these two themes in greater detail.

1.3 COMPETITIVE ADVANTAGES

In the face of increasingly powerful new technologies and, even more, the ramification of interconnections between them, winning comparative advantages depends more and more on mastering the mechanisms of technical progress and innovation and being able to transform them into a significant share of world markets.

In the face of growing globalisation, enterprises have to provide themselves with specific international advantages such as size, inter-country cooperation, build-up of world-scale resources, etc.

These two major developments have forced investigators to re-examine the theory of comparative advantage and produce a

14   Competition and Strategic Capability

theory which better integrates multi-national strategies. Two important conceptual stages have been provided by Porter[8] and, more recently, Goshal[9] and it is their concepts which we shall be using in the book.

- Porter showed two main types of competitive advantage which ensure company efficiency:
    - *Cost advantage*: which can be achieved by experience or volume (scale, learning, innovation); it can be achieved by modernising production methods (e.g. automation, robotisation, CAM, CAD, etc.); ultimately productivity also depends on worker (and thus management) behaviour.
    - *Differentiation advantage*: which consists in offering the customer a product which differs from the competitor's and is better suited to the customer's needs, even though it may be more expensive; it may derive from product functions, usage, applications, distribution methods, image, after-sales service, etc.

- An enterprise which develops one of these advantages is in a position to apply strategies of volume, specialisation or niche (see appendix 7).

  A whole series of intermediate strategies is made possible by combining the basic advantages and, as recent empirical surveys have shown, enterprises do in fact tend to combine them.[10]

- Goshal[11] shows that the globalisation of competition leads a highly efficient enterprise to develop advantages specifically directed towards international competition. From this he suggests that MNCs go well beyond Porter's generic strategies and seek to create new competitive weapons. This means principally:
    - Taking advantage of presence in a number of countries and exploiting the comparative advantages they offer.
    - Achieving a size which can take advantage of world economies of scale.
    - Developing a combination of both activities and resources within the enterprise to achieve economies of scope which optimise strategic investment in, say, R&D, marketing, organisation, management, etc.

As Goshal sees it, such competitive advantages are essential if an enterprise is to attain the major strategic objectives described at the beginning of this section.

1.4 STRATEGIC CAPABILITY

Investigations carried out at Louvain[12] show that the systematic creation of strategic capability is essential to winning, maintaining and renewing the comparative advantages discussed above. Such capability rests on a number of factors which have been identified and measured and which principally comprise the following (shown diagrammatically in appendices 6 and 7):

- Clear general guidelines
- Systemised strategic choices
- Strategically oriented R&D
- Flexible, innovative structures
- Quality of management

Strategic capability also rests on far more imponderable, qualitative factors such as management/executive behaviour, staff motivation, the employer's authority, his risk propensity, the confidence he inspires in his colleagues, etc. We call this the 'black box' and place it at the heart of the diagram to show clearly that the long-term success factors do not explain everything.[13]

The principal factors of strategic capability which will be used in this book are:

1.4.1 A sound base or the importance of 'turnaround'

It is a prerequisite of competitiveness that the hard core of the enterprise must prosper and be profitable, the more so if an international strategy is to be pursued. Whilst this may sound trite, many a European enterprise, slow to appreciate this basic fact, has been taken by surprise by a slump; attempts to escape by advancing into diversification have often proved disastrous.[14]

The first step in any strategy is thus to ensure that the enterprise's principal activity is efficient, even when it relates to a traditional sector.

Recent studies on turnaround management[15] show that turnaround can be achieved more often than was thought. The studies point to the ability of older firms to regain a solid international competitive footing and even lost leadership in some cases. The essential elements are vigorous management, reduced indebtedness, cost/quality control (often by 'production technology'), improved marketing, staff motivation – in other words, the standard characteristics of an efficient company. They may have disappeared for various reasons (poor management, a very severe slump, over-rigid environment, protection, etc.) but in many cases the enterprise again becomes competitive as soon as they are restored and the industrial structure is thereby strengthened.

1.4.2 Development and management of key resources

The long-term efficient performance of an enterprise is heavily dependent on the resources for progress which it has been able to develop and which it manages efficiently: technology know-how, go-ahead professional executives and managers, motivated specialist staff, marketing networks, financial and political relations, etc. These resources are not conjured up on the spur of the moment but are the outcome of a long-term development which demands a systematic strategy and investment to create a genuine ability to enter into the competitive world. The presence or absence of this ability is a significant divide between the efficient and inefficient enterprise.

The existence of such resources is not enough by itself. Also essential is the ability to mobilise them fast in order to grasp unexpected opportunities or shed a risk which has not paid off. Viewed from this angle, key resource management becomes a decisive competitive tool and highlights the importance of R&D/innovation management (and of R&D and innovation in themselves) and the management of technical, commercial and financial relations.

1.4.3 Quality of strategic choice

Research shows that the attitude of high-performance enterprises towards important product or market choices is more systematic, more professional. Whilst the strategy content certainly varies with sector and circumstance, the way in which it is formulated seems to be a fundamental element of performance: monitoring the environment and the pattern of demand, staying 'technologically alert', knowing the market and the competition, balancing the product portfolio, etc. all derive from better organised and more rigorous methods. The strategic tools proper are used for major decision-making, notably to do with the segmentation of activities, definition of the geographical market of reference, analysis of product and customer portfolios, investigation of market attractiveness, degree of competition, etc. All this depends on the quality of enterprise management. Also clearly important are the information networks which the enterprise can tap when it wishes to analyse the evolution of its markets, technologies and competitors.

This leads us to two topics given prominence in this report:

- The advantage of an international (global) position for access to relevant information networks.
- The competitive value to an economy, a country or a group of enterprises of data banks which are not accessible to everyone.

1.4.4 Capacity for innovation and change

In a world of rapid technological progress and aggressive competition, the enterprise's creativity and speed of reaction are important elements in its strategic capability.

Many recent studies emphasise the need for flexible structures.[16] To remain competitive or to conquer new fields, reaction speed is decisive and this requires structures which are more decentralised, head offices which are less top-heavy, divisions which are smaller and, above all, staff with sufficient team spirit to accept and take part actively in change.[17]

For the large entity the most important thing is to master

18 Competition and Strategic Capability

complexity by creating subsystems and making them more open to their specific environments; this means a great capacity for internal integration and coordination[18] which cannot be improvised but is built up systematically. Competitive advantages (economies of scope) based on coordination depend on a capacity which takes time to develop. The price paid by enterprises for not developing this capacity is very high – often decline, even extinction – as has been clearly shown for England in a particularly relevant work.[19]

In the area of creativity and innovation, it is very difficult for large enterprises to keep up with the speed of technological progress. The best of them develop far more new ideas than they can cope with and many lose their more go-ahead executives who leave to set up their own businesses. A whole series of new practices and structures is being developed to deal with these challenges: 'intrapreneurship', the 'champion', 'progress groups', creating a closer R&D/Marketing relationship etc.[20] Innovation management is becoming a major competitive tool and is discussed in section 4.

1.5 THE VALUE CHAIN AND INDUSTRIAL COOPERATION

An enterprise is not always capable of developing its competitive capability and hence its competitive advantages on a world scale. This applies to many European firms, sometimes for reasons of size or because the enterprise has neglected the development of strategic capability or because of the accelerating rate of technical progress. We return to this in chapter 2.

Recent research[21] has produced the concept of the value chain, that is, the chain of functions running from R&D through design, production and distribution to after-sales service (see appendix 8).

Each function is seen as an 'enterprise subsystem'. More and more businesses have stopped feeling that they must carry out each and every function by themselves and are turning to subcontracting or collaboration. In this way they acquire competitive advantages faster and on a larger scale than they would by going it alone. This new type of behaviour aimed at expanding the global strategic capability is already evident in R&D and in every sector representing a new technological generation (see earlier; the phenomenon is shown in appendix 9 for telecommunications, computers, etc.). Cooperation is on the increase in biology; for example, between 1980 and 1983 Japanese enterprises signed 188 collaboration agreements with American SMEs specialising in genetic engineering. The importance of this type of strategy to European competitiveness is obvious and renders management of a set of alliances a key element of global performance. For this reason one section of the book is devoted entirely to industrial cooperation.

1.6 IMPORTANCE OF THE ENVIRONMENT

In a world of global technological competition national environments have a profound effect on enterprise strategy.[22]

- First, the size of the environment varies very appreciably and the size of the home market influences enterprise strategy, particularly when it comes to public procurements. The same applies to opening the European market and the tariff or other barriers which enterprises encounter.
- Second, some environments are more sophisticated than others. This applies in particular to individual incomes and consumption levels, the diffusion of innovation, the early or late success of new products or methods and the type of public procurements on which an enterprise can reckon. It also applies to education levels and the existence of specialist skills in new fields.[23]
- Third, government policy or society's requirements may be less or more interventionist. Strategic decisions are influenced by the margin for corporate or individual manoeuvre, particularly with regard to net cash flow, for example. The requirements of society as regards pollution, jobs, social welfare can vary from one country to another and also influence strategies. Two ready yardsticks for this type of influence are the overall level of taxation and the share of

20 Competition and Strategic Capability

national income represented by public expenditure. In the creative destruction process, public resources may be allocated preferentially to protecting traditional sectors or to creating new sectors; the 'pro-active' policies are primarily concerned with:

- Technology
- Financial resources
- Human resources
- International trade and opening up markets

These are enormous fields which are well understood. They are mentioned here simply to highlight three points of importance to this report:

1. They can result in significant differences in national environments and thus play a major part in the orientation of corporate strategy.
2. They constitute the interface between corporate decisions and public policy. This applies particularly to industrial and science policy.
3. For most enterprises they are an external datum; the enterprise has little control over their content or scope and has to fit in with them as best it can. Recent research shows that high-performance enterprises adopt genuine societal strategies to get the most out of their socio-political environment.[24]

1.7 CORPORATE AND SOCIETAL RESPONSIBILITIES

An enterprise's competitiveness greatly depends on its capability in the social and political field.[25]

At social level, numerous studies have shown that staff motivation is becoming a condition of long-term effectiveness. Whether productivity, product quality, creativity or capacity for change is the issue, enterprises depend increasingly on staff commitment to strategic plans.[26] There is a new mentality; nowadays company personnel want jobs which are more demanding and carry more responsibility. Over-rigid hierarchies can stifle deep-seated qualities of flair, initiative and creativity.

Today's high-performance enterprises are those which have developed a climate of initiative and responsibility.[27] At the competitive level, it seems that the most effective structures are those which foster genuine development of the human potential – these are 'living', 'participative', 'creative' structures.

The inefficient enterprise is marked by a widening gap between problems of adaptation and innovation on the one hand and structures and management styles and methods on the other; this results in bottlenecks, inertia and a paralysis which endangers the response to new competitive pressures.

At societal level, most high-performance enterprises are seeking increasingly to give thought to the effect of their activity on society at large and this involves the enterprise's relations with the community and a more apparent, more organised contribution to the general interest. Regions, states and communities expect enterprises to contribute concerted solutions to major social problems (unemployment, regional revival, international competition, technological progress, pollution, etc.) and the pursuit of economic strategies divorced from societal problems will be regarded as less and less acceptable. Growing interpenetration between economic policy and pressure-group strategy (enterprises, unions, regional authorities, ecologists, etc.) creates an environment often calling for concerted effort towards projects and objectives.[28]

Failing close agreement with enterprises it will be impossible to formulate major national or community competitive policy or apply it realistically and vigorously, and the quality of this dialogue is becoming a key element in European development. Projects like Airbus, Ariane, Esprit or Race represent a new type of concerted action which relates to objectives and strategies rather than, as hitherto, simply to methods or the share-out of results.

Cooperation between the Commission and leading economic protagonists is essential if we are to accomplish common large-scale projects which will create sufficient demand in the high-tech sectors to induce enterprises to raise their sights and broaden their strategic aims. Commission and European Business Round Table projects are moving in this direction. Here it should be noted that the advanced technology of both the great competing economic systems (USA and Japan) rests largely on public money. A European 'strategic view' must be developed to guide the choice of mutual high-tech projects.

This applies not only to future generations of technology but also to international, particularly Third World, policy. If Europe wants to retain an active role in the developing countries, it is logical for European enterprises to seek openings for creative leadership in the 'non-Triad' markets. These have specific needs and, leaving aside all political and ethical considerations, have the potential to become substantial markets.

Similarly, if the EEC wished to broaden its Third World policy beyond that of the Lomé agreements, the only way to guarantee its application in practice would be by cooperation with European enterprises. It could be a source of new-style major projects which would, furthermore, produce their own new generations.

1.8 COMPETITION: A DESTRUCTIVE OR CREATIVE PROCESS?

1.8.1

An enterprise will increase its efficiency and competitiveness if it becomes part of a cumulative development process of which it is at once the subject and the object. This process is greater than the enterprise because it incorporates the commercial, technical, political, etc. environments, and has a decisive effect on the enterprise's chances of success. On the other hand the enterprise exerts its own powerful drive and often innovative effect by seizing opportunities and continually providing new competitive impetus through strategic initiatives.

Such a process *creates competitiveness* and in the case of large enterprises is based on the following:

- Long-term *prospects* and sufficiently wide *opportunities* to justify the risk of new technological development and considerable capital investment. Prospects of this kind may be

provided by important open markets, rapidly expanding demand and certain large-scale public projects.
- Development of a *strategic capability* which suffices for an enterprise to embark on a world scale in the major profitable markets:
  - Bolder, longer-term strategic choices and therefore improved strategic methods and anticipation procedures.[29]
  - Development of key resources for progress: human resources (skills, management, internationalisation, etc.), technical know-how, relations, finance.[30]
  - Wider functions at international level, either alone or through alliances and cooperation; (in this respect the formation of a world distribution network is particularly important).[31]
  - Greater capacity for innovation and change by a better integration of R&D into competitive strategies plus improved mastering of complex structures.[32]

- Acquiring *competitive advantages* at international level by virtue of this increased strategic capability:[33]
  - Potential for taking advantage of the differences and comparative advantages of one country relative to another combined with faster adaptation to their evolution.
  - A size which provides the enterprise with economies of scale and a cost advantage which can be decisive in many activities; here the effect of experience becomes a decisive competitive weapon.[34]
  - Adequate combination of activities and of key resources so as to optimise strategic investment in, say, R&D, marketing, organisation, management, etc.[35]

- Sufficient *profitability* to cover development costs, the cost of becoming international and the risks attendant on this strategy. It is axiomatic that the profitability of day-to-day operation (sound basis) must be continuously monitored to keep it high enough for strategic needs and that turnaround is on-going rather than an emergency reaction. In turn, profitability allows the enterprise to grasp opportunities offered by the environment and to rise to the prospects of a longer-term future. The 'virtuous circle' is initiated and the process becomes a dynamic one which creates competitiveness as shown in figure 1.1.

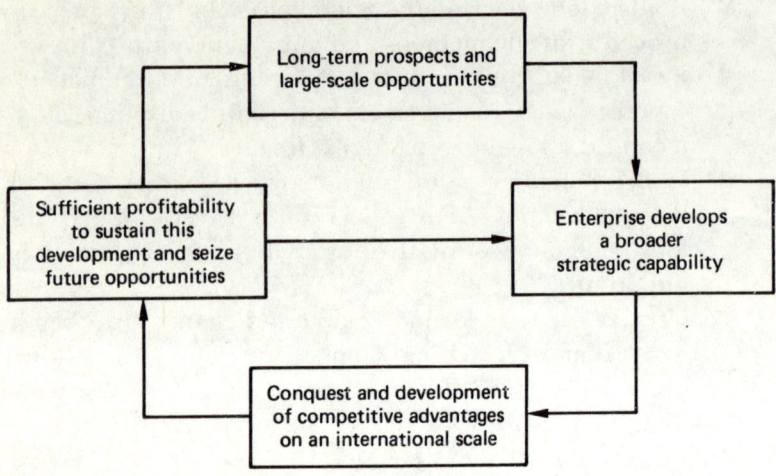

Figure 1.1 Process enhancing competitiveness

1.8.2

The chances of success of an enterprise being unable to benefit from this type of creative process are reduced, and if the process destroys competitiveness they become remote. In response to this apparent paradox it may be argued that the enterprise must then do everything in its power to escape the destructive mechanism but this assumes that the enterprise has complete freedom of action and can escape completely from its environment, which is not the case.

In very broad outline, a process which destroys competitiveness can be described as follows:

- The *prospects* are short-term and most of the *opportunities* are local or national. This is a common situation where a firm is badly behind in high-tech know-how and world markets

have already been taken up, or where sectors depend on small or medium-size government procurements favouring 'national champions' or, finally, where, because of market barriers, the market open to the enterprise is too small to justify developing an international strategic capability.
- The strategic capability developed is then purely local or, at best, national (national champions) and lacks the muscle to fight world or dominant competitors: less R&D, fewer and less internationally-minded executives and managers, scant external relations, inadequate distribution networks, little capacity for innovation, etc.
- No potential for creating international advantages, those created being simply national; only major world competitors can take advantage of economies of scale, the effect of experience and combined coordinated action.
- Profitability suffers and there are insufficient funds to develop capability or seize future opportunities; at worst, existing activities decline and enterprise survival is threatened; essential turnaround may come too late because the enterprise is slow to perceive its weakened state and the application of corrective mechanisms is tardy and sluggish. Sometimes the enterprise may seek state aid and if the state responds with defensive measures to protect ailing enterprises/sectors it reduces its potential for launching major international projects; the vicious circle closes. This kind of intervention has a highly negative effect on competitiveness because it slows down or inhibits the process of creative destruction and the large-scale operations it involves.

A further negative effect of the destructive process is the way it limits competition in order to protect national champions; this maintains market barriers and further restricts opportunities and prospects (see figure 1.2 below).

26 Competition and Strategic Capability

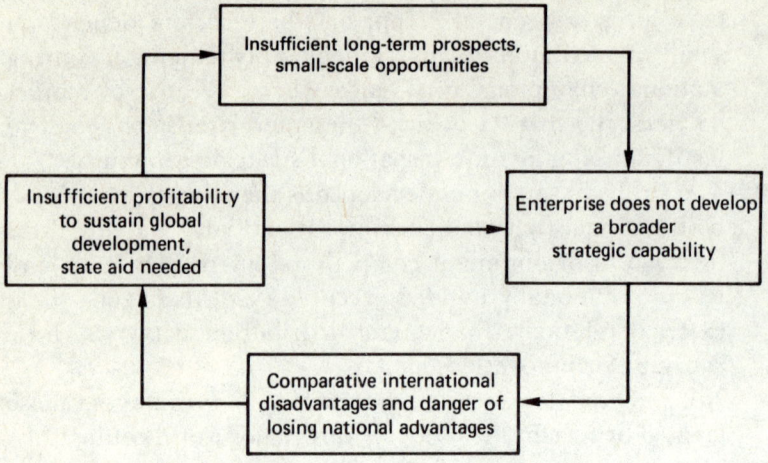

Figure 1.2 Process destroying competitiveness

NOTES

1. Adapted from Young, J.A., President of the US Commission of Competitiveness.
2. Goshal (1987).
3. Schumpeter (1949).
4. GM spent more than $40 billion in the last 5 years on creating factories of the future. IBM spent $3 billion p.a. on computerising its production processes (Source: *Economist*, 23 August 1986).
5. Stopford and Turner (1985).
6. Ohmae (1985). The Triad powers are Japan, the USA and Western Europe.
7. Clearly, this is not absolute; many products lie outside this levelling process but for others it is becoming more and more marked (Ohmae).
8. Porter (1980; 1985).
9. Goshal (1987).
10. Hall (1980); Grinyer (1986).
11. Goshal (1987).
12. de Woot and Desclee (1984); Arenas (1986); Lambin (1986). The concept of strategic capability has also been used by Doz and Prahalad (1987).
13. Buigues (1985); Godet (1987); Sallenave (1984); Sicard (1987).
14. Stopford and Turner (1985).

Competition and Strategic Capability 27

15 Bibeault (1981); Grinyer (1986).
16 Peters and Waterman (1983).
17 Crozier and Friedberg (1977); Archier and Serieyx (1984); Saias and Hall (1980); Kayser (1986).
18 de Woot and Desclee (1984).
19 Stopford and Turner (1985).
20 Pinchot (1985); Kanter (1983); Drucker (1985); Albach (1983; 1985).
21 McKinsey in Ohmae (1985); Porter (1985).
22 Jacquemin (1984); Saias (1985); EFMD and EIASM (1981); Albert and Ball (1983); Ergas (1984).
23 See chapter 4, p. 136, table 4.7.
24 EFMD and EIASM (1981); Saias and Hall (1980); de Woot and Desclee (1984); Saias and Montebello (1980).
25 EFMD and EIASM (1981); de Woot (1968).
26 Crozier and Friedberg (1977); Argyris (1964).
27 Archier and Serieyx (1984); Peters and Waterman (1983); de Woot and Desclee (1984); Page et al. (1987).
28 See Fondation Europe et Société, Cahiers 1 à 5, Paris 1986–7.
29 Ansoff (1979).
30 de Woot and Desclee (1984).
31 Stopford and Turner (1985).
32 Lawrence and Lorsch (1969).
33 Goshal (1987).
34 Boston Consulting Group (1982).
35 Ohmae (1985); Porter (1985).

2

Some Thoughts on the Competitiveness of European Enterprises

The topic has been examined in numerous studies, particularly by FAST,[1] and our report aims not to provide a summary but rather to add a specific point of view, namely that of enterprise strategy as described conceptually in the previous section.

Our consideration is limited to certain sunrise sectors for which European firms are insufficiently competitive and we go on to seek an enterprise-centred explanation. As we have seen, the enterprise is simultaneously the subject and the object of a process which can create or destroy competitiveness.

2.1 UNEQUAL COMPETITIVENESS

2.1.1 World leaderships

Fortunately the European picture is not all gloom since many enterprises have achieved and maintained world leadership and in some sectors have proved more competitive than their foreign rivals. This is notably the case in several traditional sectors in which Europe acquired competitive advantages very early and has managed to hold on to them by adopting a global strategy.

- We find large *chemicals and pharmaceutical* enterprises in this position. Our competitive export positions have held steady at figures well above the OECD average (see table 2.1). Two

The Competitiveness of European Enterprises

Table 2.1 Biotechnology R&D budgets for the biggest companies (in M$)[a]

Du Pont (USA)	120
Monsanto (USA)	62
Eli Lilly (USA)	60
Schering-Plough (USA)	60
Hoffman La Roche (Switzerland)	59
Genentech (USA)	32
Cetus (USA)	26
Biogen (USA)	8.7
Genex (USA)	8.3
Sumitomo (Japan)	6
Ajinomoto (Japan)	6
Suntory (Japan)	6
Takeda (Japan)	6
Hybritech (USA)	5
Hoechst (FRG)	4.2
Schering AG (FRG)	4.2
Elf-Aquitaine (France)	4

[a] 'New biotechnology enterprises'. Figures for the United Kingdom not available.
The high performance of European chemical enterprises on the world scene fits well into the pattern outlined in chapter I: world demand and creation of a strong strategic capability (R&D, people, Marketing) allowing the acquisition of global competitive advantages and the generation of adequate profitability. It is noteworthy that when turnaround was called for, it was carried out vigorously and in time, particularly in the case of Ciba-Geigy, Rhône Poulenc and ICI.
Source: OTA, Commercial Biotechnology.

European names head the list of principal world pharmaceutical groups and five appear in the top ten though there is the disturbing feature that biotechnology R&D budgets are far higher in the USA (excepting Hoffman La Roche); the Japanese firms are thicker on the ground and more active than their European counterparts (see table 2.1).[2,3]

- Also in this position are the *glass and cement* industries. European enterprises have won world leadership in both these sectors and shown the capacity to maintain and develop it. Even today they are pursuing bold strategies towards world-scale development. In the cement sector, European enterprises (Lafarge-Coppée, Blue Circle and Holderbank) lead the world and Saint-Gobain and Pilkington are prominent in glass.

Here again enterprises have succeeded in developing systematically a strategic capability which has enabled them to acquire global competitive advantages; they have achieved turnaround forcefully and quickly enough and their profitability has been such as to constitute a driving force in the process which creates competitiveness.

- In the *motor industry* European enterprises experienced a falling-off in international rankings during the 1970s but most have recovered to regain competitiveness by successfully pursuing Porter's three generic strategies:
  - *Cost* control by increased automation of production, robotisation, CAM, CAD, etc.[4]
  - Product improvement by speedy application of *technical advances*; electronics, fuel economy via lighter vehicles and improved engines and so on and development of sharply differentiating models: UNO, R5, Golf, Peugeot 205, etc.
  - The *niche* strategy which is successfully pursued by several manufacturers, e.g. Mercedes, Volvo, Jaguar.

Here too, turnaround operations have had a decisive effect. Most European enterprises have regained a sound basis for development by dint of strenuous effort to restore competitiveness, extracted by 'tough' employers with all the hallmarks of 'sharpbenders'.[5] This is notably the case with:

- Volvo: Gyllenhammar
- VW: Schmücker
- Fiat: Agnelli, Ghidella, Romiti
- Jaguar: Eagan
- Peugeot: Calvet

and, to a lesser extent, with Renault (Besse) and Rover (Edwardes).

Interestingly, mergers have not been a success: Peugeot-Chrysler, Fiat-Citroen, Renault-American Motors, BL. 'Mergers of lively equals never work; both are unwilling to be the one that sinks from sight. ... Economies of scale are often better translated as "if you will join me, we may both be able to stay inefficient longer"'.[6]

The Competitiveness of European Enterprises 31

A number of motor companies have opted for diversification:

- Volvo: energy, trading, aircraft/ships' engines, foods
- Mercedes: advanced technology (Dornier, MTU, AEG)
- Fiat: defence and robots
- GM: aviation and systems (Hughes Aircraft, EDS)

This is a highly controversial issue; several such diversification ventures have failed and recent studies show both that it is hard to diversify sucessfully and that diversification is no guarantee of effective performance.[7]

- European enterprises have achieved world leadership in other sectors, particularly: certain *services* such as tourism (Club Méditerranée), major retailing (Marks and Spencer, Carrefour), hotels (Neckerman), communal catering (Accor) and *creativity*.[8] It is also the case with the *luxury* industries (fashion, perfumes, wines, etc.) and the *food* industry where enterprises such as Nestlé, Schweppes, Gervais-Danone and Rowntree-Mackintosh have won global competitive advantages. All the successful examplars share certain features:

- They belong to relatively old sectors where Europe has long-held strengths.
- They are directed at the open market and do not rely on public contracts.
- They do not control future generations of technology (apart from the biotechnology subsector).
- They often represent sufficient added value to justify a world strategy.
- Their executives have managed to apply that strategy by creating world-scale competitive advantages.
- The enterprises have stayed at the forefront of technology.

In this way the high performance enterprises in these sectors have established themselves in a process which creates competitiveness and within it have achieved remarkable success.

The mature sectors therefore will offer significant potential. 'Mature industry has more technical variety, more scope for imagination, more ways to survive and more ways to put together a winning product than ever before.'[9]

2.1.2 Disturbing lags

Unfortunately the prospect is not so bright with regard to the major future technologies, particularly those which the meta-technologies command: electronics, biotechnology, opto-electronics and advanced materials. Here, despite a few spectacular breakthroughs, Europe is losing ground precisely where it matters for the future.

- Some brilliant successes have certainly been achieved: Ariane, Airbus, telecommunications, some robots, the 'Prolog' language, the 'Rita' network, Minitel, fighter aircrafts, defence electronics, TGV,[10] etc. but these are often partial, sometimes shaky and rarely global. Moreover, it cannot be denied that overall we are losing ground to our Japanese and American competitors. Generally speaking, it is only in the sectors mentioned earlier that our enterprises have managed to achieve this kind of strong international position. In the major future technologies and many high-tech activities our enterprises do not seem to have developed an adequate strategic capability to acquire decisive competitive advantages at world level. A few facts should be stated before we go on to explain why.
- In most high-tech sectors our international position is worsening. Tables 2.2 and 2.3 show the European decline.

Table 2.2 Decline of European industry (index of specialisation 1973 and 1980)[a]

	EEC		USA		Japan	
	1973	1980	1973	1980	1973	1980
Electrical equipment	1.16	1.06	1.03	1.07	0.15	1.20
Telecommunications equipment	0.95	0.71	1.31	1.32	1.55	1.96
Optics and photography	0.78	0.84	1.11	1.27	0.95	1.36
Vehicles	1.31	0.84	1.00	0.73	0.47	1.69
Other equipment and transport	0.78	1.04	1.47	2.33	1.32	0.91
Chemicals	1.21	1.23	1.14	1.14	1.38	0.25

[a] IFRI (1986). The table should be read as follows: 1 is the OECD average for exports of various products. Countries scoring better than 1 are above average and vice versa.
Source: EEC, DG III, quoted by Petrella (1983).

The Competitiveness of European Enterprises 33

Table 2.3 Export of high-technology products[a] by selected countries: % of total output of six countries[b]

Country	1972	1976	1978	1980	1982	1983[c]
Germany	26.3	21.7	21.6	20	17	14.5
France	11.1	10.9	10.4	10.3	8.1	8
United Kingdom	13.8	11.5	11.7	12.6	11.1	10
Switzerland	3.5	3.6	4.1	3.6	3.2	3
Japan	13	18.2	18.5	18.2	20.3	25
USA	32.2	34.1	33.7	35.3	40.2	37

[a] Dataprocessing, telecommunications, electronic valves and transistors, measuring instruments, medical equipment.
[b] *Business Week*, Euro-Business, 1983.
[c] Partly estimates.
Source: Deutsche Bundesbank. Annual Report for 1983.

- In the area of technological know-how, evaluations made variously by industrialists, researchers and officials all rank Europe generally lower than its competitors (table 2.4). Appendix 12 shows an evaluation recently made by Japanese industrialists.
- In the key strategic capability resource of R&D, Europe also lags behind in terms of intensity and development.[11] Whilst

Table 2.4 Evaluations in advanced technology[ab]

Sector	USA	Japan	Germany	Scandinavia	UK	France
Computers	1	2	3	4–5	6	4–5
Electronics	1–2	1–2	3	4	6–7	6–7
Telecommunications	1	2	3	4	5–6	5–6
Biotechnology	1	2	3	4	5	n.d.[c]
Chemicals	1	2	3	4	5	6–7
Metals and alloys	2	1	3	4	5–6	5–6
Design, study and development	1	2	3	4	5	6
Manufacture	1–2	1–2	3	4	5	6
Robotics	2	1	3	4–4	6	5
Mean	1.3	1.7	3.0	4.2	5.4	5.8

[a] Classification drawn up by more than 200 European chief executives who submitted their individual views of the hierarchical ranking of 6 western nations in 9 areas of technology.
[b] IFRI (1986).
[c] n.d. = not available.
Source: Management and Technology, *A Survey of European Chief Executives, 1984*, jointly sponsored by the *Wall Street Journal*, Europe, and Booz-Allen and Hamilton.

34 The Competitiveness of European Enterprises

its R&D spending is still far higher than that of Japan in absolute terms, certain figures suggest that our productivity in this area is low (appendix 1) (see also table 2.5).

Table 2.5 Development of gross domestic R&D spending

	1981 MUS$	%	1983 MUS$	Actual growth rate 1981–3
USA	73,678	46.4	88,329	3.8
Japan	25,574	16.1	33,493	8.2
EEC	47,690[a]	30.4	52,346[b]	2.5

[a] 11 countries.
[b] 5 countries.
Source: OECD.

- All this has an effect on *profits* and the European enterprise's capacity for profit is generally lower than that of its Japanese and American competitors. Although these figures are relatively old, they demonstrate how far Europe is lagging behind in certain areas, since it is the profits of yesterday that should be creating the strategic capacity of today (see figure 2.1).

This is important for our explanatory model; in fact profit is a

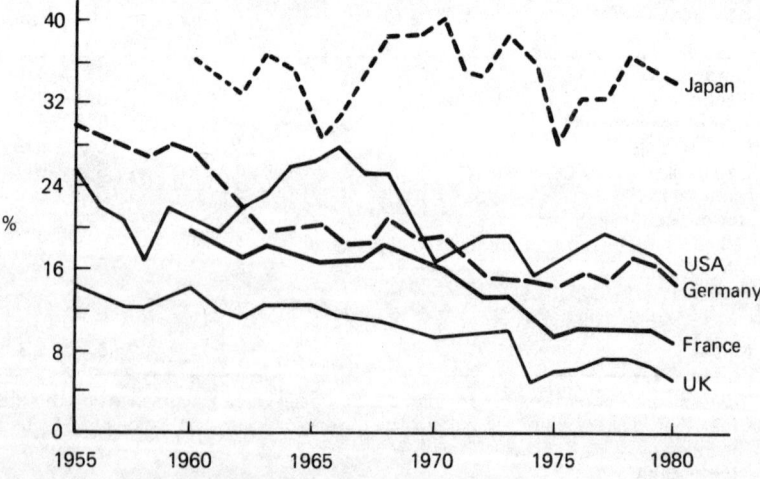

Figure 2.1 Return on assets, 1955–1980
Source: OCDE, CEPII.

driving force in the process which creates competitiveness. While it is the result of better competitiveness it is also the source of corporate strategic capability. The development of human resources, R&D and networks is the basis of global strategy and such resources can be created only if profits are high enough. Profit also allows an enterprise to take the risks involved in longer-term prospects and wider opportunities.

2.2 A PROCESS DESTROYING OR ENHANCING COMPETITIVENESS?

The analytical model presented in chapter 1 aids our understanding of Europe's relative failure in high-tech sectors for it shows that European enterprises are involved in a process which destroys their competitiveness whereas their Japanese and American competitors have managed to fit themselves into a process which creates competitiveness. As we said earlier, the key elements of this process are:

- The existence of long-term prospects and large-scale opportunities.
- Corporate development of a wider strategic capability.
- Acquisition of international competitive advantages.
- Sufficient profitability to sustain this development and seize future opportunities.

In all four key areas the American and Japanese development models are far more dynamic and effective than the European model.

2.2.1 The American model

Prospects and opportunities

American enterprises enjoy an environment which offers long-term prospects and continental, even world opportunities.

- The first opportunity is, of course, the existence of a large, unified market of 240,000,000 consumers; this is well known,

perhaps, but is absolutely fundamental. Today, no international enterprise in a high-tech sector can afford not to be in the American market.
- Another important high-tech opportunity is the existence of large projects directed at the future and, hence, very large public contracts: both space and defence have played a significant part in broadening the prospects and opportunities open to American enterprises. More than half of American R&D is funded by the US government and here the role of defence is important; the USA accounts for 71% of the defence expenditure on R&D by OECD countries (Europe 26%, Japan 6%).

    The conquest of the moon injected over $60 thousand million into firms and universities and the SDI budget is forecast at $26 thousand million.
- Underlying the American industrial fabric is an extraordinary scientific creativity thanks to the existence of science-based SMEs having close links with the universities – the examples of Boston's Highway 128 and Silicon Valley are well known and there are at least a hundred 'campuses' of this kind. We shall return to this in chapter 4.

    The development of risk capital has greatly favoured this 'technological burgeoning' and has contributed to the existence of far more American than European or Japanese high-tech entrepreneurs. It is because of them that American industry remains at the forefront of progress in virtually every area (appendix 12).
- The existence of very large multi-nationals in the high-tech sectors is a key element of the industrial set-up for they are in a position to take the opportunities offered by major public contracts. In this way they represent an enormous market for science-based SMEs.
- Finally, the American market is much more sophisticated than its European counterpart, infrastructures are more developed, there are more research workers and its financial strength far outweighs that of Europe or Japan (appendix 17).

Multinational strategic capability

In the sunrise sectors the USA has major enterprises with world-scale strategic capability. A few names suffice to convey the quality and extent of this development for Europe has nothing to match IBM, Xerox, ATT, Boeing, Motorola, United Technologies, etc. Recent studies show the degree to which they have created the elements of strategic capability and the rate at which they renew, rejuvenate and adapt them to match the latest developments.[12] This applies not only to methods and resources but also to attitudes and behaviour: capacity for change, taste for action, entrepreneurship are all systematically created and any shortfall gives rise to criticism and often outspoken questions.

Competitive advantages at world level

Because the big American enterprises enjoy large-scale opportunities and rest on a strong strategic capability they have managed to win competitive advantages in virtually every high-tech sphere; we shall be analysing some of these in the next section.

At times the advantages are so great that they result in a superiority and dominance which endanger European enterprises. IBM's strategic capability, for example, is such that the company's word is law in a number of fields, notably standards. Boeing is the only company in the world which can offer a complete range of civil aircraft.

As for the 'systems of the future' such as integrated information services (taking information services as 'ultra-tech': computers + office and accounting equipment + robotics + telecommunications), all major new groupings tend to centre round the leaders, IBM and ATT (appendix 9). This will enhance their strategic capability and enable them further to broaden their prospects and seize large-scale opportunities.

Performance

The *profitability* of these companies is high for, as we shall see in the next section, they are generally very efficient. In computers, for example, IBM's ROS (Return On Sales) for 1983 was four times that of Olivetti, six times that of Siemens and ICL and twelve times that of Philips. The profitability of every American computer company is greater than that of its European or Japanese competitors (appendix 3) and forms a link in the 'virtuous circle of success'. It guarantees the dynamic of the process which creates competitiveness, makes for a continuous strengthening of strategic capability (investment in skills, R&D, commercial and financial networks, etc.) and in fact constitutes a primary loop. It also enables enterprises to seize wider opportunities (ultra-tech, SDI, etc.) and broaden yet further their opportunities in space and time, thereby providing a second loop.

The American model is thus dynamic and allows enterprises to slot into a process which strengthens their world competitiveness.

In the context of a large, highly sophisticated home market the principal driving forces in the process are large high-performance enterprises, highly inventive SMEs with close university links, public authorities and huge defence contracts which greatly contribute to widening prospects and opportunities. Good interconnection between these four key elements has made for strong rapid growth in the high-tech sectors.

The principal strengths of the model are:

- A spiral of progress in the defence and space sectors.
- Marked ability in integrated systems and complex architectures.
- Exceptional inventiveness backed by powerful basic research leading to breakthroughs in new, barely foreseeable areas.
- Continuous creation of new products and the ability to match these precisely to highly specific needs.

The weakness of this kind of model derives from over-concentration on defence and space. Too low a proportion of technical progress is directed at consumer goods and the Japanese have leapt into the breach. In fact most of the big enterprises are heavily involved in (cost plus) defence contracts and are somewhat reluctant to plunge into commercial ventures carrying much higher risk. In turn, many of the innovative SMEs work for major groups and abandon the huge SME market with its need for simple, cheap, ready-to-use equipment.

The Competitiveness of European Enterprises   39

The Japanese ability to convert costly innovation into cheap mass production had enabled them to seize this opportunity.

The American model continually renews its superiority by new technical advances based on fundamental research, the creativity of its innovating SMEs and the strategic capability of its large diversified enterprises. This is particularly true of customised chips, ultra-tech (information services, bionics) and all large highly complex systems (SDI).

The USA is seeking to remedy its weakness in advanced mass consumer goods by increasingly promoting industrial and scientific cooperation and by restructuring SMEs around the major groups (see above).

Schematically the American model may be shown as in figure 2.2 below.

2.2.2 The Japanese model

Prospects and opportunities

- An important feature of the Japanese environment is the existence of a large home market of over 100 million consumers. It is a highly nationalist market for the Japanese tend to buy Japanese and, with few exceptions, have not up to now been over-receptive to foreign goods. None the less it is a very competitive market which favours fierce struggles between Japanese enterprises.
- Pointers to long-term prospects are to be found in certain major national objectives which are established, by consensus, under the subtle but powerful influence of the MITI. Objectives since the 1950s have included the conquest of foreign markets starting with textiles, then steel, colour TV and shipbuilding to be followed by cars and more recently by high technology (appendix 13).

Another well-known objective has been to turn Japan into a computerised society and, more recently, the more general aim, though centred on the sunrise industries, of making Japan a technologically advanced country with mastery of every major advanced technology:

40 The Competitiveness of European Enterprises

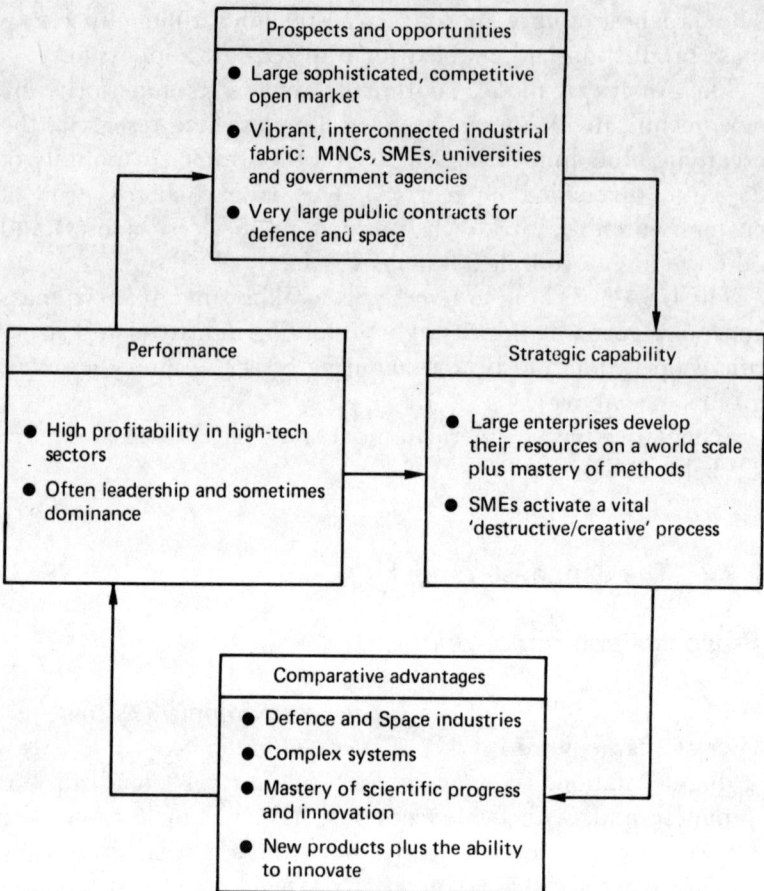

Figure 2.2 Outline of the American development process

- Communication/information systems
- Robots and factory/office automation
- Opto-electronics
- New materials

MITI influence is not at all that of a central planning authority but consists rather in drawing executives' attention to future key areas (based on very advanced studies) and trying to establish consensus on major priorities. The result of these studies and discussions is a reference document entitled 'MITI Vision for the 1960s, 1970s, 1980s'.

The Competitiveness of European Enterprises   41

Once the priorities are established a whole range of incentives, aids and contracts is organised round them to assist the efforts of enterprises committed to pursuing strategies in line with the choices. Thus, the priorities flash a signal to the banks with regard to credit policy and to the authorities with regard to public contracts, subsidies and research or development contracts. Commitment to MITI (Ministry of International Trade and Industry) priorities also brings tax concessions (e.g. special depreciation rates), exemptions from environmental regulations, non-tariff protection, etc.

Further, MITI to some extent distributes the tasks and risks between the big enterprises. It also influences the content of large 'national' projects, e.g. artificial intelligence or new telecommunications systems. In the latter area, Japan's planned investment is comparable to that for the SDI.

As far as her new digital network (Information Network System) is concerned,[13] Japan is about to invest $80–120 billion over the next 15 years and this will probably trigger some $250 billion private investment in the manufacture of PBX-type equipment and linked computers.[14]

Furthermore, MITI promotes the creative destruction process. It seeks to encourage enterprises to leave the less-profitable sectors for sunrise sectors and restricts any defensive intervention which might unduly prolong the life of declining sectors.

Finally, it is worth recording that the Japanese government has a very low military budget, public money being directed more towards civil activities with strong potential demand.[15]

The industrial picture is made up of very large, diversified industrial groups which control virtually all R&D. There is very little public presence in R&D in Japan and the universities are often directed by aged professors cloistered in their ivory towers.

Many SMEs exist but they lean towards subcontracting or craft industry and in no way play the innovative role of their American counterparts; the true driving force is that of the large, high-performance industrial companies or major trading companies, the latter contributing to the development of world distribution networks. The difference in output per man between the most modern and the least efficient sector is a factor of 88 in Japan, 41 in the FRG and 14 in the USA.[16]

MITI microchip policy is a good example which has been particularly effective in the modernisation of the Japanese consumer electronics industry (consumer electronics, TV, hi-fi, video, etc.). To disseminate this vital technology to the maximum range of activities MITI promoted domestic production of VLSI (Very Large Scale Integrated Circuit) circuits by designating them the key to the future and a condition of the country's industrial survival. Starting with protection of the home market, MITI followed this up by persuading enterprises to take part in large government research projects aimed at developing Japanese VLSI circuits, one conducted by NTT (the Japanese postal and telegraph authority) and the second by MITI itself.

Urged on by a national objective and by the investment banks, electronics enterprises made a massive investment which resulted in surplus capacity and thence a wealth of medium-price circuits; this in turn facilitated micronisation of the entire consumer electronics industry which then found itself in a position of world leadership. As a by-product, Japan became an exporter of microchips.[17]

- In terms of infrastructure and equipment the Japanese market has become as sophisticated as its European counterparts and in some sectors e.g. robotics, has surpassed the EEC and even the USA. It has greatly developed training in engineering as well as its own infrastructure and power (appendix 11).

International strategic capability

The big Japanese industrial and commercial enterprises have risen to the major opportunities and long-term prospects offered by their environment. They have developed any number of R&D resources, management skills and national and international relations and have adopted methods and structures which enable them to do business at world level. They have found a way of motivating personnel sufficiently to achieve levels of productivity and quality unequalled in the world.

The size, diversification and efficiency of Japanese groups bear witness to their mastery of complex structures and their ability to adapt quickly to important developments in markets and technologies.[18] In the field of consumer electronics, for

The Competitiveness of European Enterprises

example, enterprises such as JVC, Sony, Panasonic and Technics are of an international class and in the chips sector the same holds good for NEC, Hitachi, Toshiba and Fujitsu.

Competitive advantages and leadership

The practice by large Japanese enterprises of strategic methods taught in the leading business schools has been exemplary and their voluntary but systematic creation of competitive advantages truly remarkable. They have acquired cost advantages over a range of sectors by exploiting the effect of accumulated experience, even anticipating it by a policy of dumping abroad as in the case of steel, motorcycles, watches, cameras and, more recently, consumer electronics and chips. The formula for the rule of accumulated experience mentioned in chapter 1, which was first expounded by the Boston Consulting Group, is as follows: in the manufacture of product x, for each doubling of corporate experience there is a significant drop in production costs (often 20–30% at the start of the product's life). The cost reduction is due to the combined effect of economies of scale, the learning curve and new or improved procedures.

The rule does not apply in every sector but does hold good for large-volume activities and, on a more limited scale, for many specialist activities. The importance here of large-scale output and speedy conquest of major market shares is obvious. Appendix 14 shows the effect of experience on some past and present high-tech products.

This strategy is the key to most of the competitive advantages won by Japanese enterprises which, aided by MITI, have gone for sectors where they could still exploit the effect of experience and apply their strategic strengths to the full. In older sectors they often sought to achieve the volume effect by a pre-emptive pricing policy and to this end sold abroad at well below cost in order to increase their share of the market and hence their output; as output rose, costs soon dropped below prices. During the waiting period the difference was offset by higher prices at home or cross-subsidisation (high-profitability goods paying for futures).

In newer sectors, Japanese enterprises have had increasing

recourse to innovation to improve production procedures, no longer relying on economies of scale alone but on the extraordinary potential for manufacturing progress which the new technologies represent. Advanced production technology (automation, robotisation, CAM and CAD) was quickly introduced and firms developed an astonishing ability to turn new products into mass-produced goods and thus conquer a range of large new markets not only for consumer electronics but also for equipment (chips, robots, etc.).

When all this goes hand in hand with total quality strategy and the personnel training which it requires, it becomes clear that they have pursued the experience policy in every possible area: volume, innovation and the learning curve.

By this method, Japanese enterprises have gained competitive advantages on a world scale. True, unlike the American advantages, the advantages won by Japan tend to be specific but they have been good enough for the Japanese to achieve international high-tech leadership and, more important, to hold on to them.

Performance

Japanese corporate profitability is high and, as we show in the next section, Japanese enterprises are more efficient than their European counterparts in many high-tech sectors. The comparative profitabilities in general industry shown at the beginning of this chapter favour Japan as do measurements of investment productivity. Appendix 15 shows the marginal efficiency of investment to have been three times that of Europe for the years 1980–82. The situation may be affected by a dearer yen but the Japanese seem to react by increasing their investment abroad and this will further strengthen their international strategic capability. Their profitability is high enough for the major Japanese enterprises to develop their strategic capability. As we have seen, they were able to finance a substantial share of R&D, innovation and worldwide commercial networks thus providing the first loop towards creativity in the 'virtuous circle of development'.

The profitability of Japanese firms also enhances their ability to take bigger risks and hence allows them to rise to the wider opportunities and longer-term prospects held out by the major national objectives, thereby forging the second loop in the whole process. Like the Americans, the Japanese have succeeded in winning dominant positions which do not please their trading partners, notably in the case of video (95% of the world market) and other electronic goods. From this it follows that the Japanese model too is dynamic. It favours enterprise development on a world scale and in the sunrise sectors, and is therefore a process which creates competitiveness. In the context of a large home market which, though somewhat protected, is none the less competitive, the chief driving forces of the process are large efficient enterprises and the presence of national objectives at the heart of financial, commercial and scientific options.

Interconnection is achieved by the flexible coordination of a complex entity (incorrectly dubbed 'Japan Incorporated') in a way which provides stimulus. The operation of this system which is interconnected but competitive, decentralised but guided, directed but not programmed, is too subtle for total analysis or, doubtless, for translation into other cultures.

The main strengths of the model are:

- Mastery of: applied research, development of improvements and continuous advance, foreseeable technologies.
- Superior production technology both in methods (automation, CAM, CAD, CIM) and in management (total quality control).
- A progressive spiral in advanced sectors suitable for mass production: consumer durables, particularly electronic goods and standard equipment products such as chips and robots.
- International marketing and highly efficient distribution networks.

The weaknesses of the model lie in basic research and significant scientific breakthroughs. What the Japanese process lacks is the scientific creativity, product innovation and vigorous progress provided by the USA's university-backed scientific SMEs. This leaves it vulnerable to American breakthroughs in science and the American ability to change the competitive scene and raise the stakes by streams of new discoveries.

Finally, the absence from the Japanese scene of the thriving creativity which in America allows the dynamic coexistence of SMEs, universities, large enterprises and the public contracts which shape them into a flourishing whole meeting rigorous specifications, also means that Japan lacks mastery of large complex systems since this is based on cross-fertilisation between technologies and trades. Schematically the Japanese model may be shown as in figure 2.3.

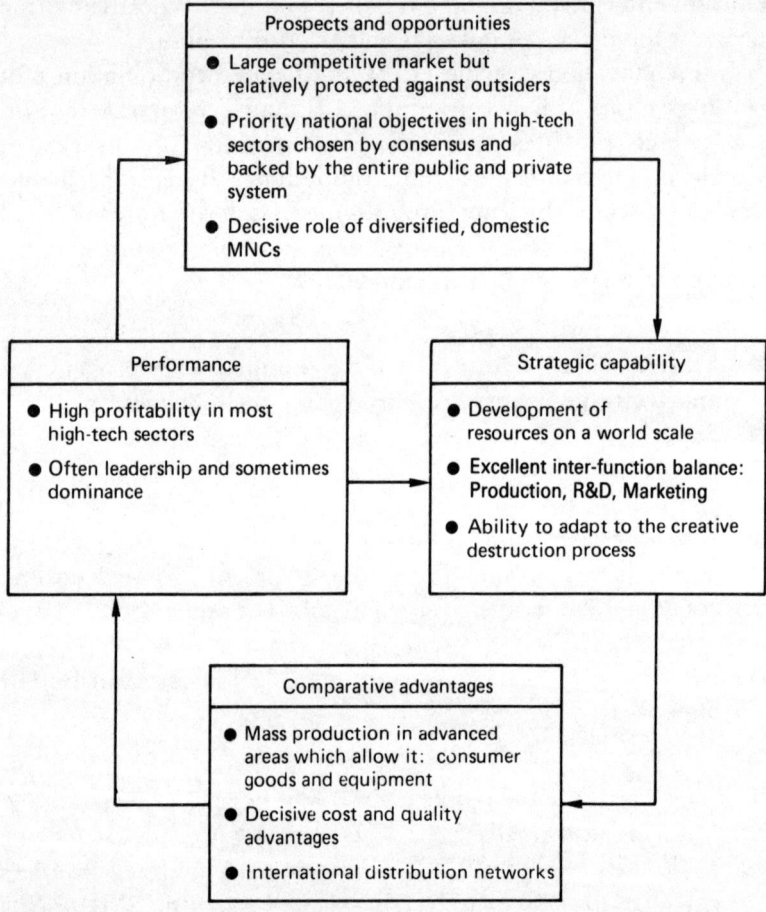

Figure 2.3 Outline of the Japanese development process

2.2.3 The European model

Prospects and opportunities

The European high-tech market is often compartmentalised and fragmented. It is competitive at national level but barely so on a European basis, a fact which dramatically reduces the prospects and opportunities open to enterprises. Too often non-tariff barriers, lack of unified standards, the presence of national champions and public contracts prevent enterprises from taking advantage of the potentially large common market which the 320 million population of Western Europe represents.

This is particularly serious in the case of activities where the enterprise needs large-scale public projects or a huge home market if it is to match up to world competition and this applies to many high-tech sectors and most major technologies for the future. It is also serious because the onslaught of major international competitors is far more destructive within the narrow confines of a state than it would be in a genuine common market. National industrial policies vary from one country to another but they all contribute to market division and are all more or less interventionist (France more, Germany less) and more or less defensive or inspired by social or economic considerations. None of this is decisive in our field, however; what is important is the extent, the nationalism and the defensive character of national industrial policy.

To take *extent* first: government spending accounts for 50% of the GDP of virtually every European country compared with some 30% for the USA and Japan (see appendix 16). This not only reduces the scope for enterprises to manoeuvre strategies of innovation and progress but limits the ability of ordinary households to buy at a more sophisticated level.

European *nationalism* hinges on practices which reduce corporate prospects and opportunities:

- *Unwillingness to specialise*: with slight exaggeration, the European nations could be described as wanting to keep their options open in every major new technological field and for this reason they support many 'small' projects in all the high-tech areas rather than concentrate on success in a few decisive breakthroughs.

- *Protection of 'national champions'*: the champions enjoy public favouritism in research, public contracts, aid and a range of subsidies and are able to survive because they lie under the public wing, safe from the rigours of international competition.
- A *policy of public contracts* focused, naturally, on existing or potential national champions; the policy further reinforces market division and takes physical form in different standards, regulations, infrastructures and tariff systems.

Ultimately this approach destroys opportunity for progress at regional or sub-regional level because even the largest European countries cut a provincial figure on the great world markets.

Thus we have here the first link in the process which destroys competitiveness. It tends, unfortunately, to be an on-going situation, because in too many areas the refusal to specialise encourages the elevation of national champions who remain too small to face up to international competition. Their need for state support to protect them against foreigners exacerbates unwillingness to specialise and the first vicious circle is completed.

Such nationalism precludes unified standards and, as far as new products and technologies are concerned, impedes access to a large European market.

This is, of course, an over-simplification but, unfortunately, it is based on accurate premises. We cannot deny that European cooperation has been known, as has European success in the international sphere, particularly in space and aviation, and we shall discuss this in greater detail in the next chapter. European projects like Esprit, Race, Brite and Eureka also exist and are a step in the right direction but are not enough to break the negative spiral of nationalism. It is not inappropriate here to recall that 80% of the Commission budget goes on the common agricultural policy.

Finally, the *defensive nature* of several of these policies has greatly reduced our enterprises' competitive capabilities. Too

The Competitiveness of European Enterprises   49

often governments have tried to protect ailing sectors by giving them a generous share of public resources; they have thereby delayed and even prevented drastic turnaround or necessary disinvestment.

As we saw above, favouring national champions shelters them from the realities of competition – but it also removes them from mainstream action. This has happened in sectors where national enterprises had the muscle to obtain this kind of protection. In the other sectors, as more advanced or dominant multi-nationals forced their way in, they found the opposition to be made up solely of medium-sized enterprises.

Given this environment, the creative destruction process is built up less quickly and less well than in the USA or Japan. Long term, European practices are more conducive to destruction than creation as shown in the destruction of jobs over recent years.

At the core of the European model we are forced to postulate the absence of large projects comparable with those of Japan or the USA. Our enterprises enjoy nothing comparable to the American defence or space contracts or the large-scale national priorities of the Japanese. In terms of corporate strategy in high-tech sectors this means that our firms do not have the prospects and opportunities which are open to their big international competitors; they are forced to work a narrower furrow.

- Despite its wealth, the industrial fabric is far less vigorous than that of the USA or Japan. In the case of high-tech activities, the fact that markets are compartmentalised and enterprises small reduces trade, inhibits cooperation and limits outlets.

  Unlike their American counterparts, the SMEs do not see before them an enormous open market or big enterprises waiting to take up their most advanced discoveries and innovations.

  The universities are far more active and dynamic than their Japanese counterparts but their relations with this industrial fabric are still not close enough; it is too divided and does not put forward major priority projects.

- Finally, the European market is far less sophisticated than the American market in terms of equipment and infrastructures; the Japanese have more engineers and more installed robots than we have; as for the financial aspect, the Europeans are now dwarfed by the gigantic USA and all-but gigantic Japan (see appendix 11).

Multi-national strategic capability

Lacking adequate opportunities and prospects in the main sunrise industries, most European enterprises have so far failed to rise to the level of the great American and Japanese firms. However, of the many important high-tech names – such as Philips, Siemens, Thomson, CGE, Olivetti, Bull, ICL, GEC, Plessey, Ericsson, AEG – not one has yet succeeded in dominating a complete set of new technologies as IBM, ATT or Boeing are doing. Similarly, few have managed to take any decisive share of the world market for consumer goods or advanced equipment as JVC, Sony, Fujitsu or Toshiba have done. Most show a profitability well below that of their world competitors (see appendix 3 for computers) and when they are efficient, as in the case of Olivetti, they team up with gigantic firms ten times their size. Many have gone in heavily for diversification and as a result cannot concentrate large resources on the important products of the future. As we saw earlier, none of this applies to chemicals and pharmaceuticals, although their biological development seems slow and inadequate.

The strategic capability of many European enterprises remains limited. Key resources are developed in an overly national perspective; for example: IBM'S R&D budget for 1983 equalled Bull's total turnover. In terms of executives and international networks there seems to be much still to do. Recent work shows that European management systems are still too traditional, enterprise climates too feudal and methods somewhat archaic. This description must, of course, be qualified; enormous differences exist between one business and another. Moreover the same work shows that many enterprises have recognised the management lag and are trying to modernise. Yet the weight of the past, ingrained habits of working agreements and protection,

The Competitiveness of European Enterprises 51

ill-defined strategy and distrust of the workers all conspire to make such change more difficult.[19]

In a general way it is fair to suggest that many European enterprises have not yet developed their strategic capability to world level because of inadequate opportunity, because national protection has softened the edge of competition and because structures, methods and mentalities have therefore been unable to develop at the same rate as those of their competitors.

To put it more forcefully, too many enterprises are losing the competitive struggle because they are confronting twenty-first-century problems with nineteenth-century weapons. The strategic capability demanded by the universalisation of competition and the accelerating speed of technical advance are on a new and different scale compared with what was needed for the conquest of national markets.

Competitive disadvantages at world level

Lacking adequate opportunities and prospects or a world strategic capability, European enterprises in high-tech sectors too often find themselves in a position of inferiority. As we shall see later, this applies to virtually the entire electronics sector, with the exception of telecommunications, professional equipment, medical electronics and instrumentation which represent, however, only 30% of the overall world turnover for electronics and even here a number of European advances are under threat. As far as the 70% balance is concerned Europe lags behind the USA (particularly in computer hardware and software) and Japan (mass electronics, components, office equipment and robotics). As we have seen, Europe is behind its international competitors in the new areas of opto-electronics and biotechnology which, with advanced components, constitute the key areas of the great future technological generations.

Aviation presents a more positive picture, for here, thanks to international cooperation, we see the beginnings of a vigorous European response and the same can be said of space where a number of major projects are making European enterprises competitive at international level. We may thus suggest that European enterprises are already, or are likely to find

52 The Competitiveness of European Enterprises

themselves, either excluded from vast sectors which control the future of industry or tackling them from a position of inferiority (see figure 2.4).

More immediately, we observe that our enterprises have not so far managed to become sufficiently competitive either in the areas of large complex systems and continuous innovation at which the Americans so excel or in the mass production of the most advanced products which is the Japanese forte. What is left

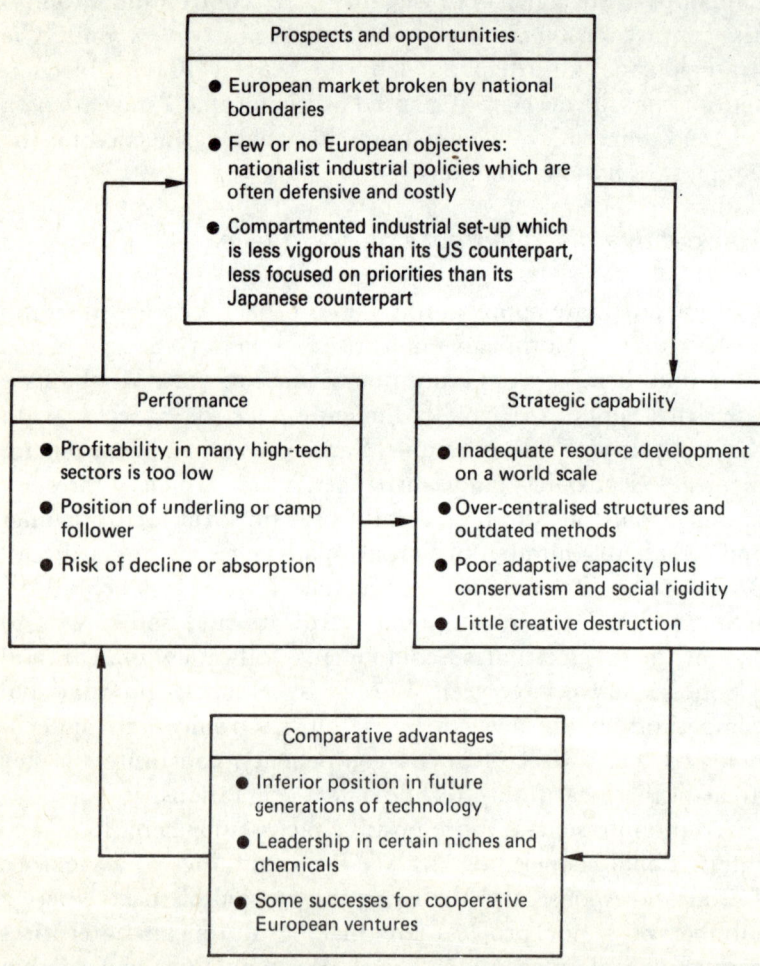

Figure 2.4 Outline of the process of European non-development

The Competitiveness of European Enterprises 53

for Europe if their competitors dominate these fields of action? Niches are still open and it is here that Europe has succeeded in a number of high-tech areas, notably in electronics as mentioned above. But can a great continent be satisfied with mere high-tech niches and not risk losing control of the great. We shall return to this.

A cooperative strategy also still remains open and whenever this has been practised with resolution it has produced positive results; it is one of our major weapons and will be discussed in the next section.

Performance

The profitability of European high-tech firms is too often lower than that of their international competitors (see appendix 5, dealing with computers).

The poor performance of our enterprises is attributable to the absence of decisive world-scale competitive advantages and this has a very adverse effect on developing improved strategic capability: investment in R&D, skills and networks is too low to create these competitive advantages and thus constitutes a first link in the negative chain.

Low profitability has a second negative effect in that it prevents enterprises from expanding their ambition and seizing bigger or longer-term opportunities. The inadequacy of 'national' projects and the dearth of European ones constitutes a second link in the negative process of non-development. The European model thus lacks the dynamism of the previous models; our enterprises are too often caught in a process which destroys competitiveness from which they find it very difficult to escape in the high-tech areas.

2.3 EXAMPLE OF THE ELECTRONICS INDUSTRY

We use this sector as our illustration because it is one of the keys to the future and has already become sufficiently established in the economy to allow analysis of strategies and competitiveness.

In 1985, total electronics represented a market of $485

billion, 4.7% of the world gross product; by the year 2000 it will represent 8% and is thus a sector with very high growth potential. However, what makes it so important is that it controls a number of important future generations, e.g. telecommunications and, even greater, the information services which the Americans refer to as ultra-technology par excellence as they tend to interconnect a whole range of high-tech sectors such as computers, office equipment, robotics, etc. and bring these into virtually every human activity, particularly the service industries.

The sector is important, finally, because the future generations of technology which it commands will be essential to the creation of even newer, more complex generations by cross-fertilisation between highly different technologies. This is already happening with opto-electronics and will doubtless happen in the bionics field too with its dependence on electronics, new materials and biotechnology.

2.3.1 Europe lags overall but has some successes

In the first part of this chapter, we described the decline of European competitiveness in the leading high-tech sectors, most strikingly in the case of electronics. Our export positions are worsening and an assessment of our scientific and technological capacities classes us overall after the Americans and Japanese (see also appendix 12).

The figures which follow confirm how Europe has fallen behind and is moving in the wrong direction. In 1983, Europe was trailing behind the United States and Japan:

- 97% of patents used in European computers were American or Japanese, as well as:
- 66% of integrated circuits and computer-assisted equipment;
- 75% of component-making machines;
- 100% of powerful computers; and
- 95% of microprocessors used by Europe (see table 2.6).[20]

Import penetration is as follows: Europe imports 29% of requirements, the USA 20%, Japan a mere 9%.[21]

The Competitiveness of European Enterprises 55

Table 2.6 In the electronics sector, European enterprises' share of world production and exchange is in continuous decline

	1980	1985
● *Production*		
EEC	26%	21%
Japan	15%	21%
USA	46%	47%
● *Trade deficit ($ billion) with:*		
Japan	3.9 (79)	8.5 (84)
USA	5.6	10.8

Source: Electronics International Corporation: *L'Electronique dans le monde*, quoted by Eric Le Boucher, *Le Monde*, 29 April 1986, *Le Triangle de l'Electronique*.

● Whilst the overall European position is declining and in deficit, some electronics sectors are not; in certain areas, European enterprises are more than holding their own. We must therefore analyse this enormous field in greater detail and the figures provided by Electronics International Corporation are very enlightening.

Table 2.7 shows clearly:

● The enormous Japanese lead in consumer electronics in conjunction with impressive breakthroughs in components,

Table 2.7 Trading surplus and deficit in the ten electronics sectors, 1984 (in $ million)

Sector	% of total electronics industry	EEC	USA	JAPAN
Consumer electronics	11%	−4,110	−9,260	+15,210
Computers	24%	−6,550	+5,050	+ 4,360
Software and services	10%	− 700	+1,950	− 300
Active components	7%	−2,500	−2,500	+ 4,330
Passive components	7%	− 270	−2,300	+ 3,810
Measurement and instrumentation	7%	+ 420	+3,110	+ 370
Medical electronics	2%	+ 550	+ 300	+ 340
Professional electronic equipment	13%	+1,690	+4,170	+ 880
Telecommunications	8%	+1,400	−1,000	+ 1,600
Automation devices	6%	− 900	+1,000	+ 900
Office and accounting machines	5%	−1,110	−1,600	+ 4,000

Source: Electronics International Corporation, *L'Electronique dans le monde*, quoted by Eric Le Boucher, *Le Monde*, 29 April 1986, *Le Triangle de l'Electronique*.

56 The Competitiveness of European Enterprises

computers, office machines, automation and telecommunications. With the exception of software Japan shows no deficit in any sector.
- The very strong American position in computers, software, measurement and instrumentation, professional electronic equipment and automation.
- The weak position of Europe in 70% of sectors, her strong position in medical electronics and telecommunications and average position in instrumentation and professional electronic equipment. However these sectors account for only 30% of electronics and, as we shall see, some of these positions are shaky.

More detailed sub-division is needed but this first analysis clearly reveals the competitive advantages which American and Japanese enterprises have achieved. It also highlights this aspect of our development models: American leadership in large systems, complex architectures and related software which are particularly relevant to defence and space; Japanese leadership in mass-production areas such as mass electronics, components and certain computers. Overall, Europe lacks strength in both directions and, with the exception of telecommunications to which we shall be returning, its relative successes lie rather in niches.

A very brilliant case is Philips' leadership in the compact disc business. In this field, Europe is at the top of the world production league, as figure 2.5 shows.

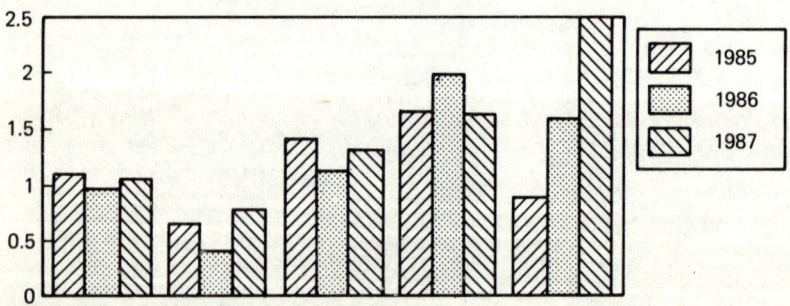

Figure 2.5 World production of compact discs, 1985–1987
Source: CPE, Bulletin 33, 33–8, December 1986, p. 60.

2.3.2 Computers

- Overall, European enterprises have not won comparative world advantages over the Americans or the Japanese. Europe's deficit in 1984 was $6.5 billion compared with a surplus of $5.5 billion for the USA and $4.3 billion for Japan.
- Our analytical model attributes this failure to inadequate corporate strategic capability:

    - Taking size alone, of the top 100 computer firms in the world, 72 are American, 19 European and 8 Japanese. Of the top 20, 13 are American, 4 European and 3 Japanese. Whilst this may seem a very rough measurement, it does give a first indication of relative strengths, and sector shares.

- A less crude way of measuring is to use net financial surplus because it shows enterprises' financial capacity to take on high-risk ventures. In table 2.8 the net financial surplus is calculated conservatively as 40% of net profit. It therefore does not include amortisation and genuinely shows each enterprise's discretionary power; in fact, after everything has been paid (costs, amortisation, finance charges and dividends) the balance can be used to finance future resources and take the risks of progress. Net surplus constitutes true financial backing for continuous strategic development. The figures for 1985 (a normal year) in appendix 3 provide a fairly clear picture of comparative strategic capability and productivity. Table 2.8 shows two key figures for 1982.

Taking 1982 as a normal year we see that:

- All the very profitable enterprises (ROS) are American.
- IBM achieves net surpluses which are mostly more than ten times those of its largest competitors; the comparison with European enterprises is very illuminating.
- Profit-making competitors have specialised in niches (Apple, HP, DEC).
- The biggest European net surpluses barely exceed the surplus of a mere IBM subsidiary; European strategic

The Competitiveness of European Enterprises

Table 2.8 Profitability of main computer manufacturers in 1982

Enterprises	Return on sales ROS %	Net surplus (40% net income) $ millions
IBM	12.8	1,760
DEC	10.7	280
Apple	10.5	30
HP	9	153
IBM (UK)	8	72
IBM (FRG)	7	106
IBM (J)	7	56
IBM (F)	6	82
Control Data	3.6	62
Olivetti	3	30
Ricoh	3	19
Burroughs	2.9	46
Siemens	2	111
ICL	2	8
Philips	1	64
CII-H.B.	(–)	(–)

Source: University of Louvain (UCL) and *Fortune*.

capability is markedly provincial except when a niche strategy is pursued. Furthermore, Siemens and Philips are highly diversified and their surplus cannot be exclusively applied to computers.
- Although its return is not very good, Olivetti heads the European enterprises because it is the most specialised.

The same key figures for 1985 are as shown in table 2.9. They illustrate that:

- IBM's net surpluses represent a past and future strategic capability which gives it a better grasp than any other on the key technologies of the future (e.g. telecommunications) and this on a world scale; the differences in 1986 are nearer to a factor of 20 than 10.
- Olivetti has matched the best returns on the back of a particularly spectacular turnaround; it is targeted to lead Europe, and in net surplus is catching up on the far more diversified Siemens and Philips. It has signed collaboration

The Competitiveness of European Enterprises

Table 2.9 Profitability of main computer manufacturers in 1985

Enterprises	Return on sales ROS %	Net surplus (40% net income) $ millions
IBM	13.1	2,622
IBM (UK)	10.1	160
Olivetti	8.2	106
IBM (J)	8.0	122
HP	7.5	196
NCR	7.3	126
Digital	6.7	178
IBM (FRG)	6.5	116
Fujitsu	5.7	146
Sperry	5.0	114
Burroughs	4.9	99
Nixdorf	4.3	23
Honeywell	4.3	112
Canon	3.9	62
Apple	3.2	24
Ricoh	3.1	27
Siemens	2.8	196
Philips	1.5	110
Bull	0.7	5
Wang	0.7	6
Control data	(–)	(–)

Source: UCL and Fortune.

agreements with ATT and Toshiba in the knowledge that it will not become a world force on its own.
- No European company seems equipped to pursue a world strategy in a major area of new technology; on the other hand they are level with specialist American and Japanese enterprises.
- Our many references to IBM's dominance are clearly borne out by the figures. The company has 60% of world sales and doubtless 70% of gross margins and will be difficult to dislodge. Simon Nora's report on information technologies was already emphasising the potential threat which this situation represents and went so far as to suggest that only an alliance between the European nations/major enterprises and ATT could create a strategic capability to compare with IBM's.[22]

The foregoing figures show that IBM is way ahead in the computer sector but that there is fierce world competition, particularly in the sectors of the future; the profitable computer companies realised that it was better to aim to win tomorrow's battles than to fight rearguard actions for sectors which were already lost. This was particularly the case with DEC, Apple and Olivetti.

It must also be stressed that IBM itself systematically updates the competitive advantages which it wins. Its strategic capability is such that it can adapt fast to technical developments, face up to multiple competition and update its approach and methods in a way that defies the forebodings of its detractors. Appendix 17[23] summarises the doubts expressed at various times.

Though IBM undoubtedly embodies many elements of dominance (particularly the way in which it so often manages to impose its own standards), we must emphasise the existence of an effective, powerful, up-to-date strategic capability which, despite all, lies at the heart of the matter. A recent book maintains that IBM's success is in large measure attributable to monopolistic practices; it is fairly convincing but is based on relatively old material.[24] In any case, every technological or commercial advance confers a degree of monopoly (Schumpeter) but it has first to be won and IBM's successive strategies suggest that the monopolies are far from permanent. The most significant thing for our purposes is the fact of a genuine strategic capability which is far superior to any wielded in Europe.

- It is interesting that most of the collaboration agreements in computer areas are reached in the USA and Japan rather than in Europe.

2.3.3 Components

- As everyone knows, integrated circuits are the key to every sector of electronics and here too European enterprises have failed to acquire world competitive advantages. In active components, both Europe and the US showed a $2.5 billion deficit in 1984 compared with a Japanese surplus of $4.3

billion; in passive components Europe had a $270 million deficit and the US a $2.3 billion deficit against a Japanese surplus of $3.1 billion.
- On the European market four European firms (Philips, Siemens, SGS-Ates and Thomson) make a reasonable showing against their foreign competitors as table 2.10 shows.

Table 2.10 Top semiconductor companies in Europe*

Company	Sales 1988 ($m)	% increase over 1987
Philips (Holland)	1002	7.7
SGS Thomson (France/Italy)	650	21.0
Texas Instruments (US)	636	29.3
Motorola (US)	616	28.9
Siemens (W Germany)	571	20.2
Intel (US)	485	71.4
National Semiconductor (US)	390	13.0
NEC (Japan)	370	48.6
Toshiba (Japan)	349	85.6
AMD (US)	279	18.7

* By European sales
Source: The Economist, 18 February 1989.

- In terms of production capacity, and therefore of experience and cost advantages, there is only one European firm in the top ten (table 2.11). American enterprises are still in the lead but the Japanese are catching up fast. It shows how far we have very largely failed to win major international markets. This measurement is interesting because in microelectronics the experience curve drops away rather sharply; the annual fall in costs, at least for the first few years, is around 30%; given the short product life, the importance of high-volume output and therefore large market shares is immediately apparent.
- A more detailed breakdown shows that American firms are maintaining powerful leads.
  - This applies to the design of mcps which provide the intelligence for advanced electronic equipment such as PCs and engineering work stations. These components

62   The Competitiveness of European Enterprises

Table 2.11   World's top semiconductor companies*

Company	Sales 1988 ($m)	% increase over 1987
NEC (Japan)	4534	34.6
Toshiba (Japan)	4302	42.0
Hitachi (Japan)	3506	33.9
Motorola (US)	3035	24.8
Texas Instruments (US)	2741	28.9
Fujitsu (Japan)	2359	31.0
Intel (US)	2350	57.6
Mitsubishi (Japan)	2278	52.7
Matsushita (Japan)	1886	29.4
Philips (Holland)	1764	10.1

*By worldwide sales.
Source: The Economist, 18 February 1989.

represent an annual market of $2.75 billion which breaks down as follows:[25]

USA: 43%
Japan: 34%
Europe: 18%

American enterprises seem set to maintain their dominance in the up-market ranges[26] but are beginning to lose ground in mass components, e.g. Motorola's 68000 and 68020 mcps which the Japanese produce under licence and more efficiently.

- European firms are ahead in ISDN-type telecommunications components; this is the case for Siemens and Standard Elektrik Lorenz, an ITT subsidiary.
- Japanese enterprises lead the field in memories, with control of 67% of the DRAM market ($1.65 billion p.a.). According to some experts,[27] there is no way that the American SMEs can fight the Japanese giants in components with increasingly complex structures and systems, which suggests that in certain areas the big Japanese enterprises could become more creative than the American science-based SMEs. These have reacted by seeking financial sponsorship and closer relations with big business, as in the case of Intel and

The Competitiveness of European Enterprises 63

IBM, and this is a new strategy which marks a development of the American model described earlier. Between 1980 and 1983, integrated groups accounted for a share of components supply which rose from 28% to 57%.[28]

Elsewhere, European enterprises have accepted the challenge at the Commission's request and Siemens and Philips have collaborated in the development of a new generation of integrated circuits which should enable them to by-pass the Japanese.

Philips will be producing a megabit chip (capacity = 1 million characters) in the Netherlands by 1987 and Siemens a four megabit chip (capacity = 1 volume of an encyclopaedia) by 1989. Each enterprise is investing $400 million and the same amount is being provided by each government. This is an interesting illustration of a European offensive strategy based on cooperation, research and clear objectives.

- The Americans have clear leadership in VHSIC and are developing a circuit which is planned to carry 35 million transistors compared with 1 million in the most sophisticated models of today. This is a TRW development with Motorola assistance under a national defence priority VHSIC programme with a 1 billion-dollar budget.
- The components branch is relevant because it confirms in general terms the development models shown earlier:

  - Japanese enterprises are pursuing a strategy of mass production and occupation of the world market.
  - American enterprises are benefiting from the inventions and technical creativity of a dynamic industrial set-up in conjunction with very large R&D contracts.
  - European firms risk being 'caught between two stools'.

However, the components market also shows the models to be changing in the interest of increasing the large enterprises' comparative advantages; the Japanese are stepping up their R&D; the big American enterprises are forming closer relations with high-tech SMEs and speeding up collaborative arrangements.

In conclusion, the example reveals a new European strategy; technical cooperation between large firms, with government encouragement, in pursuit of a European objective.

2.3.4 Telecommunications[29]

● As we know, telecommunications are one of the major technologies for the future. Turnover for the sector in 1982 was $57 billion and is expected to be around $80 billion by 1987. The LANs[30] market alone is expected to expand from $400 million for 6,500 offices in 1985 to $56 billion for 60,000 offices in 1990 and European enterprises have managed to secure significant competitive advantages in this particular field.

It is one of the few electronics areas in which Europe has a trading surplus ($1.4 billion in 1984); the Japanese also showed a surplus ($1.6 billion) and the USA a $1 billion deficit but they have far and away the largest output and a domestic market representing almost 50% of the world market. The starting positions thus look good but the rules of the game change very quickly and unless Europe reacts swiftly its position could be at risk. Some experts are highly pessimistic:

> Telecommunication in Western Europe is a disaster waiting to happen. Europeans distressed by their failure in computers and chips have found consolation in their $2 billion trade surplus and handsome 25% share of the world's telecom equipment market. They are kidding themselves. Americans and Japanese are hard at work, knocking the props of that prosperity out from under Western Europe.[31]

Two major factors have upset the earlier situation: technical progress and the deregulation of the American market.

■ Technical progress is the result of the transition of electromechanics to electronics. Relations between the telephone industry and the computer industry are closer; both depend on microchips and the quality of their software. Starting from there the most different items of equipment can be connected to each other; telecommunications control information efficiency and vice versa. If we add the progress achieved in optical fibres, satellite networks and ISDNs, the discontinuities which enterprises will be confronting become obvious. Figure 2.6[32] shows clearly the expanded frontiers and structure of this new family of systems (see also appendix 8).

From this point of departure there have been numerous major new developments; these are the subject of highly aggressive private strategies in conjunction with public attitudes which vary markedly from country to country. The greatest stake in contention is the development of networks and their various potential applications. A number of products and services are involved, the most important of which are shown in table 2.12.[33]

■ The second major cause of upset is the deregulation of the American market which has opened up the competition and made it more universal. The American market had long been a monopoly market. ATT provided an up-to-date service but was not really under pressure to innovate and ITT's growth was outside the USA. There were no offensive or even competitive strategies. This market was demonopolised and deregulated a few years ago, long-distance calls being opened to competition in 1977 and ATT broken up into separate companies in 1982. This giant enterprise thereby shed its down-market low-profit services (local calls are now handled by seven independent companies) but has retained its up-market high-profit services (long-distance calls) and is authorised to go into new sectors such as computers and office machines.

The *public network* carries local services (a monopoly everywhere except in the USA) and long-distance services. It uses a number of transmission channels (copper or optical fibre cables, satellites and earth stations) and central switching facilities to link voice and data transmissions (computerisation of these facilities is a major stake in the competitive game).

Deregulation has made it possible to by-pass the public services and some of their equipment (see earlier diagrams).

★ The privatisation of services means that a public line is rented out for private needs, particularly multiplexed data transmission.

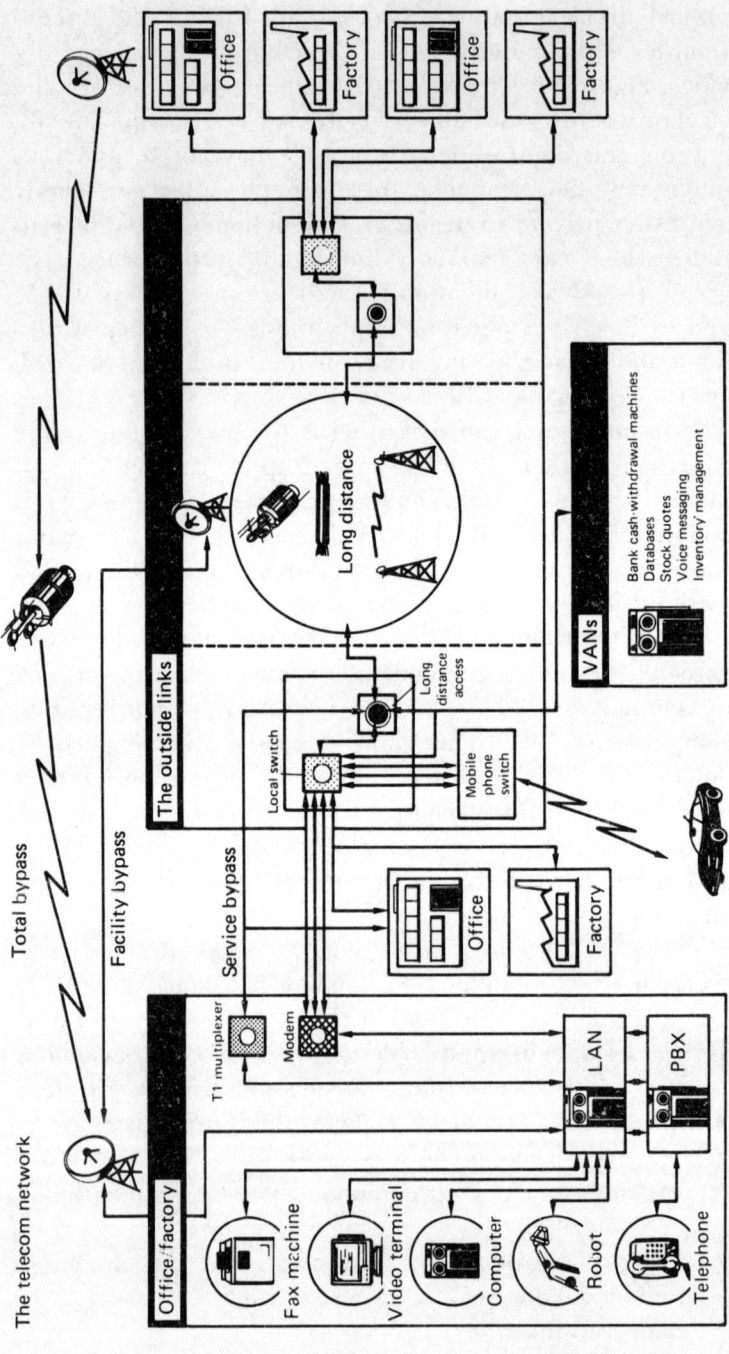

Figure 2.6 The telecom network

Source: *The Economist*, 23 November 1985

The Competitiveness of European Enterprises 67

Table 2.12 Telecom equipments and services (annual sales in 1984 $ billion)

	United States 1984	United States 1989	Western Europe[a] 1984	Western Europe[a] 1989	Japan 1984
Private markets					
Terminal equipment (e.g. telephones, fax, voice-data workstations)	2.5	4.1	1.2	1.9 ⎫	
Data communications equipment (e.g. modems, multiplexers)	2.4	6.0	0.7	1.2 ⎬	3.6
LANs	0.5	2.5	0.05	0.6 ⎭	
Switching equipment (e.g. PBXs)	6.5	9.0	3.2	3.8	0.6
Attached network functions (e.g. protocol converters, voice messaging)	0.6	1.9	0.02	0.2	n.a.
Total private market	12.5	23.3	5.1	7.7	4.2
Public markets					
Transmission equipment (e.g. earth stations, microwave)	2.9	5.2	2.7	4.4 ⎫	2.4
Switching equipment	2.8	2.9	2.4	3.1 ⎭	
Public telecoms services			69.3	117.0	21.9
Local service	69.4	129.9			
Long-distance service	39.8	57.1			
Public data networks	0.3	0.6			
Cellular car telephones	0.5	4.2	0.02	1.0	n.a.
Total public market	116.0	200.0	74.4	125.5	24.3
Total market	128.5	223.3	79.5	133.2	28.5

[a] Figures are for the 26 members of the CEPT, the European telecoms authorities association. Figures for output: equipment output for calendar 1984, services for year ending March 1985, n.a. Not available.
Sources: America and Europe: Dataquest. Japan: Communications Industry Association of Japan. Ministry of Posts and Telecommunications and *Economist* estimates.

★ The privatisation of networks may be partial (calls sent direct via any point on the public service) or total (public services are by-passed and calls are direct user-to-user).

Private telephone systems are mainly found in enterprises and interconnect office/works equipment such as telephones, computers, video terminals, robots and fax machines. LANs and PBXs provide the link.

Finally, the *new VANs* (Value Added Networks) are largely taken up with electronic mail, data banks, banking services, etc.

- A central feature of future strategy is the race between two complementary technologies which have advanced to differing degrees: ISDN and the more specialist VANs.[34]
  - The ISDN is a single network which would carry any transmission of any kind. It has been made possible by digitalisation which enables the network to carry out a range of activities formerly carried out by connected equipment (e.g. Centrex v PBX, Public Network v VANs). ISDN development leans towards the 'technology push' type.
  - VANs derive from a different concept: specialist high-value added-service networks which transmit and process sophisticated calls. They can be connected to the public network but private enterprises provide the service. This is a 'market pull' type development and has reached a more advanced stage than the ISDN.

What is really at stake is the respective roles of the central network and the specialist networks.[35]

The real problem is to determine which parts of ISDN 'intelligence' should be incorporated in the public network and which left to network-linked equipment supplied by outside suppliers.
- Generally speaking, the public monopolies would like the network to serve as many subscribers as possible and as much intelligence as possible to remain with the central system.
- The equipment manufacturers (computers, telephones, etc.) and VAN subscribers would like to retain as much intelligence as possible at their terminals and push the interface as far as possible from the end customers.

Here too, standards are involved. Ideally the ISDN should be world-compatible and there should be standards to ensure its compatibility with all telecommunications/office/electronic production equipment. At present there are two major norms: IBM's SNA (system network architecture) and OSI (open standards interconnection) which is in process of definition and is backed by Europe, ATT and NTT in concert.

It will be recalled that IBM dominates the market in the

The Competitiveness of European Enterprises 69

essential area of mainframe computers and in terms of IBM-compatible equipment its standard represents 80% of the world supply; more than 20,000 SNA networks are already installed.

- Telecommunications are thus clearly tilting towards the broader complex of the new technological chain of 'information services'. Numerous cooperation agreements are being signed and these are tending to centre round a few giants such as ATT and IBM, as shown in appendix 9.

This provides the framework within which strategy must be located and relative competitiveness assessed. Several important points emerge:

- Giants like IBM and ATT have already entered the race and are seeking to widen the opportunities and prospects. Their very powerful strategic capability, drive towards cooperation and ability to set the standards make them a force to be reckoned with. This kind of major manoeuvre could jeopardise European successes.
- The giants are a magnet for large European and Japanese enterprises; in VANs, IBM is the focal point of cooperation agreements with British Telecom, Nippon TT and Mitsubishi; in equipment, ATT has the same role in a coalition which already involves Philips, Olivetti, Mitsui and Toshiba. Cooperation is becoming a key strategy which operates at the Triad level and so far no European firm constitutes a focal point.
- Deregulation favours decentralised telecommunication strategies. It provides significant stimulus to the activities generated, e.g. VANs (specialist networks), LANs (Local Area Networks), PBXs (Private Branch Exchanges), etc. which seem to be developing faster than ISDNs.
- The American market is the largest and most sophisticated in the world and deregulation is stimulating corporate competitiveness by providing the enterprises with a test bench for a whole range of new activities.

Demanding though the market is, it is dynamic, and within

it enterprises can achieve important progress. The effect of experience here is spectacular and costs fall rapidly (10% p.a. for PBXs and small systems, 7% to 10% p.a. for private switching facilities).

Unless our telecommunications enterprises have a presence on the American market they are committed to a provincial role. It has become a priority market for Siemens and NEC; BT is trying to acquire MITEL (PBX) in Canada; Olivetti has its foot in the door through ATT; in the CGE-ITT joint venture the European enterprises involved will have easier access. For the moment North American enterprises are in very strong positions. The PBX market divides as follows.[36]

Northern Telecom (Can.)	21.2%
ATT	18.9%
Holm	18.4%
Mitel (Can.)	10.2%
NEC (J)	6.9%

ATT and Northern Telecom still have a firm hold on network equipment (central exchanges and transmission systems) but deregulation is attracting European and Japanese enterprises. The VAN market is dominated by GTE Telenet and Tymnet (a McDonnel Douglas subsidiary).

European enterprises' strategic capability will have to improve to this level if they want to win their share of the world market and from this point of view the USA is a good testing ground: 'The American market is unforgiving – Sweden's L. M. Ericsson, so successful elsewhere, has had an especially rough time there – but everybody who wants to be anybody has to chance it'.[37]

- Faced with this new competition which is global in terms of both geography and systems, European enterprises will find themselves ill-served by the model of non-development which derives from lack of European unity.

In fact the Japanese and American models which create competitiveness, as shown earlier, seem to be holding good for the new telecommunications strategies.

The Competitiveness of European Enterprises 71

■ America's rate for progress and her spurt in telecommunications are based on a lively dynamic industrial fabric. By deregulating this immense market the government has made it attractive for enterprises to apply at speed the very wide range of recent technical advances in electronics most of which, as we know, are the outcome of major defence and space projects. All the evidence shows that the enterprises which apparently intend to lead this commanding technology have great international strategic capability.

It will be recalled that the two leaders' net surpluses for 1985 were:

	$ million
	2,622
ATT	623

Furthermore, they are no longer going it alone; as we have seen, they are seeking to strengthen their capacity by a whole set of international alliances. In giving priority to decentralised telecommunications they are tackling the end customer, having apparently learned the lesson of mass-production strategy from the Japanese.

Decisive competitive advantages on the most demanding market in the world are there to be won by dynamic firms. As we have seen, cost advantages are already being achieved in many products and unless other markets are opened up the existing leaders could move further and further ahead.

Here too the Japanese remain faithful to their development model; national objectives have been clearly set. We saw MITI's avowed intention to convert the Japanese economy into an information economy, with total commitment to the creation of an Information Network System – our ISDN. The potential budgets are enormous: $80–120 billion over 15 years plus a probable $250 billion in private investment.

NTT[38] has also played a very important part through its large research laboratories and policy of public contracts. This has greatly helped Japanese electronics enterprises to grow to their present level and is currently providing encouragement for research in opto-electronics.

Starting from this modernised, well-focused base, the Japanese are beginning to deregulate their market, particularly in the VAN and office-machine areas. They are still true to the idea of internal competition but seem to be extending it to foreigners.

The Japanese are thus pursuing simultaneously the technology-push strategy of a single ISDN and the market-pull strategy of VANs and private telephone systems. The balanced combination of directed effort plus competition corresponds perfectly with their development model with one difference only: the model seems to be opening slightly more to foreigners.

The enterprises involved are major diversified groups such as NEC, Toshiba, Mitsui, Mitsubishi, Sony, etc. All have strategic capabilities that enable them to seize new opportunities and make long-term plans. Their net surpluses are sizeable albeit lower than the Americans':

Matsushita	405
Hitachi	344
Toshiba	141
NEC	110
Sony	119
Mitsubishi	77

and because of this they are pursuing a very lively policy of international cooperation.

■ When we turn to European enterprises there have been remarkable successes in winning significant technical leadership. Siemens, Ericsson, Cit-Alcatel, Bell Telephone (ITT), etc., have been in the forefront of progress in certain key areas of telecommunications, particularly as regards central switching (Systems 12 and 10), private telephone systems, videotext, remote copying, etc.

A few European enterprises are emerging as highly competitive in world equipment sales, for instance in public switching sales (1989).[39]

ATT	25.3%
Alcatel	18.5%
Siemens	13.2%
Northern Telecom	10.5%

Ericsson/CGCT   8.3%
NEC   8.3%
GTP-Stromberg   5.1%
Fujitsu   4.6%
Italtel   3.9%
GTE   2.3%

As a result of bold action at European level, it has been possible to regain the initiative in the face of international competition. Summer 1986 witnessed a major alignment of the telecommunications activities of the CGE and ITT. The Société Générale de Belgique also joined this new consortium.

The new group, Alcatel, has a European management. It will have a turnover of nearly 12,000 million dollars and will employ a staff of more than 160,000 in 75 countries. In the central switchgear sector it has the advantage of a genuine technological lead (System 12) and a range of high-performance products, notably those for which the CGE occupies a strong position on the international market: fifth place in the world league table for telecommunications, second place for mail processing and telecopying, second place for telecommunication cables and first place for videotext terminals.

As a result of this realignment, Alcatel is now number two in the world for telecommunications, with the necessary stature to face up to competition on a global scale.

This is what the league table looks like on the basis of the 1987 total turnover figures for telecommunications (in millions of ECUs).[40]

ATT (USA)	9,000
Alcatel (France + USA)	6,800
Siemens (Federal Republic of Germany)	5,400
Northern Telecom (Canada)	4,100
LM Ericsson (Sweden)	2,800
NEC (Japan)	4,400
GTE (USA)	1,000
Philips (Netherlands)	1,500
GPT (GEC + Plessey) (UK)	1,600
Fujitsu (Japan)	1,700
Italtel (Italy)	900

Other major alignment manoeuvres are currently under way: Plessey and GEC in the UK; ATT, Philips, Telefonica (Spain) and Olivetti; GTE and Siemens; Northern Telecom (Canada) and STC (UK); Italtel and Teletra have set up Telit; Ericsson, Matra and CGTC.

As the competition intensifies and becomes more global we may wonder if Europe's competitive advantages may not soon be negated unless we create a unified 'telecommunications Europe'. Indeed, in the absence of a large home market as in the USA (different national standards and regulations) or a large-scale ISDN-type project as in Japan, our enterprises will not be in a position to strengthen their strategic capability sufficiently to fight the new global American and Japanese champions.

In this respect Arthur D. Little's study for the European Commission is alarming. It brings out two major problems:

★ The regulations and practices of the postal and telegraph authorities which are completely isolating them from the market and slowing the race towards competitiveness.
★ The fragmentation of the market and the protection of national champions which, as we know, are very destructive of competitiveness.

The effect is that the development of our communications infrastructures is much slower and our most advanced enterprises are forced to go for more distant markets in which it is harder for them to recoup the cost of technical progress (developing a central switching facility today costs $1 billion and needs to be amortised by a $10–15 billion turnover over the succeeding ten years).

In these circumstances the absence of a genuinely common market is suicidal. A further negative effect is that it prevents our national champions from raising their strategic capabilities to a world scale. No European company is yet playing a world role. It seems likely that the constellations of the future will cluster around American companies. A comparison of net surpluses for 1985 (capacity for taking the risks of strategic progress) highlights the danger of the negative effect:

	$ million
Siemens	196
Philips	110
CGE	34
Ericsson	34

compared with the following competitors or partners:

IBM	2,622
ATT	623
Matsushita	405
Hitachi	344
Toshiba	141
Northern Telecom	120
NEC	110

All is not lost but the new facts of the competitive market suggest that we are in a different ball game. Even the largest Americans are operating international alliance strategies. Isolated by their inability to expand to the size of a unified Europe, can European enterprises remain competitive? If not, will they not be tempted to become part of one of the American-dominated giant constellations?

Clearly the creation of a unified, deregulated market is an essential condition of the survival of independent European enterprises; a large-scale common project is certainly another. The huge sums which the Japanese plan to invest in their ISDN shows us where international competition is heading. Unless Europe promotes both strategies simultaneously her enterprises will be trapped in a model which destroys their competitiveness, caught between the Americans, spurred by competition and an enormous market, and the Japanese, guided and supported by a grand common project.

Possibility of a major European project
In his recent book[41] Ian Mackintosh, an electronics consultant, proposes a project closely resembling Japan's to bring Europe forward from the computer age to the era of information. He suggests massive investment in the order of $400 billion (Japan: $350 billion) to create a broadband ISDN-type network which he calls Eurogrid. The investment would provide Europe with a

very advanced standardised communications system and would stimulate the entire European information-technology industry. He too, sees Europe as threatened in this area:

> Europe is in danger of slipping into a serious competitive disadvantage. The US is far ahead in its appreciation of the information society. Japan has already planned its broadband network. By comparison Europe has yet to embark seriously on the difficult and costly journey from the Computer Age to the Era of Information. With only a few exceptions, industry and commerce and governments in Europe still function on the basis of voice communication, data processing and paper records. It is slow, expensive and inefficient.

The same theme recurs in a European Round Table of Industrialists report.[42] A number of interesting features emerge from their survey of user requirements:

- Demand is growing much faster for data transmission than for voice transmission and most of this relates to trans-European services.
- There are specific complex needs for thick file or complicated drawing transmission or for transmission to very isolated addresses.
- VANs are showing very rapid expansion and are expected to grow from $0.5 billion in 1984 to $3.4 billion in 1990 for electronic mail and data bank transmission.
  Users have few complaints regarding internal services in their respective countries but are highly critical of the existing situation for trans-European calls and worry about the future:
- Coordination is lacking in trans-European telecommunication services.
- Equipment approval regulations are costly and largely ineffective; in most countries the equipment has to be rented, which prevents undertakings from operating central purchasing or equipment policies.
- Telecommunication service supplier strategies are inconsistent and the treatment the different services receive is preferential or adverse depending on the country.

The Competitiveness of European Enterprises 77

■ International standards are not compatible and efforts to remedy this are slow and badly coordinated.

The writers say that collaboration must be increased or speeded up and that Europe constitutes an excellent base as the industry is not lagging and the relevant authorities are highly competent to deal with these problems.

Furthermore, in 1985 the EEC formulated a communications policy which recognised that, despite European enterprises' technical mastery, greater cooperation was essential in the production of equipment and services if Europe wished to maintain and develop its competitiveness. The writers of the report make the following recommendations with regard to this policy:

■ Consumers should be more closely associated with formulating European business communication policy.
■ The rules governing use of user equipment in Europe should be unified.
■ Introduction of new key services in Europe should be synchronised.
■ There should be a more uniform price structure which better reflects the cost of providing each service.
■ The installation of a cheaper, more efficient European switching facility should be speeded up and medium- and high-speed lines should be made available for rental at competitive prices and within reasonable installation times.

NOTES

1 FAST, see particularly: TET 4, TET 9, SERV 4, SERV 5, SERV 7, COM 1, COM 2, COM 8, ALIM 1, etc.
2 A study of biotechnology patents shows that Europe is appreciably more creative than Japan but much less so than the United States (appendix 10).
3 RAMSES 86–87. IFRI – Economics.
4 It is worth noting that GM has already spent more than $40 billion in the last five years on this kind of modernisation; European enterprises have also responded vigorously.
5 Grinyer (1986); Bibeault (1981).

6 What Mr Fiat learnt, *Economist*, 30 August 1986, p. 9.
7 Rumelt (1982); Desclee (1988).
8 Piantoni (1986); *Economist*, 30 August 1986, p. 10.
9 *Economist*, 30 August 1986, p. 9.
10 High-speed train.
11 Télésis, Report Excerpts, Paris 1981–5.
12 See in particular: Peters and Waterman (1983); the work of P. Drucker, the cases of the Harvard Business School, the many analyses carried out by *Fortune, Business Week*, etc.
13 The West refers to this type of system as ISDN (integrated services digital network).
14 Source: *Telecommunications. A Survey, Economist*, 23 November 1985.
15 For a more detailed analysis of MITI see particularly *MITI's Industrial Policy* in the excellent Survey of Japan, *Economist*, 23 February 1980.
16 See note 15.
17 High technology Survey: Chips with everything, *Economist*, 23 August 1986.
18 There have been many investigations of Japanese group performance and we may cite here the work of the INSEAD Euro-Asia group and Ohmae (1985).
19 Stopford and Turner (1985); de Woot and Desclee (1984); Daems (1977); Channon (1978).
20 Delmas (1985).
21 Source: Electronics International Corporation, *L'Electronique dans le monde*, quoted by Le Boucher (1986).
22 Nora and Minc (1978).
23 Rodgers (1986).
24 De Lamarter (1986).
25 The high tech race, *Fortune*, 13 October 1986, pp. 28–30.
26 Dataquest estimate.
27 Ferguson, MIT.
28 Delmas 1985.
29 Much of this section is drawn from the Survey on telecommunications, *Economist*, 23 November 1985.
30 LANs = local area networks.
31 Survey on telecommunications, *Economist*, 23 November 1985, p. 20.
32 Survey on telecommunications, *Economist*, 23 November 1985, p. 7.
33 Survey on telecommuncations, *Economist*, 23 November 1985, p. 8.

34 See in particular FAST project COM 1, Laurent Gille, June 1986.
35 For the whole of this part see *Economist*, 23 November 1985, pp. 33 and 34.
36 Survey on telecommunications, *Economist*, 23 November 1985.
37 Survey on telecommunications, *Economist*, 23 November 1985, p. 11.
38 Nippon Telegraph and Telephone.
39 Source: *Financial Times*, 18 Jan. 1989.
40 Source: Northern Business Information.
41 MacKintosh (1986).
42 European Round Table of Industrialists, Clearing the lines, November 1986; Oultrement (1986).

3

International Cooperation

The globalisation of markets and the accelerating rate of technical progress are forcing many enterprises to adopt a global strategy. Failure here could mean their being overtaken, even dominated by major international competitors. As the previous chapters show, for the enterprise it is a question of creating sufficient corporate strategic capability to win international (global) competitive advantages.

Such a capability depends on a number of interdependent factors:

- A healthy base which generates adequate cash flow.
- Strategic choices which are sufficiently bold and far-sighted to place the enterprise among the emerging generations of technology.
- Development of key global strategic resources (management, R&D, networks, information).
- A capacity for innovation, change and adaptation allowing rapid response to opportunities and threats.

Unless our enterprises can improve their strategic capability to the level of world competition they will enter a process of potentially mortal decline.

3.1 DIRECT INVESTMENT ABROAD

There are a number of routes to international development, the simplest of which is independent growth. This gives an enterprise maximum freedom, control over initiatives and 100% of any profit resulting from its efforts.

It is a route often taken by enterprises having sufficient sectorial strength or advance to take it without excessive risk and has long been the main strategy of efficient large groups such as IBM, Siemens, Boeing, Xerox, Ericsson, etc., or of smaller enterprises which nevertheless lead their field like Bekaert, Benetton, Magotteaux, Apple, the Swedish robot manufacturers, etc.

If we ignore exports pure and simple, expansion by this route involves the creation of subsidiaries abroad or the acquisition of existing enterprises and enterprises employing this dominant 'direct investment' strategy[1] must therefore be stronger or more advanced than their major competitors if it is to be successful.

Direct investment is not the subject of this report and we shall just mention it briefly.

A major acceleration in the takeover of undertakings has occurred over the last few years. Takeovers have become one of the chief means of promoting growth or diversification. In the United States alone, takeovers have been increasing at a spectacular rate:

2,500 in 1984
3,000 in 1985
3,300 in 1986[2]

While this phenomenon is attributable to the growth strategies pursued by the companies, it is further accentuated by the increased activity of the commercial banks and by the presence of financial raiders, pure and simple.

A number of these takeovers have assumed considerable proportions. A list of major takeovers bids for UK companies in 1986 is annexed hereto.

The main bids were in excess of 2,000 million pounds sterling.

John Stopford demonstrates clearly how important the strategy has been since the early 1900s and figure 3.1 shows the extraordinary international growth of the USA, the recent but rapid rise of Japan and Germany and the recent comeback of the UK. The international importance of small countries such as Switzerland and the Netherlands should be emphasised.

International Cooperation

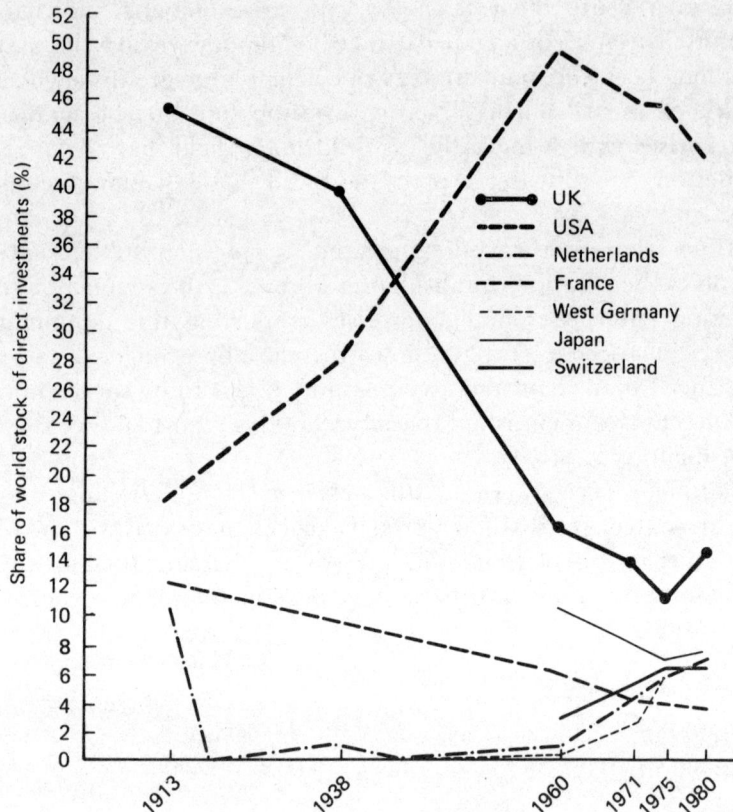

Figure 3.1 Long-run trends in the share of foreign direct investment by leading capital-exporting countries, 1913–1980[a]

[a] Stopford and Turner (1982).

Source: Data for 1913 and 1938 from J. H. Dunning (1983): Changes in the level and structure of international production: the last 100 years, in Mark Casson (ed.) (1983), *The Growth of International Business*, London, George Allen & Unwin. Data for 1960 onwards from J. M. Stopford and J. H. Dunning (1982), *Multinationals: Company Performance and Global Trends*, London, Macmillan, table 13.

- Stopford shows clearly that in recent years this kind of British corporate investment has been concentrated in the USA. The top 66 British multi-nationals are manufacturing abroad to the tune of some £100 billion and 40% of this is concentrated in the United States (see table 3.1).

Recent spectacular acquisitions in the USA are well known (Nestlé bought out Carnation, ICI bought Beatrice Chemicals,

Table 3.1 Foreign output of 66 multi-nationals by territory, 1983

	No. of firms	Foreign production (£ million)			
		Total	USA	Europe	Other
Over £2,000 million	6	59,700	21,000	21,000	17,700
£750–1,999 million	20	21,500	11,000	4,500	6,000
£450–749 million	20	11,600	4,500	3,000	4,100
£200–449 million	20	5,900	2,600	1,400	1,900
Total	66	98,700	39,100	29,900	29,700

Source: Stopford and Dunning, 1985.

British Oxygen took over Airco, Hoechst took Celanese, etc.).

Between 1980 and 1986 the pattern of direct foreign investment in the United States was as shown in table 3.2.

European market fragmentation, over-capacity in traditional sectors, the national champions policy in the emerging systems have all been significant obstacles to the creation of a solid European base for multi-nationals.

Bulldozing a path into Europe today cannot, it would seem, be

Table 3.2 Direct foreign investment in the USA, 1980–1986

Investor countries	thousands of millions of dollars	
	1980	1986
Switzerland	5.1	12.1
Federal Republic of Germany	7.6	17.4
Canada	12.1	18.3
Japan	4.7	32.4
Netherlands	19.1	42.9
United Kingdom	14.1	51.4

Source: For Sale: America, *Time*, 14 September 1987, p. 27. See also Stopford and Turner (1985); Eurostat, EEC, 1986.

achieved by acquisition on a major scale. The spirit of the Treaty of Rome does not extend to allowing control of a key national resource to slip into foreign hands, even when those hands are also European ... Economic nationalism remains a potent force and a major barrier to the free transfer of assets within the community. Only in a very few instances, such as Thomson Brandt's takeover of Telefunken's German consumer electronics activities or Philips' purchase of

Grundig, have major transnational acquisitions been permitted. Even in these examples, a major external threat in the form of the Japanese seemed barely sufficient to overcome still nationalistic resistance. If large-scale acquisition is not possible, transnational mergers or partnership seem equally difficult. The 1960s and 1970s spawned various attempts to repeat the earlier Shell and Unilever successes; all have failed or seem about to.[3]

Here we could name many unsuccessful attempts: Unidata, SGPM-Olivetti-Bull, Dunlop-Pirelli, Lucas-Ducellier, United Biscuits-Le Brun, Thorn EMI-Locatel, CGE-AEG, etc.

Total foreign investment by European enterprises between 1980 and 1984 breaks down as follows (in millions of ECU):[4]

USA	29,045	= 61%
Trans-European	17,627	= 38%
Japan	539	= 1%

Sweden also shows the same trend of a weaker European base and a stronger presence in the USA.[5]

The Europeans are investing more in the USA than in other European countries but hardly at all in Japan. Table 3.3 shows that the Japanese are the true 'triadians'. With the exception of a few very large multi-nationals (see figure 3.2) our enterprises have still not developed a sufficient global strategic capability.[6]

● As far as internationalisation of the different sectors is concerned we may advance the following hypotheses: European enterprises achieved internationalism in the mature sectors first because it was in these sectors that they had developed an adequate strategic capability. This is borne out for the UK whose foreign investment in 1963 breaks down as follows:[7]

65% on low-tech activities
11% on medium-tech activities
19% on high-tech activities

Even though the situation is changing, the change comes very late compared with American and Japanese competitors and is certainly not enough to place European enterprises in the forefront of the coming major generations of technology.

Table 3.3 Authorised foreign direct investment regions (%)

	1971	1975	1980	1985
Norway, Finland, Denmark, Switzerland	15.0	21.0	12.1[a]	15.3
Great Britain, Netherlands, Italy, West Germany, France, Belgium	32.7	36.6	26.0	21.5
USA	6.9	11.7	31.4	31.0
Canada	13.1	1.0	2.9	–
Japan	1.3	4.5	–	–
Brazil	3.0	8.0	2.8	1.0
Other	28.0	17.2	24.8	31.2
Total	100.0	100.0	100.0	100.0

[a] Excluding Switzerland.
Source: Sveriges Riksbank, Förvaltningsberättelse, 1975, 1980, and 1985; Ohmae (1985); Hedlund, 1986.

We can then suggest that in the high-tech sectors many European enterprises are not strong enough to 'internationalise' by themselves. In fact they have no continental base and started late to invest in the United States and Japan. Many of them thus lack an adequate strategic capability to conquer world markets on their own and for this reason are forced to adopt, at least in part, a strategy of international cooperation as the only means of broadening their strategic capability and making up for lost time. That this approach is essential is borne out by the way it is being adopted by the most advanced multi-nationals, e.g., IBM, ATT, Siemens, Boeing, Philips, NEC, Hitachi, etc., which had hitherto developed independently.

One disturbing feature should be noted: all the writers regard cooperation as a less desirable option than independent expansion because of the complexities involved and the management qualities which it demands.

The case of Sweden is particularly illuminating. Hedlund[8] shows that Swedish enterprises have little recourse to international

86 International Cooperation

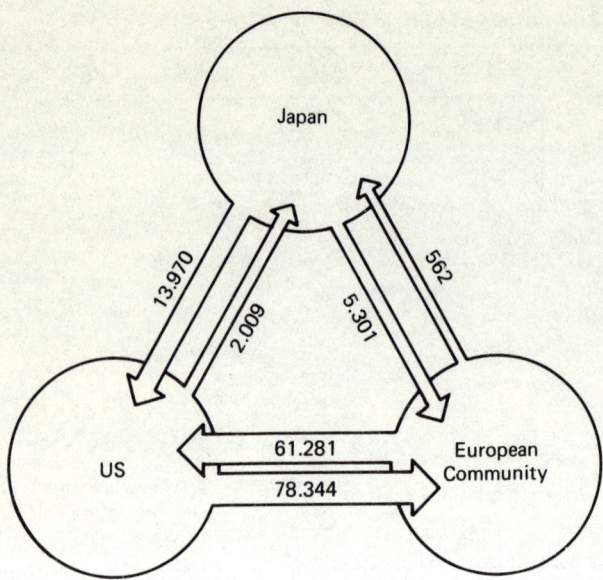

Figure 3.2 Investment interchange among Japan, the USA and the European Community (cumulative total at end of fiscal 1982; unit $1 million)[a]

Japan–USA and Japan–European Community figures represent cumulative totals as of end of fiscal 1982 on authorisation and registration basis.

European Community figures represent total for ten nations. However, in the case of European direct investment in Japan, figure represents total for six countries (West Germany, Britain, France, Netherlands, Belgium and Denmark).

[a] Ohmae (1985).

Source: Data from Bank of Japan, Survey of Current Business as quoted by Masuo Shibata, Looking Together for Tomorrow's World, *Journal of Japanese Trade and Industry*, no. 11984, pp. 19–24.

cooperation and do not seem to be developing systematic strategies in this regard. For example, ASEA Robotics is one of the very few large robotics firms not to be involved in a complex web of cooperation.[9] Swedish enterprises give priority to an independent internationalisation strategy either by their own expansion or by acquisition, thus opting for the 'first choice' and tending to regard cooperation as a last resort. Doubtless this is explained by the lack of public protection on the home market plus its small size. In order to survive in high-tech activities

Swedish enterprises are forced to export to difficult markets and develop an international strategic capability; they thus partly evade the European model. This is also true of another small country, Switzerland.

Interestingly, in their high-tech developments, Swedish firms regard the American market as more important than the European and their investment in the USA is more expansionist and more innovative. The pharmaceutical firms, for example, place very great importance on the American market which enables them to follow the latest developments. The same applies to the manufacturers of advanced scientific instruments, of equipment for the biochemical industry, of materials for high-tech applications etc., as exemplified inter alia by the strong position of Alfa-Laval in Genentech.

The current trend is for Swedish enterprises to invest in conquering large and what are regarded as technologically advanced markets. This occurs not only in America but also in the Japanese market, penetration of which many Swedish enterprises regard as essential.

By contrast, Swedish investment in Europe is more defensive. A major preoccupation in markets already won is total industrial reorganisation on a European basis – this is particularly the case with Electrolux (household equipment), Esab (welding), Esselte (office equipment). The strategy involves multiple acquisitions with an eye to rationalising the production and distribution networks.

It also involves the concentration and specialisation of production in a few factories; SKF is a pioneer in the field with its GFSS.[10] This approach gives very advanced mastery of automated production and could constitute a basis for international development in the form, for example, of exports to the USA. Volvo's recent success in turning round the White Truck Corporation was based on the same competitive advantage in production techniques.

The contrast between rationalising 'mature' industries in Europe and investing in high tech in the USA is exaggerated but genuinely reflects a basic trend. The policy pursued by Swedish multi-nationals would seem to confirm Europe's relative decline in high-tech areas as a focus of investment.

3.2 COOPERATION AS A COMPETITIVE STRATEGY

3.2.1 Different forms

Industrial cooperation takes many very different forms. In certain functions it tends to substitute behavioural patterns founded on agreement and collective action for competitive behaviour founded on rivalry and conflict. As Jacquemin suggests, cooperation varies greatly in intensity: at one extreme, tacit cooperation (collusion not cooperation), at the other, total integration of individual or collective partners who renounce all sovereignty over all or part of their activity: merger or joint venture, and, in between, any number of forms which allow divergent interests to persist. ('Within these formulas each partner seeks to safeguard his strategic advantages and the possibility, should he so wish, of regaining independence, cooperating with others or modifying the original agreements.')[11]

Specialists differentiate between traditional-type agreements and more complex forms such as networks.[12]

- Traditional types include *technological agreements*. They provide access to technical shortcuts and make it possible to catch up or diversify. For example, Japanese enterprises bought many licences to catch up on foreign competitors; nowadays they both buy and sell (Hitachi-Thomson, Matsushita-3M-Sanyo-Intel, Fujitsu-IBM, Mitsubishi-Boeing, Philips-Grundig-Sony) and their agreements increasingly go hand-in-hand with joint industrial operations, either in Japan (to protect their know-how) or abroad (to penetrate frontiers). This type of cooperation develops towards two-way exchange of know-how and joint research. Cooperation agreements in the field of semi-conductors are often of that type (appendix 21).
- Then there is *commercial or financial cooperation*. This makes it possible to extend and globalise distribution networks. The vast majority of robotics and machine-tool agreements boil down to import/distribution/maintenance contracts regardless of whether the importer also manufactures.[13]

A financial agreement makes it possible to strengthen

International Cooperation 89

the foreign partner by taking up shares (BL (Rover)-Honda, Nissan-Alfa Romeo) or to take part in an international project or joint venture as, for example, with GM and Toyota who resolved on joint production of a small car (the Corolla). This type of agreement, clearly, can lead to multiple cooperation arrangements.

Shareholding (or partial control) in foreign enterprises allows three strategic advantages to be pursued.[14]

■ By seeking new technologies through venture capital (e.g. Showa Denko's current investment in the US); here the transition from financial cooperation to takeover pure and simple is rapid.[15]

■ By seeking independence and the creation of a genuinely global group (e.g. Fujitsu's acquisition of a significant holding in Amdahl).

■ By seeking production capacity in smaller, weaker competitors (Nissan's 33%, later 65%, holding in Motor Ibérica).

● There are also *more complex agreements* which incorporate the technical and marketing aspects.

■ Here the OEM (Original Equipment Manufacturing) is becoming increasingly important.

Under this kind of agreement, manufacturer A of product X supplies manufacturer B with a finished product or components which B uses or markets under his own name. Briefly: in any OEM agreement the supplier-manufacturer gains a major outlet, benefits from economies of scale and appreciable experience, retains his know-how, penetrates a market via his partner's network with no servicing problems and finally, is in a position to discourage his partner (and even local competitors) from developing their own production; the buyer/distributor-manufacturer can supplement his output or, more generally, widen his range with a new product, which he previously lacked, at no R&D or tooling cost and minimum commercial risk ... OEM agreements may be concluded for virtually any product but are mainly found in robotics, mass electronics, computers, household electrical goods (OEM agreements are common in this area in Europe) and the motor industry (GM distributes in Australia a 1500 cc car which Nissan makes in Australia).

The products usually involved are new products for which the final vendor lacks the know-how or the appropriate R&D or production capacity.[16]

- Other complex agreements are based on the complementary nature of the partners' strengths and weaknesses in the value chain and may cover a number of functions, markets and products.

• Finally there are *agreement networks (or 'multipolar joint working')*. These may be likened to:

- The sun: the rays link the various protagonists to a single centre to serve the strategy of a central enterprise (IBM or ATT at the centre of an Information Service system: see appendix 9).

Or to:

- A spider's web: all points are interlinked to pursue a common strategy.

Whichever the case this is no longer a simple bilateral arrangement but a highly complex multiple process which is difficult to operate and vulnerable to every disagreement.[17] It also raises a new phenomenon: the alliance portfolio which must be optimised in the same way as a portfolio of products, technologies, or shares.

Many international cooperation agreements exist and are mainly concentrated in the technical commercial fields. In table 3.4 we give a breakdown by type of Japanese enterprises' international cooperation agreements:[18]

3.2.2 An external strategic weapon which can lead to dominance

The enterprises see it as offering sure strategic advantages, the first being development of their strategic capability. The value

Table 3.4 Number of contracts declared to FTC (Federal Trade Commission) by type (numbers)

		1975			*1980*			*1981*	
	Total	*Input*	*Output*	*Total*	*Input*	*Output*	*Total*	*Input*	*Output*
Technical cooperation	1,552	1,198	354	2,098	1,522	576	2,057	1,488	58
Representation	826	417	409	1,284	589	695	1,165	512	653
Joint enterprise	255	78	177	248	72	176	178	72	106
Use of trade marks	70	60	10	384	353	31	329	282	47
Finance	1,182	1,119	63	639	511	128	391	190	201
Sundry	1,284	1,156	128	1,485	925	560	1,596	973	623
Total	5,169	4,028	1,141	6,138	3,972	2,166	5,716	3,517	1,688

Input: imports of foreign know-how, capital, etc.
Output: exports of Japanese know-how, capital, etc.
Source: Turcq, 1985 p. 110.

chain concept is highly relevant here. As we saw in chapter 1, strategic capability particularly depends on a balance between the corporate functions and such a balance is the result of well-developed resources within each function plus the ability to manage them correctly.[19]

It may be that enterprises have failed to develop balance sufficiently at the international level and need cooperation in research, production or distribution in order to achieve it.

Furthermore, there is no one optimum size corresponding to lowest possible unit cost for all of a firm's activities. By contrast, there are different levels of indivisibility and optimum size depending on the function considered (production, marketing, distribution, finance, research). Given this, cooperation can allow the enterprise to reach efficient size in a given function without imposing unnecessary growth overall.[20]

Other advantages of cooperation largely relate to the question of prospects and opportunities because cooperation enables firms to seize wider opportunities and extend their planning horizon. Bringing their strategic capabilities together increases their chances of success in bolder projects and allows them to take greater risks.

Finally, it can speed up the effect of experience as it favours greater specialisation (division of work) and greater volume (more outlets).

The more dynamic enterprises are not wrong in their belief that cooperation can constitute a suitable strategic weapon for responding to global technological competition, and, in fact, they are having more and more recourse to it.

Recent original work[21] makes it clear that the effects of cooperation are not simply external but operate within the coalition on the partners themselves who, though collaborating in some aspects, are competing in others; to put it another way, cooperation is not 100% pure but is rather an extension of competition in a different form (Doz). Cooperation could thus progressively drive a weaker partner into a permanently dependent or inferior position.

Jacquemin shows that one partner may have aggressive intentions towards the other; he may aim to obtain maximum information, poach key resources, take early advantage of the learning curve so as to catch up and surpass his partner, blackmail him into changing the coalition, apply trickery, etc.

Turcq shows the need to be in control and poses clearly the problem of knowing who will benefit from working together in the long term. As he shows, the agreement may reflect a situation of very different strengths which are constantly changing. The enterprise which is more dynamic or better able to turn the agreement to its own advantage can rapidly rise to a dominant position and in Turcq's opinion Japanese international agreements often fall into this category: 'They correspond to alliance strategies aimed at strengthening the competitive strengths of the contracting parties without necessarily spreading the benefit equally between the parties in the long term.' He goes on to draw four caricature agreements:

- The stepping-stone agreement whereby one enterprise rises above the other.
- The 'prosthese' agreement whereby both enterprises survive and may one day do without the device.
- The burial agreement which foretells the death of independence and sometimes digs its grave.
- The obstetric agreement which brings a new industrial entity into being.

He also shows how aggressive, even imperialist, the OEM system can be: a corpus of OEM agreements involving a number of countries gives the manufacturer lower cost coverage of much of the world market; high profit margins, thanks to zero investment in marketing, allow him to invest heavily in R&D and production capacity and as soon as he has sufficient mastery he can decide to do the client's job himself and carry on alone.

Doz, Hamel and Prahalad take the analysis even further by showing the factors which can influence relative strengths in a strategic cooperation agreement. It is the actual functioning of the cooperative process which determines whether the balance of power between partners will be maintained or destroyed and the process itself embodies the risk of dangerous strategic encroachment by one party on the other. These factors are described below:

- *Strategic intent*: One partner's intentions may be far more aggressive or imperialist than the other's. If partner A is aiming at world leadership and partner B is pursuing a defensive strategy of consolidation, A's behaviour will be more aggressive and will seek dominance by concentrating skills and maximum added value within his own sphere by controlling know-how and relegating B to the position of a mere distributor; he will also try to extract B's distinctive skills. By speeding up the rate of new product development A will retain the investment initiative and will force B to follow him on increasingly tricky conditions.[22]

  He may also use blackmail to form new alliances or terminate them and finally, he may force his partners into proxy battles against dominant competitors – thus NEC and Fujitsu, the Japanese partners, dispatched ICL, Bull, Siemens and Amdahl to the front in their stead to do battle with IBM.

  > IBM could accept local competition in Europe which was relatively weak but enjoyed 'national champion' protection but it became much more aggressive when the European firms started to sell Japanese goods: its somewhat sharp reaction succeeded in cutting their sales and profit margins. In this case the European allies of Japanese firms were the cannon fodder in a global war and undoubtedly find themselves in a worse position than before cooperation with the Japanese.[23]

- *Transferability of contributions and skills*: Relative strengths change significantly if one partner rapidly takes over the other's resources and skills. This depends on how explicit or tacit is the nature of the skills (a tacit skill is more difficult to comprehend and capture) and on whether they are equipment-embodied or not (equipment-embodied skills are much

more easily captured). The writers suggest that Western partners' contributions are more explicit and equipment-embodied than those of the Japanese who place more reliance on *savoir-faire* and socio-organisational processes. The difference clearly places Europe at a disadvantage.
- *The organisation's learning curve*, i.e. the speed with which one partner can learn from the other, also influences the partners' relative strength. The learning curve depends particularly on the quality of an enterprise's vertical and horizontal communications. The Japanese have a long tradition of selective corporate learning and have even developed systematic approaches to it.[24]

The writers end their analysis by suggesting that international cooperation is a complex process which can lead to one partner's dominance. If relative strengths are to be understood the component factors must be considered in their totality rather than individually and should be viewed in dynamic perspective. The writers show clearly that an even balance of strength between the partners is essential in all three areas referred to if dominance by one is to be avoided. The situation becomes even more dangerous in the case of alliance or cooperation networks like those described for telecommunications or components. The principal object here is to win a central or 'nodal' position and enterprises at the periphery are more exposed to domination if the linking threads are bilateral rather than multilateral.

The existence of international agreement networks may make European cooperation more difficult insofar as global cooperation has taken place faster than European. National European firms may thus find themselves trapped in an inferior position in international alliances because of their failure to unify at European level. The presence of American or Japanese partners may specifically prevent European enterprises from drawing closer together.

3.3 MANAGEMENT OF COOPERATION

International cooperation arrangements are difficult to manage. Where the relationship between partners is simultaneously collaborative and competitive there is ambiguity and the ability to manage this ambiguity becomes an important element of the game.[25]

Because of this the enterprise has to conduct cooperation on two levels:

- It must make the agreement effective in order to achieve the external alliance objectives – this comes from day-to-day management.
- It must retain sufficient control relative to its partner to avoid being dominated – this comes from strategic management.

3.3.1 Day-to-day management

To ensure consistency, efficiency and creativity is already difficult in the context of one company; to do it within a more complex arrangement[26] and, even more, for enterprises which are foreign to each other, increases the difficulty exponentially, which is why cooperation may always be said to be a less desirable option than independent development.[27] However, as we have seen, it is a choice which is often forced on enterprises by globalised competition and accelerated technical progress.

- Principles of day-to-day management which can serve in the area of cooperation are outside our subject and we shall not discuss them in detail.

  A useful starting point is complex systems management which calls for a high degree of both differentiation and integration. Integrative devices, conflict management and familiarity with the environment and the strategic stakes are an essential point of departure.

  Day-to-day management of cooperative arrangements and consortia entails keeping a close eye on the following:[28]

  - Ensuring the presence within each enterprise of sponsors who are convinced of the usefulness of the consortium or joint venture.
  - Giving them responsibility for cooperation over a sufficiently long period for them to monitor and influence it.

- Developing within the enterprises mechanisms for communication, interchange and confrontation to different hierarchical levels: top management, operational executives and staff.
- Spending more time and effort on communication than on control.

● A recent work studies a number of organisational models for cooperation[29] from which some emerge as clearly superior to others in terms of results.

- *The pilot role structure*, the form preferred by Boeing. Here one partner takes the dominant role (leader) and exercises substantial control over the joint operations, often acting as the main contractor and subcontracting to the other international partners. Its power does not necessarily derive from its share of the contract but from the control which it exerts over certain key decisions such as choice of technology, size of output, marketing, division of labour, etc.
- *Cooperative structure* or 'task duplication' which has been used for the construction of several European military aircraft. Here leadership lies with committees of the partners' representatives. This model largely works by consensus, the partners retaining right of veto in certain important areas which can be decided only by unanimous decision. A large number of representative committees is set up to work out compromises which will satisfy all parties.

  Enterprises involved may not act without the consent of all the partners.
- *The integrated approach* or multi-national group which was the form chosen for Airbus. Here the partners create a new entity which is made the leader and given responsibility for the organisation.

  The model resembles the pilot role structure in the sense that a good deal of power is entrusted to one entity unilaterally but in the integrated structure it is an 'artificial' enterprise set up by the partners and its management team is drawn from the various members. It thus has genuine decision-making power, no longer operates by continual consensus and is not managed by a number of committees in a search for compromise (appendix 22).

The findings of studies of 11 aircraft consortia[30] are clear-cut; the cooperative structure is much less effective in terms of costs, delivery periods and objectives. Used mainly for military aircraft, it is imposed by the political will of governments.

These studies show that this type of model has favoured political as opposed to economic objectives and the negative effect for Europe can be seen. If cooperative structures originated mainly from military or political projects, our enterprises might be forced to adopt less efficient models than those of their major foreign competitors.

3.3.2 Strategic management

As we have seen, cooperation often creates ambiguity for the partners who are also competing. Control of such ambiguity becomes an important strategic weapon because it enables an enterprise to take over leadership of the coalition and avoid domination by its partners. There must be a balance of corporate strength, theoretically from the outset though this is not always the case, and the balance must be maintained throughout the period of the agreement.

A number of important factors have recently been highlighted.[31]

- The agreement must fit into the enterprise's global strategy. It is not simply a question of short-term maximisation of results; cooperation must also be used as a weapon in its global strategy as a means of developing its own strategic capability and gaining international leadership.
- The management of inter-partner relations must be dynamic and detailed; a balance of skills and resources must be maintained; relative strengths must not be allowed to alter to the detriment of one; each partner's dynamism must be the

same; close watch must be kept on the danger of domination by one partner.
- A key feature of strategic management is control of transfers of technology. The enterprise's core technologies must be sufficiently protected for it to retain its competitive advantage.[32] It is also important to develop R&D resources systematically and to update the portfolio of know-how fast, whether emergent, specific or even basic technologies are involved.[33]
- The relative weights of the individual contributions must be managed throughout the life of the agreement, for if contributions are too small, the external strategic objective may not be attained and if they are too big, one partner may be tempted to appropriate the skills and resources of the other.
- Finally, one enterprise's receptivity and openness must be developed at least as fast as the other's. The structure's ability here may benefit from systematic learning and cumulative experience.

From this it follows that control of the cooperative game will greatly depend on the strategic capabilities present. An enterprise having relatively unambitious guidelines and strategic choices, a 'local' dimension and tardily updated competitive advantages will find itself in a genuinely inferior position relative to a more advanced or more international partner.

3.4 COOPERATION AND COMPETITIVE MODELS

Our earlier discussion of the development models which create or destroy competitiveness allows us to suggest that European enterprises are more vulnerable than their major foreign competitors in cooperation agreements. This is because the Japanese industrial system, based on subcontracting and shared priorities, leaves Japanese enterprises well-equipped for and significantly ahead in this area, while the American model has created such a technical lead and such large enterprises that American firms have a good chance of controlling the cooperative game and often of exerting dominant influence.

3.4.1 The Japanese model

This model favours cooperation and the development of aggressive cooperation strategies.[34] Turcq's work shows that, in Japan, cooperation is located at the point where voluntarist industrial policy meets corporate policies aimed systematically at greater internationalisation and this approach has created strong national cooperation agreements which constitute a solid base for international alliances. We know that MITI guides the Japanese economy towards the introduction and spread of new technologies; this often involves technical cooperation agreements between Japanese and with foreigners.

In addition, encouragement for the formation of Japanese coalitions has led to relatively loose-knit oligopolies. In computers, for example, the cooperation agreements are organised as follows:

- Fujitsu-Hitachi for IBM-compatible equipment
- NEC-Toshiba for non-compatible equipment
- Mitsubishi-Oki for peripherals

MITI does not manage the agreements but still wields its own particular brand of influence; it negotiates with industrial companies to ensure that they reach agreement on minimum contributions to collaboration (e.g. the creation of joint research laboratories). Thereafter, though the results are available to all, the parties compete with each other in any consequent commercial developments.

From this already solid starting point and backed by a range of incentives (public contracts, easy credit, export aids, etc.), Japanese enterprises launch out into major international cooperation agreements and enter into more complex networks. Their increased strategic capability based on their positions at home increases the likelihood of their attaining a sufficiently central position in such networks to avoid domination and sometimes even to take control. International cooperation agreements can take the form shown in figure 3.3.

In telecommunications,[35] when NTT was privatised and lost its monopoly, three groups were formed to compete with it in VANs:

International Cooperation   101

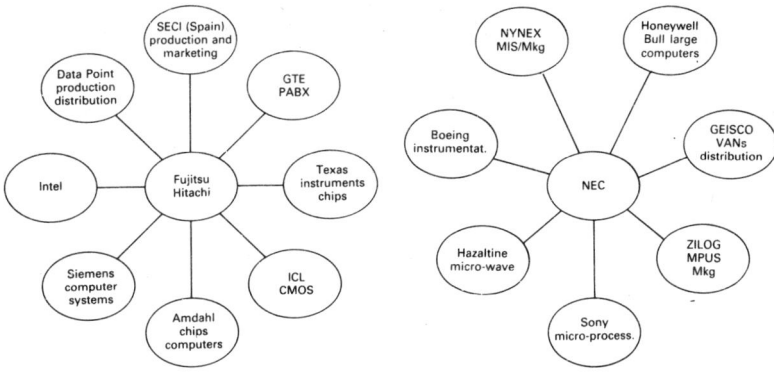

Figure 3.3 International cooperation agreements
Source: Doz et al. (1986).

- The first is organised around ATT, Mitsui and the Industrial Bank of Japan: it combines 14 other Japanese enterprises which include Sony, Nissan, Toyota, Dentsu (the foremost advertising agency in the world), Asahi Shimbun (the premier Japanese daily newspaper);
- The second comprises 12 potential users of ATT's VANs and includes Sumitomo Trading, the Bank of Tokyo, Nomura Securities, Nisho Iwai (a trading company), etc.;
- The third is the IBM-Mitsubishi Trading Group.

In addition, at the bottom of the agreement pyramid lies a very close-knit subcontracting network. In Japan, 85% of large Japanese enterprise production costs are located outside the enterprise.[35]

From this we can appreciate how well placed are the big Japanese firms for cooperation; they practise it on the local, national and international scale; they are supported by a powerful domestic base and follow convergent courses towards certain major technological advances; they have thus been able to create sufficient strategic capability to tackle international cooperation dynamically, even aggressively.

To some extent international agreements are then an extension of national agreements with the same twofold problem of alliance as to base knowledge and of competition as to developments. The object of international agreements is to form groups which by their very size can impose certain standards and to allow 'innovators' who control the know-how to work together with 'developers' who make only minor modifications to the product but control the production and 'followers' who control the distribution.[36]

Can it be by chance that Turcq's conclusion uses the word 'control' three times?

3.4.2 The American model

This model also favours cooperation and the development of aggressive strategies within it. We saw how well developed are relations between science-based SMEs, large multi-nationals, universities and government defence and space agencies. We also saw how the model promotes control over complex systems and continuous technical advance.

It is not surprising, therefore, that most of the American multi-nationals manage the coalitions which they are beginning to form. They usually tend to be the leaders and control relative strengths to their own advantage.

We have seen the role of IBM and ATT in telecommunications alliance networks and the position is the same for aviation. Boeing will not cooperate unless it is in control and the big aircraft engine companies like GE or Pratt & Whitney retain absolute control over their core technology (as does RR).

Japanese–American agreements studied by Turcq show that the Americans tend to seek Japanese enterprises already having powerful strategic capability, as with IBM and Matsushita and Mitsubishi or GM and Toyota. Both sides seem to be strong enough to avoid either being too far outweighed or dominated by the other. Turcq's work suggests that the game is played between evenly balanced teams even if the leadership lies with the larger, more advanced enterprise.

Does this denote a 'new form of cartel between different countries' companies'[37] – here Japan and the USA? Turcq thinks not in the caricatured form of a joint will to win. He does, however, fear a simpler reality: American and Japanese enterprises have long been accustomed to working together and reciprocal holdings are common. They often represent the largest national industries in the free world; by and large each provides the other with its principal foreign market. 'They have therefore tended to draw closer together. This closeness is today a source of joint action towards winning world markets. It allows them to achieve industrial and commercial intellectual 'critical mass' ... and American–Japanese technical standardisation of high tech products.[38]

3.4.3 The European model

Will the European model allow our enterprises to enter into international cooperation without risking loss of control or domination? This is highly unlikely unless we can change the compartmentalised, nationalist model in which our enterprises are too often trapped. Already cooperation is a second choice to independent expansion into which many European enterprises are forced because they lack adequate strategic capability; this must not be further compounded by their entering international alliances in a position of weakness.

The greatest European successes in collaboration have been based on joint European projects as in aviation, space or advanced research (Esprit, etc.). This approach has broadened the prospects of the enterprises involved and has stimulated development of improved strategic capability. Outside such projects we tend mainly to cooperate with non-European firms in relationships where relative strengths may be to our enterprises' disadvantage.

Some figures

● A survey[39] of 212 European enterprises which have concluded research agreements shows that:

- *30% were with enterprises of the same nationality*
- *Of the remaining 70%*
  26% were intro-European
  74% were with non-Europeans
- *70% involved two enterprises*

104   International Cooperation

- *30% involved more than two enterprises*
- *As far as the agreements with non-Europeans were concerned*:
  55% were with an American enterprise
  17% were with a Japanese enterprise
  23% were with enterprises of other nationalities
- *77% took the form of a simple agreement*
  23% created a joint company
- *24% were in chemicals*
  23% were in electrical and electronic products
  13% were in computers
  12% were in energy
  8% were in the motor industry

The list shows the low incidence of intra-European agreements, the preponderance of trans-Atlantic agreements and the low incidence of agreements with Japanese companies.

- Out of 197 joint subsidiaries set up in the EEC between 1982 and 1985:[40]

  - 24 were national operations
    35 were EEC operations
    41 were international operations
  - 75% were industrial
    25% were commercial

Again we see the preponderance of international over intra-European agreements. Another point which should be stressed is the relative lateness of commercial agreements.

- A Bocconi University study[41] of 1883 cooperation agreements reached by Italian enterprises between 1982 and 1985 also shows a low proportion of intra-European agreements (see table 3.5).

  Over and above the low proportion of European agreements, the study also shows the major extent of cooperation with the USA, almost one-half of agreements involving an American enterprise. Finally, the triad is involved in 78.1% of the agreements studied.
- Turcq's research[42] into agreements concluded by Japanese

International Cooperation

Table 3.5 Cooperation agreements reached by Italian enterprises, 1982–5*

%	Nationality of partner in Italian agreement
18.7	USA
15.0	Europe
3.1	Japan
21.9	Europe and USA
8.6	USA and Japan
10.8	Europe and Japan
21.9	Other

* Sinatra (1986).

enterprises shows the dominant position of the USA as single partner compared with a scatter of Europeans.

Almost 50% of agreements are with American enterprises. Were the EEC a single entity (same standards, regulations, networks, etc.) Euro-Japanese agreements would represent 40% of the total. This is significant because European fragmentation prevents such agreements from leading to a genuine globalisation of our enterprises. In fact, if we take the analysis a little further we find an uneven distribution of agreements between types:

- *Technical cooperation*
  50% with the USA
  40% with the EEC

- *Commercial cooperation*
  56% with the USA
  33% with the EEC

- *Joint ventures*
  66% with the USA
  26% with the EEC

Agreements with Europe are mostly technical (the Japanese have an eye to our research) whereas agreements with the USA lead to far more broadly based cooperation.

One major fact emerges: European cooperation is developing far more slowly than international cooperation. This is dangerous for European enterprises:

- They do not constitute a sufficiently broad base for 'domestic' cooperation; the scale of their strategic capability remains

national and is not developing sufficiently to the continental scale achieved by Japanese and American enterprises.
- They lack experience of managing cooperation arrangements and the inherent internal power strategies.
- They thus risk entering into international alliances less powerfully armed than their partners. Faced with 'competitor-allies' employing aggressive strategies they could find themselves lacking in resources and know-how and be rapidly reduced to a dependent position.

The compartmentalisation of the European market and the fact of inappropriate laws differing from one country to another have had a very negative effect. These laws have obstructed industrial reorganisation to meet international competition and have favoured the conclusion of agreements between local and international enterprises to the detriment of European groupings. For example:

> it is conceivable that Thomson's failure to strengthen its presence in Germany in 1983 because of a veto by the German Anti-competition Commission blocked the way to a strengthened European mass electronics industry and encouraged European industrialists to seek agreements with Japanese or American partners. The Japanese who, largely thanks to a state-controlled industrial policy from the 50s to the 70s, had succeeded in organising competition at home into oligopolies, were better placed than many others to pursue a policy of international agreements. In fact the stock onto which the policy was grafted was formed of relatively stable domestic competition (the monopoly laws prohibit over-concentrated oligopolies) which already comprised very powerful groups having a strong position in any negotiations.[43]

3.5 THE CASE OF THE AVIATION INDUSTRY

The case is of interest because it illustrates both the need for cooperation policies and the advantage here of a European base. It further shows the importance of major European projects and, finally, it highlights the essential nature of cooperation management.

3.5.1 Vital need for cooperation

Civil aviation is enjoying rapid *expansion*. It is a major market for our enterprises; forecast expansion up to 1990 is in the order of 6.7% with 5.5% from then to the year 2000.

World forecasts outside the Communist bloc predict more than 4,000 orders for 100-seat and larger aircraft over the next ten years to a value of $135–210 Billion. Over the next 20 years, commercial aircraft sales are expected to approach $500 billion of which more than 50% would go to Boeing.[44]

Technical progress is very rapid and mainly relates to engine/airframe ratio (weight, materials, room, range, etc.). It entails rising development costs; $3 billion for a new commercial aircraft (of which $1.5 billion each for airframe and engine) and the normal payback is eight years. In embarking on the development of a new aircraft, an enterprise gambles with its life.

Given the additional factor of very fierce competition, it is hardly surprising that one-quarter of the 6,400 commercial aircraft currently in service were sold at a loss and only 6 out of 20 made a profit (all 6 were American).

In one form or another every aircraft manufacturer has depended on large public contracts. American military orders have been a powerful support for enterprises in this sector and the figures given in table 3.6 are a good illustration of the

Table 3.6   American defence contractors*

The top ten in fiscal 1985 Company	Prime contract awards ($ billions)
McDonnel Douglas	8.8
General Dynamics	7.4
Rockwell	6.2
General Electric	5.8
Boeing	5.4
Lockheed	5.1
United Technologies	3.9
Hughes	3.5
Raytheon	3.0
Grumman	2.7

Source: US Department of Defence
* *The Economist*, 3 May 1986

American high-tech development model as we have described it.[45]

It should be noted in passing that America's 1984 defence budget was $300 billion, i.e. four times greater than the combined French, UK and German budgets. Despite military contracts, sector reorganisation was essential and was achieved through competition; great names like Northrop, General Dynamics, Rockwell and even Lockheed simply stopped working on civil aircraft.

In Europe, reorganisation took place within the narrow confines of individual countries and, though fairly drastic within these limits, was not enough to keep our enterprises in contention. Three years ago, for example, 10 airframe manufacturers and 5 engine manufacturers were still in business in the UK; today only one of each remains. This kind of national reorganisation was not enough and European enterprises found themselves forced into cooperation.

Lack of a European base had virtually destroyed the competitiveness of our enterprises; the gaps had become too wide and become startlingly clear if we take the simplistic approach of overall strength (see table 3.7).

Joint leader with BAe of the European aircraft industry, Aérospatiale is crushed by its American competitors whose

Table 3.7 Comparison between Aérospatiale and the American steam roller

Company	Turnover FR (000 million)	Payroll 000
United Technologies (United States)	118.7	184
Boeing (United States)	103	104
McDonnell Douglas (United States)	86.7	97
Rockwell (United States)	86.1	123
Hughes (United States)	46.8	80
British Aerospace (Great Britain)	28.7	75.5
Aérospatiale (France)	24.6	35
MBB (FRG)	18.9	35
CASA (Spain)	2.3	9
Aérospatiale+MBB +British Aerospace+CASA	74.5	154.5

Source: Le Nouvel Economiste, no. 555, 29 August 1986, p. 36.

average strength is four times its own. The only way to counter this imbalance is by allying with other European groups.

A more detailed analysis which compares models aimed at the same market slot shows the imbalance clearly:

	Aircraft sold[46]
Boeing 727	1,832
Lockheed Tristar	232 (Lockheed has given up)
BAC 1-11	234
Trident	117

Comparing aircraft by payload capacity gives the same result:

	Aircraft sold[47]
DC 9	1,166
Boeing 737	1,070
BAC 1-11	234

This is the result of competition between the United States and the European countries taken separately. If, by comparison, we turn to an area of competition in which there has been soundly based European cooperation, again taking comparable aircraft, we obtain the following result:

	Aircraft sold[48]
Airbus 300	252
Lockheed 1011	102
Boeing 767	104[49]

A striking contrast. The national champion policy could not hold its ground without cooperation; the strategic capability of our industry remained fragmented compared with that of its world competitors.

Let us compare these enterprises' net surpluses (1985) which, as we saw, give a measure of discretionary power to take the risks inherent in progress and grasp wider, longer-term opportunities.[50]

	M$
Boeing	226
Lockheed	160
McDonnell Douglas	138
BAe	66
Aérospatiale	24

The net surplus figures for the aircraft engine manufacturers are as follows:

GE	934
United Technologies	125
Rolls Royce	40

Of course, the latter figures should be qualified as GE is far more diversified than the other two enterprises; none the less GE is formidably strong.

Of the 8443 commercial jet aircraft built since 1958,

7082 were American
1361 were European

Cooperation was the only way for European enterprise to survive; the first results of adopting this strategy seem positive.

3.5.2 Airbus: an example of successful cooperation

- As we know, Airbus Industries is the product of cooperation between Aérospatiale (France), British Aerospace, Messerschmidt-Bolkow-Blöhm MBB(FRG) and CASA (Spain).

  The consortium opted for the integrated or 'multi-national group' model in which the partners create a new entity which acts as leader and takes responsibility for the organisation. As we saw earlier, this is one of the most efficient cooperation models.
- The effect was soon felt. Without going into details, the following points are worth noting:

  ■ Airbus chose the market niche showing fastest growth and went ahead of its major American competitors. The Boeing 767 did not come into service until eight years after the

A300. Cooperation thus made it possible to regain the initiative in this sector.

- Enough airbuses have been sold for it to join the international front-runners despite its small size; by the end of February 1986 firm sales were as shown in figure 3.4. As the figure shows, in its particular market Airbus has achieved global size; it has taken a significant share of the American market and its customers include such prestige airlines as PanAm and Eastern Airlines.
- Market prospects look very good as shown by figure 3.5.
- The aircraft supplied are technically tried and tested and compare favourably with the most advanced products in the sector. Airbus rapidly incorporates new know-how and the A320 will go even further ahead in this respect. Europe is thus perfectly capable of competing with its international competitors in technology, proving that know-how was not the cause of our aircraft manufacturers' decline. As far as fuel consumption is concerned, Airbus even leads its competitors.

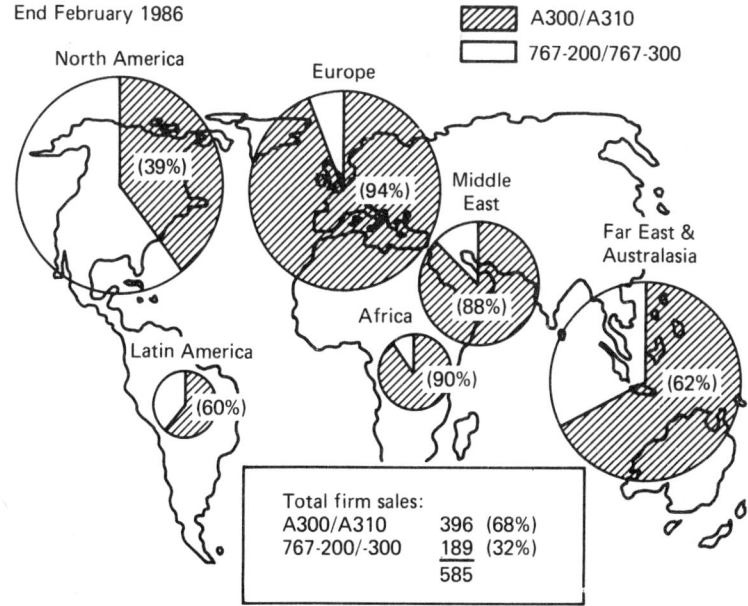

Figure 3.4 World penetration by the A300/310

Source: Airbus Industrie.

112 International Cooperation

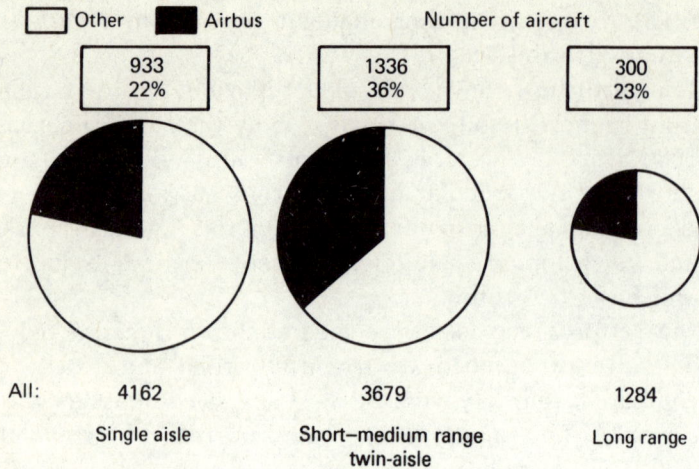

Figure 3.5 *Airbus Industries market forecast, 1985–2004*
Source: Airbus Industrie.

- In the very tricky area of product range, work has started on developing an Airbus 'family'. Of course, much remains to be done and the construction of medium- and long-haul models (respectively the A330 with 9,000 km range and the A340 with 13,000 km range) is of the greatest importance. These aircraft are intended to compete with the currently unrivalled 747, the long-haul, high-payload carrier which is Boeing's major profit-maker.

  Currently (1986), Boeing is alone in offering the full commercial range from 110-seat (737-200) to large 500-seat (Jumbo Jet) aircraft. The task of developing a full range is difficult and risky but it is probably necessary to expand the family in order to stay in the race once the existing products start to age. The mere fact that the prospect can even be discussed in European terms shows how far cooperation has helped to globalise the strategic capability of European enterprises.

- State assistance has been very substantial; the Americans say that the figure of $4 billion in direct government subsidies for Airbus announced in the course of the last 15 years should be doubled. Precise evaluation is difficult but two considerations are relevant: (1) American defence and space orders are for very

International Cooperation 113

much higher figures and their spin-offs have greatly benefited firms like Boeing, Lockheed and McDonnel Douglas; (2) any large-scale European project must involve a launch-plus-comeback phase requiring government support and we have seen that the Japanese and American models which create competitiveness are a determinant feature of their operation.

Prior to European cooperation our enterprises were dying; market shares had collapsed, losses were growing and resources were in danger of melting away. A joint industrial/commercial project has been enough to revive them; it attracted the necessary funds to allow them to carry on.

The case of *Aérospatiale* is significant[51] and closely resembles that of the other European manufacturers. Without cooperation the company was moribund; backed by alliances it has virtually doubled its exports in the last 10 years and has a world product in Airbus. Financial figures for this kind of set-up appear long after the event but the situation is beginning to look healthy again.

By 1985 the 1983 loss of FFr 357 million had been turned into a FFr 454 million profit,[52] the enterprise's indebtedness was down, its capacity for self-financing improved and its R&D effort up to FFr 6.8 thousand million or 28% of turnover. The Airbus project provides work for 7,000 of Aérospatiale's 13,000 employees in Aircraft Division. These figures relate to a short period and should not be regarded as authoritative but they justify us in at least suggesting not only that European cooperation has enabled Aérospatiale to survive but that it is now allowing the enterprise to globalise its strategic capability.

The figures shown in table 3.8 demonstrate the importance of cooperation to an enterprise such as Aérospatiale. Interestingly,

Table 3.8 Importance of cooperation

Division	Divisional turnovers in 000 millions FFr	Turnover achieved by cooperation (%)
Aircraft	6.8	70
Tactical weapons	7.8	52
Missiles and space	4.1	22
Helicopters	5.7	17

Source: Le Nouvel Economiste, no. 555, 29 August 1986.

the cooperation strategy uses the 'integrated' model discussed earlier. It also involves ad hoc cooperation in several areas with different partners[53] and here the network concept is clearly visible:

- Aircraft Division is working at 70% capacity because of cooperation, i.e. Airbus and ATR (a small regional transport aircraft launched with Aeritalia in 1984).
- Space Division's most notable products are Ariane and the TDF, TV, SAT, Eutelsat and Arabsat satellites. Cooperation predominates here: for example, the enterprises working on Ariane are drawn from 11 countries. For the most part only European partners are involved but there are a few exceptions, e.g. Ford Aerospace in Arabsat.
- Tactical Weapons Division depends on cooperation for 52% of its work principally the Hot, Milan and Roland missiles with MBB.
- Helicopters is the most independent division and is only 17% dependent on cooperation.

● One fact which should be emphasised is the need to continue along the same road and broaden the prospects further in this environment of lively competition.

As we have seen, this raises the issue of aircraft family and the possibility of launching out into a medium- and a long-haul aircraft (the A330 and A340). It also raises the issue of space cooperation; if Europe decides to take part in the Ariane 5-Hermes-Columbus combination (latest rocket-plus-shuttle-plus-station in orbit) its annual space expenditure will double from 1 to 2 thousand million Ecus, which indicates the importance of major European projects and their strategic character en route to becoming internationally competitive again.

● What Airbus makes even more apparent is the strategic character of management in the cooperation field.

In a cooperation agreement it is important that the partners be of equal or, at worst, of roughly equal strength. In fact, arbitration is essential and cannot be envisaged from a position of weakness. One danger of cooperation is loss of skills.

This is the reverse of transfers of technology. Thus, even

International Cooperation 115

though Aérospatiale management categorically denies that the Germans could assemble the future long-haul A330 and A340 at home, there is no doubt that the MBB engineers have partly made up their lag in know-how through Airbus. Again, because of the division of tasks Aérospatiale no longer works on wings; responsibility for this essential feature of the aircraft's success, lies with the British (Airbus) or the Italians (ATR). This kind of sacrifice is an unavoidable consequence of cooperation unless there is recourse to a ruinous revolving system.[54]

Airbus executives also emphasise the importance to the consortium of specialist, highly professional management, with particular reference to clear definition of objectives, explicit agreement on a joint programme and the need to delegate programme management to an organisation responsible for its execution.

Difficulties in agreeing the joint programme (general characteristics, aircraft accessories and delivery schedules) set the A 320's commercial launch back by two years.

3.5.3 The importance of management models: the case of military aircraft

Examples of cooperation in this area highlight in their own particular way the dangers inherent in inappropriate or inadequate management of alliances and consortia. Louvain's work[55] shows clearly that the management model which a consortium adopts can greatly influence its results in terms of costs and delivery periods.

The 'association of partners'/'task duplication'/'cooperative' model produces far less efficient results than the 'pilot role' or 'integrated' models. In this approach, as we have seen, the individual members retain right of veto over a range of important decisions and this leads to the practice of unanimity. A large number of committees is set up to find a basis for consensus and propose compromise when necessary. The model is often adopted when governments seek to exert political influence and operate fine control over joint project progress. The result is expensive task duplication in the assembly lines and in compo-

116   International Cooperation

nent or subsystem provisioning based on nationalist attitudes of governments still aiming to protect and favour their national champions in any project-related area.

This occurred notably with the Tornado, Jaguar and Transall projects.

- The *Jaguar* (Sepecat consortium) is a ground-attack aircraft built by British Aircraft (now British Aerospace) and Dassault-Breguet.

  Delivery periods were far exceeded; according to the original schedule the aircraft was to come out in May 1970, with the first delivery of 400 at the end of 1975. Engine development troubles and continual government modifications of the specification set this back by two years. By the time the plane appeared it was May 1972 and delivery of the first 400 began in the late 1970s, to reach completion in December 1981.

  Costs were far higher than budget which predicted a unit cost of £374,000 compared with the true cost of £1.9 million for the combat plane and £1.7 million for the trainer.[56]

- The *Tornado* was built by the Panavia consortium set up by MBB, BAe and Aeritalia.

  The R&D and production tasks were split between the three countries on the basis of their buying commitment but production of the most expensive items was not 'duplicated'. Even so, there were three final assembly lines and the consortium took the 'association of partners' form.

  The technical results were first-class but the economic performance was poor. There were significant production *delays* as a result of the political colour of the negotiations and of the compromise which had to be reached on orders, suppliers, specifications, etc. The several-year delay entailed $550 million additional finance, not to speak of the loss in potential orders and the head start gained by competitors.

  The *costs* far and away exceeded those of the competitors; the unit cost of the Tornado is put at $37 million[57] as against an estimated average cost of $29 million for the competing Grumman F-14 and A-6.[58]

  It should be added that the aircraft has not so far achieved a real commercial breakthrough.

The *Transall* offers more or less the same pattern and results. This was a military transport aircraft built in cooperation by two German and two French enterprises (respectively Blume and Hamburger and Mercier and Nord Aviation). Here again Transall was a technical success, though the competing Hercules is superior except for short take-off and landing, but the project was inefficient in terms of costs and delivery. In the latter respect it was four years behind because of political problems and sluggish decision-making. The total cost was double the original prediction.

Analysis of the aviation consortia which opted for models other than the 'association of partners' shows them to be far more efficient as to cost and delivery. Without going into details, for example:

- pilot role models:
  * the F-16: General Dynamics+Belg+Nl+Dk+Nw
  * the F-28: Fokker+Shorts (UK)+VFW+HFB (FRG)
  * the Harrier AV-8B: McDonnel Douglas+BAe

- integration models:
  * Airbus: Aérospatiale+BAe+MBB+CASA
  * ATR 42: Aérospatiale+Aeritalia
  * SF-340: SAAB+Fairchild

Studies of this kind bring out the negative nature of one of the three models, namely the model variously known as 'cooperative', 'an association of partners' or 'task duplication'.

It is not conducive to economic efficiency because it is too involved in politics. This provides an unequivocal guideline for European projects.

Having accepted that cooperation is already an inferior option to independent expansion it must be wrong to make it even worse by opting for the least favourable management model. The danger lies in the model's popularity with politicians who see it as safeguarding their influence and providing the means to 'protect' their enterprises.

The most efficient model is the 'pilot role' structure in which one enterprise acts as leader. This is the least popular with politicians because it leads to professional management which gives very high priority to economic considerations. Furthermore, one enterprise conducts the whole operation and can thus overshadow the other national champions. All this explains why it is preferable for the major partners to be of equal strength.

3.6 BRIEF DESCRIPTION OF OTHER CASES

3.6.1 Importance of strategic cooperation management: the case of the computer

This is no place to consider complex arrangements like the Olivetti-ATT-Toshiba or Bull-NEC-Honeywell alliances.

However, we can include them in our analytical chart to highlight yet again our working hypothesis that international competition is moving faster than European unification; that our high-tech enterprises cannot afford to wait and are forming alliances with major non-European firms in order to survive; and that in doing this they enter into unequal relationships and risk domination by their partners.

- If we take the case of *Olivetti*, we see that the alliance network is wide but that the American and Japanese are the key partners (appendix 23).

Olivetti is an excellent example because it is a very efficient enterprise. It achieved a strikingly successful turnaround and it completely fulfils the first condition of solid strategic capability in having a healthy base.

Between 1980 and 1985 it virtually tripled its turnover, reduced its indebtedness from 200% to 15% of own capital and lifted its ROS from 4% (1980) to 7% (1984). R&D investment rose from 3.4% to 5% of sales and the number of people engaged in it from 2,535 (4.8% of the total payroll) to 3,223 (6.8%).

Olivetti's share of European markets makes it a European front runner. It has moved dynamically and efficiently towards computers: mechanical as opposed to electronic products accounted for 66% of its sales in 1980 and a mere 10% by 1984.

Olivetti thus represents a jewel in the European crown and is, moreover, in good health and enjoying systematic development of its strategic capability (R&D, skills and networks). It inspired thoughts of a European picture having Olivetti as one of its axes.

Instead the company opted for the 'triad' as the direct route to globalisation and has turned notably to ATT and Toshiba as its partners and whilst this does not necessarily exclude European alliances, they are not central to its network.

The issue immediately raised is that of relative strengths. If we accept net surplus (40% of net profit) as the measure of an enterprise's ability to take the risks inherent in progress the difference in strengths is clear:

Net surplus 1985 ($ million)
ATT   623
Toshiba 141
Olivetti 106

Without going so far as to suggest such an alliance cannot yield very positive results, one cannot help wondering which enterprise will be best placed to take the strategic initiative, speed up the rate of progress and make its word law. Moreover, ATT has 18,000 people in its laboratories against Olivetti's 3,000.

The alliance announced between *Bull*, NEC and Honeywell is too recent to allow discussion in any great detail.

Here too a European enterprise, with an apparently successful recent turnaround, has preferred to give priority to a non-European basis for cooperation and once again we see the pitfalls and constraints of the European model. The failure of Unidata in 1975 ended a first serious attempt to form a European-based computer alliance (Bull, Siemens and Philips). It was followed by a second attempt involving Bull and Olivetti under the SGPM aegis but the French government decided otherwise.

In order to globalise its strategy Bull recently took both the initiative and the leadership in forming a genuinely triadic computer group. A computer company has been jointly set up by Bull (42.5%), Honeywell (42.5%) and NEC (15%). The company will comprise the personnel, customer base, industrial potential and R&D strength of Honeywell Information Systems. Bull is the only group to work exclusively in computers and will have the controlling vote on the Board. Honeywell has the right to reduce its share to 19.9% after two years.

The new company plans to market its complete range of universal computers, mini-computers, mcps, software and services in the USA and other foreign HIS markets. It will also market Bull and NEC products and the existing range of HIS products including all three shareholders' compatible systems.

The company is the fruit of 16 years' cooperation between the three companies. The people managing the agreement all refer to the value of the operation in strengthening their competitiveness at world level.

Looking at the figures, we find that the combined sales of the three partners will make the new company the third largest manufacturer of computers and office machines in the world (see appendix 24). Their combined net surpluses for 1985 amount to $227 million, which ranks second in the world after IBM ($2,622), ahead of Siemens ($196 million), HP ($196 million) and DEC ($178 million).

The promoters make the following points:

- A genuinely global size with an effective operational presence in Europe, the USA and Japan.
- The perfect complementarity of products and services as a result of more than 15 years' cooperation.
- Bull's dominant role which has enabled a European company to take strategic leadership of a world entity.
- The enhanced strategic capability, notably in terms of financial, technological, industrial and marketing resources.
- The creation of competitive advantages on an international scale.

Several points are worth underlining in the context of our analysis chart:

- The initiative has been taken by a European enterprise which has thereby improved its strategic capability, taken a share of the American market and strengthened its Japanese alliance.
- Globalisation comes late and in a period of over-capacity and falling profitability; it could have been achieved much earlier in Europe had the difficulties and constraints been less.
- The case is a good illustration of the dynamic nature of

cooperation as after 15 years it has led to a clear leadership for Bull over HIS. This is a further reason for keeping a close eye on alliances with NEC whose net surpluses are far greater than Bull's.

■ Adequate integration of approaches, methods and cultures will require strenuous effort and highly professional alliance management.

3.7 SME COOPERATION[59]

Many SMEs make products for the international market. For them a solid European base can constitute a strategic priority. Because of their size they see the countries of Europe as offering greater interest by virtue of their geographical proximity and cultural affinity.

SMEs are not always adequately equipped to 'Europeanise' by themselves and it is here that cooperation comes into its own. J. C. Jarillo has been conducting a large-scale investigation into efficient SMEs. His conceptual framework fits well with our own and complements this report in the SME area. He puts forward the idea that global strategy may be essential to an SME whenever the threshold of economies of scale goes beyond the national limits.

In such a case the only way in which an SME can create genuine competitive advantages is by broadening its horizons, for example by Europeanising; this is often true for products with high technical or marketing content.

At present the decisive choices for SMEs are:

● Which part of the value chain should they concentrate on or specialise in?
● Which type of structure should they adopt to coordinate European activities? Should they decentralise by country or create a very strong unit with central management?
● In which European regions should their various activities be located?

The answer to the first question is often to specialise in one part of the value chain for this in fact facilitates the acquisition of competitive advantages in terms of cost and quality. The SME will then be led to form a cooperative alliance with other European enterprises to complete the value chain.

This first type of cooperation leads to a similar solution in response to the other questions (structure and location).

The enterprise will thus be faced with the possibility, even the necessity, of forming an alliance network which will allow it to pursue a global strategy. Jarillo refers to a 'strategic network' because the choice and constitution of the network become a powerful competition weapon.

In this context the creation and management of a network become a key element of competitive strategy. Becoming/staying competitive depends more on the SME's ability to find its place in the right alliance network than to make a direct approach to the market on its own.

In this perspective, Lorenzoni[60] did some research on the reorganisation of the textile industry in northern Italy. The industry had suffered splintering on a massive scale – the 700 firms of 1951 becoming 9,500 by 1976 and average payroll falling from 30 to 5 whilst total jobs in the population sampled doubled over the same period. The industry is one of the most competitive in the world and extremely prosperous. Lorenzoni shows how the evolution towards clustering went through phases: the reaction or 'realised constellation' phase, the search-for-efficiency or 'rationalised constellation' phase and the strategic efficiency or 'planned constellation' phase. Here we have a genuine strategy in which the partners set out to create competitive advantages by specialisation, cost-reduction and greater flexibility.

This kind of network strategy is being employed increasingly in Europe and examples include the franchise explosion in the UK and the creation of supplier networks on a pan-European basis.

3.8 THE CASE OF ENGINEERING[61]

The engineering sector is relevant for several reasons: its orientation is international; it is a major vehicle for new technologies; by this fact it is susceptible to cooperation. Professor Gallo's work shows that a strengthened European base is not currently a priority objective for Spanish companies but that it might become an essential strategy whenever high tech is involved.

His analysis of 53 Spanish enterprises shows that the most international of these have managed to gain an international competitive advantage in a specific technology. He further shows that most companies having international contracts purchase or subcontract some contractual elements from enterprises in technologically advanced countries, usually by forming consortia which enrich the value chain. Spanish companies seeking to internationalise would like to be involved in consortia but are sceptical of the potential for creating a European base given the over-capacity in any medium-tech activity and the fact that public contracts go to national enterprises.

Their current objective is therefore not to create a strong European base for their overall activities but rather to turn to Latin America and Africa in a 'super-domestic' approach.

They do, however, recognise that a European dimension may be essential to the more specialist engineering companies using more advanced technology but will take this road only if the conditions favouring the pursuit of global strategy are satisfied. Otherwise they would rather cooperate with companies from America, Japan, Brazil etc.

The importance for Europe of cooperation in this area is obvious. If European integration continues for too long to lag behind the globalisation of competition, all chance of carrying out major international high-tech engineering projects will be lost.

In fact the lack of integration:

- Discourages European cooperation
- Inhibits the emergence of major exportable technologies
- Reduces our competitive advantages on world markets

NOTES

1. 70% of direct Swedish investment abroad takes the form of acquisitions: Hedlund, G., Swedish MNC's strategies for Europe, Penelope, 1986.
2. Source: *Financial Times*.
3. Stopford and Turner (1985).
4. Source: Eurostat, EEC, 1986.
5. Hedlund (1986).
6. Ohmae (1985).
7. Stopford and Turner (1985).
8. Hedlund and Zander (1986).
9. Ohmae (1985).
10. Global Forecasting and Supply System.
11. Jacquemin (1984); Jacquemin et al. (1985).
12. On this topic see Turcq (1985). This section draws largely on this work and also on Doz et al. (1986).
13. See note 12, p. 37.
14. Turcq (1985).
15. All but two of the small European ion implantation firms were taken over by the Americans and a few years later all but one of the American firms were taken over by the Japanese.
16. Turcq (1985) pp. 43–5.
17. For example Dainichi Kiko's transition from producing robots to producing complete automated factory systems involved 28 cooperation agreements. In computers NEC and Fujitsu have set up networks of extremely complex alliances: Doz et al. (1986).
18. Turcq (1985).
19. de Woot et al. (1971); de Woot and Desclee (1984).
20. Jacquemin et al. (1985); Jacquemin and Spinoit (1986).
21. See particularly Doz et al. (1986). See also Turcq (1985); Jacquemin (1984).
22. This is what happens with JVC and European partners such as Thomson and Thorn-EMI.
23. Doz et al. (1986).
24. Jacquemin and Spinoit (1986) carry out an analysis of this kind. To explain asymmetries in the power game they posit the following factors: future weight, number of partners, degree of specificity of the agreement, contractual rules, effect of the learning curve, ethics and the effect of reputation.
25. Turcq (1985); Doz et al. (1986).

International Cooperation 125

26 de Woot and Desclee (1984).
27 Doz et al. (1986).
28 Ohmae (1985).
29 Spreen (1986).
30 Atlantic, Transall, F-28, Jaguar, Airbus, Tornado, Alpha Jet, F-16, Harrier AV-8B, SF-340, ATR 42.
31 Doz et al. (1986).
32 This was the case in the cooperation agreements between GE and SNECMA and between Pratt & Whitney, RR and a Japanese consortium. 'The hot core of the joint product of GE and Snecma, the CFM 56 engine, is provided by GE while the "cold" parts are provided by Snecma'. 'Similar restrictions apply to the transfer of Rolls Royce's and Pratt & Whitney's know-how to the Japanese' (Doz 1986).
33 Arthur D. Little.
34 This passage draws on Turcq (1985).
35 Source: Nomura Research Institute, quoted by Turcq.
36 Turcq (1985).
37 Bayen M., *CPE Report*, Etude no. 90, Mars 1983, Caracterisation des Coopérations entre sociétés americaines et japonaises dans le domaine des technologies critiques.
38 Turcq (1985).
39 Jacquemin et al. (1985).
40 Source: 15th Report on Competitive Policy, EEC Commission, Brussels, 1986.
41 Sinatra (1986).
42 Turcq (1985).
43 Turcq (1985) pp. 66–7.
44 Estimate by companies:

	1984	1995 (Units)	2004	$billion
Airbus			9,125	471
Boeing		4,005		135
McDonnel Douglas		4,716 (1998)		210
Pratt & Whitney		4,200		178

Source: Survey, *Economist*, 1 June 1985.
45 *Economist*, 3 May 1986.
46 *Economist*, 1 June 1985.
47 *Economist*, 1 June 1985.
48 *Economist*, 1 June 1985.
49 The aircraft came into service eight years after Airbus which suggests that Europe has regained the initiative in this particular market.

50 Net surplus as calculated here is 40% of net profit. Source: *Fortune*, April–August 1986.
51 Jacquier (1986).
52 Jacquier (1986).
53 Jacquier (1986).
54 Jacquier (1986).
55 Spreen (1986).
56 French National Assembly Finance Committee's figures. These are disputed by the British who maintain that the cost rose from £555,000 to £1 million.
57 *Economist*, 21 June 1986.
58 *Economist*, 21 June 1986.
59 Jarillo (1986).
60 Lorenzoni (1986); Lorenzoni and Ornati (1987).
61 Gallo (1986).

4
Research and Innovation[1]

We showed in chapter 1 how the process which creates competitiveness rests on four essential features:

- A long-term view and the creation of international-size opportunities.
- Development of sufficient strategic capability to be in a position to seize opportunities and embrace longer-term prospects.
- Acquisition of global competitive advantages.
- Sufficient profitability to keep to this route.

In this chapter we consider one key factor of strategic capability: the mastery of technological progress as a source of innovation and competitive advantage. We shall seek to justify the proposition that European countries still have a highly creative research potential but put it to poor use; the potential is not being converted sufficiently into a globally competitive weapon. In high-tech sectors our enterprises seem to suffer not from poor know-how but from difficulty in making rapid use of R&D and innovation in offensive strategies which would give them sizeable segments of international markets. As we have seen, this is not the case with the chemicals industry nor, in a more qualified way, with the motor industry.

Based on this, technological cooperation looks to be a priority strategy for our enterprises to control future technologies. For many enterprises, cooperation is now a necessary condition of survival in high-tech sectors. None the less, it is not the definitive answer and cannot replace the existence of a large open market or large-scale joint projects.

4.1 MUCH EUROPEAN R&D BUT LITTLE EXPLOITATION

- Europe's position is good as far as R&D investment is concerned (see table 4.1): 30% of OECD research spending, less than the USA but far more than Japan.

Table 4.1 Evolution of gross domestic spending on R&D

	1981 MUS$	%	1983 MUS$	Real growth 1981–3
USA	773,678	46.4	88,329	3.8
Japan	25,574	16.1	33,493	8.2
EEC	47,536[a]	30.4	52,346[b]	2.5

[a] 10 countries.
[b] 5 countries.
Source: OECD (1986).

If we look at the number of research jobs created by these budgets (table 4.2) we see that our R&D productivity is far lower than that of Japan, bearing in mind the figures in the previous table. The figures also show the slower growth of our research effort.

Table 4.2 Number of research jobs

	1981 Full-time	%	Real growth 1979–81
USA	683,700	41.8	5.5
Japan	392,625	24.0	3.9
EEC[a]	414,640	25.5	3.5

[a] 10 countries
Source: OECD (1986).

- We should also stress that public financing of R&D is everywhere on the rise. Though in absolute figures American public spending on R&D is far higher than the other countries', proportionally it is the lowest; from this it follows that American enterprises' R&D effort is far greater than that of their foreign competitors (table 4.3).

Remembering their technological superiority in virtually every high-tech area (see chapter 1), we can posit that they have

Table 4.3 Shares of industrial R&D: EC, US, and Japan (%)[a]

	Total industrial R&D		Industry-financed R&D	
	1967	1977/8	1967	1977/8
EC-9	23.7	32.9	31.1	32.8
US	71.5	52.6	60.1	47.5
Japan	4.8	14.5	8.8	19.7
Total	100.0	100.0	100.0	100.0

[a] Ergas (1984).
Source: Pavitt, K., Les perspectives du développement technologique en Europe face aux nouvelles contraintes internationales, Science Policy Research Unit, University of Sussex, 1983.

succeeded in using R&D as a major competitive weapon and this corresponds well with the model presented in chapter 2.

When we turn to exploitation of R&D and innovation as a competitive weapon, the weakness of our enterprises in high-tech sectors becomes only too evident (table 4.4).

Comparison of all these tables shows that the real problem is our enterprises' inability to use R&D for global product and market strategies.

Table 4.4 Market share: manufacturing industries

	High intensity			Medium intensity			Low intensity		
	70	80	84	70	80	84	70	80	84
USA	35.4	30.5	31.2	26.0	22.5	20.5	16.1	15.4	14.3
Japan	15.0	21.3	28.8	10.1	17.1	21.5	15.7	13.7	15.5
EEC	33.0	33.4	26.1	40.1	39.4	33.9	34.4	37.9	34.8

Source: OECD (1986).

Our R&D effort is not converted into international competitive advantages in the high-tech sectors. This is partly explained by its orientation as R&D in Europe concentrates more on the older sectors such as the motor industry, chemicals and mechanical engineering.

However, as we shall see, the major reason is the dearth of prospects and strategic opportunities – once again, the price we pay for a non-unified Europe!

130 Research and Innovation

- Europe's technological balance shows a fairly constant deficit, Japan's has markedly improved and the USA's shows a massive surplus (table 4.5).

Table 4.5 Technological balance of payments (MUS$, prices at 1975)

	1973			1983		
	Rev.	Exp.	Bal.	Rev.	Exp.	Bal.
USA	3,582	456	3,126	4,328	132	4,196
Japan	231	1,035	−804	646	750	−103
EEC	1,505	2,478	−873	1,926	2,734	−771

Source: OECD (1986).

Despite the problem of data in this area, due to the heterogeneous nature of technological payment balances and the poor comparability of international figures, we none the less feel that the above figures indicate a real trend. Ignoring America's outstanding position we see that Japan has tripled its revenue and reduced its expenditure whereas Europe's position has hardly improved.

As percentages of the OECD total, the figures show increased European technological dependence (table 4.6).

Table 4.6 Technological dependence of Europe

	% of OECD total	
	1973	1983
European revenue	27.6	26.9
European expenditure	26.9	58.4

Source: OECD (1986).

- Ergas's study of the major industrial countries'[2] innovative capacity leads him to rank them as follows:

  - The USA are far ahead; though Japan is tending to catch up, America is in a dominant position in the OECD.
  - Europe's position is improving but not to the same extent as Japan's.

Research and Innovation   131

- European positions vary with sector; strong in chemicals and biotechnology; less so in electronics, information technology and aviation.
- The European countries form two contrasting groups of which one (FRG, Scandinavia and Switzerland) is markedly more innovative than the other (UK and France).

4.2 THE REASON LIES MORE WITH THE CORPORATE STRATEGY THAN THE R&D

The fact that European research is not being turned sufficiently to international competitive advantage does not mean that it is poorer than Japanese or American research, as Airbus, Ariane, telecommunications, Olivetti, the chemicals industry and Scandinavian robots prove. The quality of our science is not at issue.

Studies of corporate strategy suggest that the reason lies rather in the inadequate strategic capability of our enterprises. In this respect Louvain research is quite explicit.[3]

4.2.1

R&D and innovation constitute a factor of competitive success only if they are part of a total strategy which exploits and guides them. To be a factor of success R&D needs the 'strategic vehicle' to carry it into the process of creating competitive advantages. If R&D and innovation are not part of such a strategy they are likely to yield nothing more than an isolated change or an economically unproductive 'invention'.

- There is no direct relationship between quantity of R&D or innovation and an enterprise's competitiveness. In the population considered there was no correlation between number of innovations or R&D spending over the last 10 years and corporate profitability. It is only through the medium of a product and market strategy that R&D influences profitability.
- There is no correlation between number of innovations or R&D spending and quality of product policy. In other words, R&D does not guide strategy; in fact the reverse is

true. Good research is useless without a well-defined strategy. Research for research's sake does not enhance corporate competitiveness. Where the strategy is 'provincial' the effect of R&D will also be provincial.
- On the other hand, R&D spending does correlate with quality of innovation. The quantity of R&D has a direct effect on the nature of the change or technical breakthrough at which the enterprise aims. Whether we consider the degree of novelty or simple technical quality of an innovation, the R&D effort plays a significant part. This is relevant to any activity in which the companies are involved in non-stop technical competition.

From this we see that even when the resources devoted to R&D and innovation are efficient in terms of technical advance, they do not necessarily contribute to increased corporate competitiveness.

What counts for the competitiveness is not the quantity of R&D or innovation but the enterprise's ability to integrate technical advance into a strategy. Only in this way can an innovation become effective in competitive terms. Otherwise it remains isolated, detached from the remainder of the enterprise. It does not become part of a strategic process designed to translate it into competitive advantage and market share but remains simply an inadequately exploited invention, an advance without a future because it has no major effect on the important markets. Strategic capability is thus a necessary condition of the economic efficiency of R&D and innovation.

In summary: the important thing is the ability to convert research results into a new product or process which creates a decisive competitive advantage. It is not the number of innovations which matters but their effect on the market, a sufficiently marked effect to contribute to the creative destruction process which is the nub of competition. The motor industry provides a good illustration if we confine ourselves to major innovations.[4] There have been three decisive breakthroughs in the history of the car:

- The first was made in the USA around 1910 with the changeover from small scale to mass production.

Research and Innovation 133

- The second was made in Europe in the late 1950s when enterprises managed to combine mass production with differentiated models.
- The third was made in Japan in the late 1960s when costs were slashed but high quality was retained.

4.2.2

Strategic capability is the key to competitiveness. Louvain research has clearly identified the component factors. Corporate strategic capability depends above all on:

- Systematic product policy.
- Well-developed resources in marketing, production, R&D and management and a good balance between them.
- The internal and external information systems to which the enterprise has access.

If these factors have been developed just to a national or local level the enterprise will be unable to create sufficient competitive advantages over its major foreign competitors. This is precisely the point we are making with regard to European enterprises in high-tech sectors.

Chapter 2 showed Europe's lag in strategy in these sectors.

- *Product policy* is the combination of the decisions and choices which enable an enterprise to compete successfully. The choice may be more or less ambitious, bold, open. If the enterprise is protected (national champion) or lacks international opportunities or long-term prospects (fragmented European market) its strategic decisions will necessarily be local or national in nature, its ambitions will be confined to smaller markets and a more restricted horizon and it will tend to protect its older products longer and to react to rather than lead the competition.
- *The development and balance of its strategic resources* depends on the enterprise's ambitions. In a protected, compartmentalised environment the systematic creation of key factors to efficiency will be pursued less boldly and less professionally than if the enterprise has access to major international markets and is forced to face world competition.

Recent research has shown clearly the importance of these strategic resources sometimes referred to as the enterprise's skills base. This means not just technical resources but also commercial ability (marketing, distribution networks, promotional skills, etc.), manufacturing skills (automated production, quality, cost control, etc.) and quality of management (management methods, behavioural patterns, climate).

Studies also show that it is essential to establish some balance between resources and major functions. For example, great technical mastery without the equivalent marketing skill will not produce a competitive advantage in the market place. Louvain shows that an enterprise's strategic capability is global and that its quality is determined by the weakest link in the value chain, which might explain why the significant R&D effort made by European enterprises so rarely results in global competitive advantage.

- *The quality of the internal and external information systems* depends on the type of strategy pursued. An enterprise pursuing a world strategy has to widen and refine both its information network and the requisite data-gathering and processing skills. An enterprise pursuing a more local policy will have less powerful 'radar', executives less capable of thinking globally and more traditional management tools. Studies point to the risk of paralysis in this area. In fact, lacking an ambitious strategy the enterprise has no incentive to seek highly complex, highly international or highly detailed information on global markets, major competitors or market developments. It therefore does not develop more powerful, more sensitive, more intelligent management tools and the absence of these dictates that the enterprise will perceive and seize only short-term opportunities with low strategic significance.

By relating these findings to the European model shown in chapter 2 we can posit that this kind of model does not favour the development of an international strategic capability. Because opportunities in the emerging systems have not been wide enough or the prospects long-term enough, European enterprises have not developed their strategic capability on a sufficiently large scale to do business at world level. With few exceptions they have remained national, i.e. provincial. They have failed to achieve global development of their product/market strategies, of their resources in skills, networks and alliances or of their information systems. As we have seen, most of our enterprises in high-tech sectors are incapable of crossing the size/complexity/endurance thresholds which characterise world competition today.

4.3 EXTERNAL INCENTIVES TO COMPETITIVE INNOVATION

By and large Ergas's work[5] confirms our hypothesis concerning the influence of the models which create or destroy competitiveness and allows us to study in greater detail the first element of the model, namely the opportunities and prospects open to an enterprise caught up in the development process. His findings show that innovation depends on interaction between:

- Sufficient demand (market) to spur the enterprise.
- Technological opportunities with a potential for progress from the existing situation.
- An industrial structure which relates market pull to technology push.

The European model can be shown to leave our enterprises at a disadvantage in all three cases as compared with their Japanese and American competitors.

4.3.1 The market or demand

- Ergas starts from the idea that because innovation is both risky and expensive the larger the market the greater the incentive to innovate.

Work at Louvain reaches the same conclusion concerning *market size* but more in terms of outlet than incentive. In fact many European enterprises innovate but launch their innovations in restricted markets only. As we have seen, this is the case with certain national champions in high-tech sectors. Yet it is indisputable that for large-scale, long-term, high-risk projects the absence of a major market inhibits innovation in a way which only public finance can overcome.

The central issue is not whether a large market is important as an outlet or as an incentive; the main concern is that European enterprises are at a disadvantage in this area. The lack of a large unified European market often prevents them from innovating or from converting their innovations into international competitive advantages (table 4.7).

Table 4.7 European lag in modern infrastructure (1980–1981)*

Installed base per 10.000 Hab.	USA	Japan	Europe
Telephones	7,700	4,200	3,500
PABX Lines	1,445	483	485
Televisions	6,350	2,450	2,300
Photocopiers	17	20	10
Computers	10	4	3
NC Machine Tools	32	42	25
Robots	0.15	0.70	0.10
CT-Scanners	0.05	0.01	0.01
Nuclear Electr. (KWH)	1,308	735	826

Source: ATT, NRI, Financial Times, UN Statistics, Jetro, Maptec, Télésis Estimates.
* Ergas (1984)

The many aspects of the fragmented European market are too well known for us to dwell on them here. We have already emphasised the importance of public contracts, of technical barriers and of the absence of common standards. Worth highlighting is the fact that in terms of economic strength a European market would more or less equal its American counterpart and be double the Japanese.[6]

Demand for high-tech products in Europe remains on a small scale, however, because potential users, particularly governments, adopt a nationalist stance: according to estimates, public purchasing represents 17% of GNP;[7] more than 90% of public purchases are made from national enterprises, despite the obligation to open purchasing up to all European enterprises.[8]

- In any case, market size is not the only factor; the *degree of market development or sophistication* is another and a number of indicators exist to measure it.

  ▪ One is the modernity of the infrastructure equipment and

here the European market is less sophisticated than the others in most areas.[9]
- A second indicator is average consumption level. In 1981 this was:

  USA $8000
  Europe (EEC) $5500
  Japan $5000[10]

- A further indicator of interest is density of scientific information. The data base is an important feature of information systems and in this area we find appreciable differences (table 4.8).

Table 4.8 Data banks: bibliographic references (in millions of references)

Producer origin	Private producers	Public or non-profit-making producers	Total
USA	33.2	41.9	75.1
EEC (inc. EC)	4.9	16.3	21.2
Rest of the world	0.8	6.2	7
International organisations (excluding EEC)	–	1.5	1.5
Total	38.9	65.9	104.8

Source: Ergas (1984)

A recent EEC survey of data bases and data banks to which European users have on-line access shows that 56% of accessible systems are of American origin compared with 26% of European origin. Whereas American and European 'production' are substantially equivalent as regards numbers of bibliographical and factual data bases, the USA has five times as many digital data banks.[11]

- As we have seen, high-tech demand depends heavily on public contracts. For American enterprises, defence contracts are a powerful stimulus to innovation. We show below the distribution of military spending on high-tech R&D between the OECD countries in 1982:

  USA   71.3%
  EEC   26.3%
  Japan 6.0%
  Other 1.8%

138   Research and Innovation

American government contracts for high-tech products and services in 1981 were in excess of $40 billion.[12] As we well know, this type of contract has been a decisive spur to American enterprises since the 1950s. We discussed earlier the budgets planned for the SDI. Current estimates of total 1980–85 expenditure suggest $100 billion on defence priorities in electronics: communications, remote controls and intelligence.

4.3.2   Technological opportunities or supply

This denotes the scientific–technological base on which the enterprise rests and the rate at which it develops. Gaps in a country's technical skills or sluggish development of its scientific resources reduce the capacity of enterprises to innovate proportionately. Conversely, great technological creativity with rapid widespread diffusion provide enterprises with opportunities for progress and backing for their creativity. Ergas suggests two important indicators: (1) training and (2) the links between industry and the universities.

- In the present context, *training* denotes education in pure and applied (engineering) science. Despite difficulties of comparison, the figures show situations which are sufficiently contrasted to reflect real differences (see figures 4.1, 4.2 and table 4.9).[13]

Ergas's work shows clearly the various dimensions of training policy: its diversity, range, response to industry's needs and quality. The research establishes that, typically, in the more innovative countries, training is better matched to industry's needs.

> Higher education is not everything. Nowadays the educational and training qualifications of workers and employees are of crucial importance. This is one of the strengths of West German industry. In the Federal Republic, 60% of the workforce have acquired a qualification as a result of systematic programmes and written and oral examinations, whereas in the United Kingdom the figure is only 30%.[14]

Research and Innovation

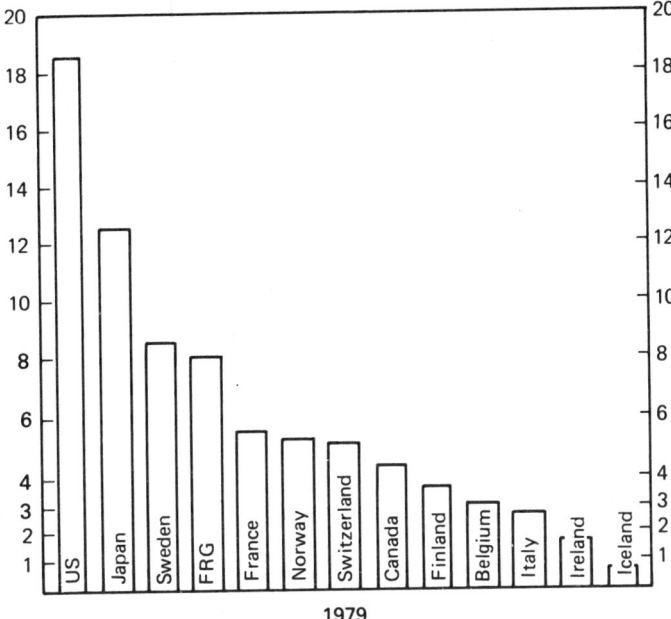

Figure 4.1 Research scientists and engineers per 1,000 manufacturing employees (including university graduates), 1979

Source: Ergas (1984).

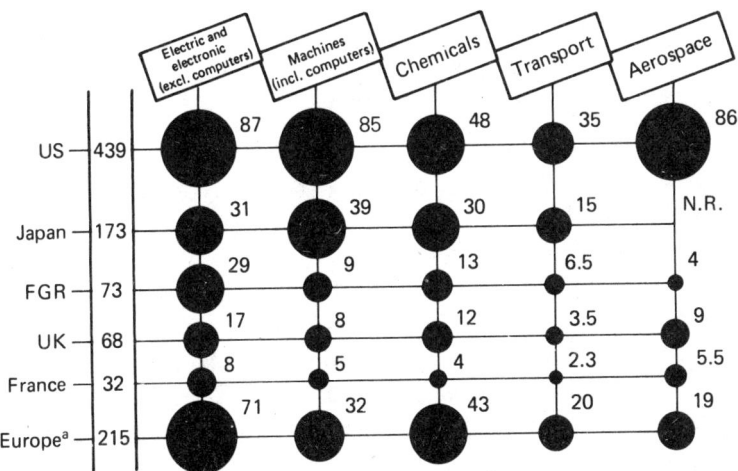

Figure 4.2 Estimated number of R&D scientists and engineers in selected industries, 1979 (thousands)

[a] EC and Sweden, Switzerland, Austria and Norway.

Source: NSF, MITI, RDI, MRI, Télésis (1985).

Table 4.9 Number of graduates in 1979 (thousands)

	Engineering sciences	Natural and cognitive sciences
US	100.4	120.3
Japan	82.9	13.5
UK	18.6	22.3
France[a]	10.0	15.0
FRG	6.4	7.9

[a] Estimated.
Source: OCDE (1984).

- The links between industry and the universities are a powerful catalyst of creativity and innovation. As we have said, the first such link is dialogue on the kinds of skill which enterprises need. Ergas investigates other features too, such as:

  - Enterprise funding of university research; in the USA it is as much as 6–7% which is far higher than anywhere else.
  - Enterprise use of university consultancy.
  - Science parks or multiple developments, e.g. Highway 128 or Silicon Valley.
  - Communications networks set up for specific projects between the university, industry and a public agency.
  - Innovation centres which the National Science Foundation has been setting up since 1973.

Although the United States seem well ahead here, Europe has not been idle. Once again, however, its initiatives are fragmented and national, and they vary greatly from one country to another.

Japan, which lagged for so long in this area, has greatly improved its record and today Japanese enterprises are helping to provide the universities with ultra-modern equipment. There is also a major effort to spread scientific knowledge to the SMEs and give them technical support.

4.3.3 The industrial structure

This is an important factor in our development model, namely the dynamism of the industrial set-up or the thrust of the creative destructive process. Ergas stresses the competitiveness of the industrial structure and its potential for cooperation.

Whether an economy is *competitive* depends on the presence of enterprises strong enough to take the risks of progress and sufficiently under threat to remain innovative and efficient. Thus, to compare the vitality of industrial structures we must analyse the size of the enterprises involved, the degree of competition and the regeneration of structure by the continuous arrival of new enterprises.

Size differences are much less than they were, as we can see from the work of Dunning and Pearce quoted by Ergas (tables 4.10 and 4.11).[15]

If we exclude oil companies from the top 25 largest enterprises we find that American firms are no longer bigger than European ones.

Table 4.10 Sales of x largest US firms as % of sales of x largest non-US firms: 1962, 1967, 1972, 1977 (non-US = 100)

	1962	1967	1972	1977
x = 25	224.6	228.2	167.3	143.2
x = 50	212.5	210.6	147.1	129.5
x = 100	196.2	192.7	139.8	123.0
x = 150	189.1	187.1	138.8	121.2
x = 200	186.3	183.9	137.6	119.9
x = 250	n.a.	n.a.	136.7	118.6
x = 300	n.a.	n.a.	135.6	117.4

Source: Dunning and Pearce (1981).

Table 4.11 Sales of firms ranked x_i to x_j in US samples as % of firms ranked x_i to x_j in non-US sample: 1962, 1967, 1972, 1977 (non-US = 100)

	1962	1967	1972	1977
x_i to x_j = 1–25	224.6	228.2	167.3	143.2
x_i to x_j = 26–50	184.0	174.2	107.1	98.2
x_i to x_j = 51–100	155.3	152.0	121.3	104.5
x_i to x_j = 101–150	150.3	157.7	132.8	109.8
x_i to x_j = 151–200	159.8	155.8	127.1	107.1
x_i to x_j = 201–250	n.a.	n.a.	123.8	101.1
x_i to x_j = 251–300	n.a.	n.a.	116.4	94.2

Source: Dunning and Pearce (1981).

142 Research and Innovation

- Ergas takes corporate price policy as the indicator of intensity of competition. Using recent studies he comes to the following conclusions:
  - Japan is typified by very great flexibility of industrial prices both in absolute terms and by comparison with the other OECD countries.
  - The UK is at the other extreme with very little price flexibility, particularly in the most highly concentrated sectors; France also seems to have little flexibility.
  - The USA, FRG and Sweden lie between the two.
- Regeneration due to the influx of new enterprises. Without going into a discussion of the birth and death rates of industrial firms in general, we concentrate on the formation of new enterprises in high-tech sectors.

The available figures suggest that this is far more marked in the USA and Japan than in Europe. Ergas gives a detailed analysis of factors which may influence the formation of new enterprises and makes a number of points which are of interest to us, including in particular:

- The potential profit margins.
- The network of entrepreneurs (mostly engineers and researchers).
- The abundance of risk capital.
- The existence of mobile specialist labour.
- Access to specialist equipment and specific components (Silicon Valley).
- Ease of access to large markets.[16]
- Ease of divestment.

Studies of Highway 128 and Silicon Valley in California confirm the existence of these conditions and the resultant creativity.[17]

The European policy of supporting national champions has slowed or blocked the influx of new enterprises. By placing orders solely with such firms national governments have indirectly helped to restrict the potential supply of know-how.

To take some examples: more than 80% of UK aid to the micro-electronics industry went to 5 firms and one firm received more than 50% of the total.[18] We find a similar situation in

France: the Hannoun Report made much of the heavy concentration and low efficiency of government aid to industry and showed that more than 50% of all aid to industry was divided between just 6 firms.[19] More recent studies confirm this for France: in 1984 most of the approximately FFr 12 thousand million State funding for enterprise R&D went to aviation (50%) and electronics (32%); 79% of this benefited enterprises in the public sector, i.e. a few very large enterprises, and only some 5% went to SMEs employing less than 500 people. Furthermore, government customer-orders wrote off 20–30% of enterprise R&D investment.[20]

4.4 R&D COOPERATION

We saw that European demand for high-tech products is low because of market fragmentation and the absence of joint projects comparable with the American SDI or the Japanese 'information society'.

This shows the importance of an R&D cooperation policy at Community level if innovation supply and demand are to expand. This applies not only to the markets for technology but also to any activity which can make use of the results of joint research.

In fact, it is easier to escape national market constraints and reach a pan-European market in areas such as aerospace, telecommunications or defence equipment where the new technology and resultant products are the fruit of cooperation.

International cooperation is one of the subjects on the agenda of the European Commission; a number of projects have been launched and their success proves that enterprises are aware of their utility and wish to be involved. The Esprit project is a brilliant example; the Brite and Race projects also resulted from cooperation. These are major poles which have been sufficiently described and analysed elsewhere[21] and we do not propose to discuss them here. Two significant points should be made, however:

- Within the selected new generations of technology the enterprises themselves decide on the priority choices and by

that very fact the approach demands a strategic perspective.
- All the evidence shows that this type of cooperation is one answer to the problems which arise in this kind of work; cooperation is essential and represents a move in the right direction but is not enough in itself to globalise the strategic capability of European enterprises; it must become part of a wider policy which includes large-scale joint projects and speedier unification of the European market.

It is clear from the last chapter that the Japanese have a long history of industrial cooperation, notably in the field of R&D. A similar trend can be detected in the United States:

> According to William Norris, President of Control Data, the American undertakings detested cooperation, and the anti-trust laws provided them with a very good pretext for avoiding cooperative partnerships. This led to a scandalous and unnecessary duplication of work in the field of R&D.
>
> In recent times the situation has been clarified. Partnerships are legal, provided that they comply with the National Cooperative Research Act adopted in 1984. Forty Joint R&D Ventures have sought to take advantage of it as a means of meeting international competition, sharing the costs of R&D or attracting the best research staff. Initially, these partnerships confined themselves to granting research bursaries; more recently, they have been carrying out their own research in their own laboratories. However, the undertakings have shown an unwillingness to assign their talented research staff to these partnerships for the simple reason that human resources have become their most precious commodity.[22]

4.4.1 Motivation for R&D cooperation

A recent survey shows that there is a will to cooperate in R&D.[23] The mainsprings of motivation have been well identified:

Information exchange

One of the original reasons for R&D cooperation was to exchange information in order to stimulate new ideas and widen the basis of thinking and research. The need to use such information more systematically and on an international scale led enterprises in certain areas to pool certain base data. In the face of an ever-increasing corpus of information, international cooperation makes it possible to set up faster, wider and more efficient systems.

A good example is the Diane Euronet. This was set up at the instance of the Commission to promote interchange of scientific, technical and socio-economic data between EEC member countries.

Shared resources

We have shown that R&D is becoming increasingly expensive. Many enterprises are expressing the need to share equipment, staff, know-how, etc. and this, of course, applies to very complex systems or major technological projects. Where the R&D cost reaches the heights already mentioned for aviation and communications it becomes difficult for one enterprise or one country to finance such projects. The individual approach is still possible if the project is highly specific or extremely advanced but is becoming less and less likely in more general or major emerging technologies.

- In the development of semi-conductors, for example, 20 major international cooperation agreements have been reached in the last 10 years (appendix 21).
- A second example is the Prometheus project which was submitted under the Eureka programme by 10 European enterprises, most of them in the motor industry. It is designed to develop assisted steering by means of an on-board electronic device. The programme is planned to run for seven years and will call for FFr 300 million per annum.[24]
- A further example of this collaboration which is so essential to the pooling of resources is Ariane. Since 1973 Europe has

succeeded in perfecting a heavy (250 T) first-stage rocket which has been taken up by ten European countries. France's Centre National d'Etudes Spatiales is responsible for project management and the tasks have been split between seven principal contractors: Aérospatiale, Architecture Industrielle, Société Européenne de la Propulsion, Matra and Air Liquide (France), ETCA (Belgium), Contraves (Switzerland), ERNO (FRG). In turn these enterprises put much of the work out to some 60 European subcontracting firms.[25]

Furthermore, pooling resources also spreads the risk: first and foremost the financial risk (risk spreading), followed by the technical risk (risk pooling) because the enterprises involved can try different technological approaches to one and the same problem.

Extended market

In many high-tech activities the cost of R&D is excessive relative to the total foreseeable turnover deriving from the product. Such massive investment can be justified only if the market can be

Table 4.12 Ratio of R&D expenditure to turnover, 1983

Company	Ratio %
TeleSciences	31,6
Policy Management System	26,6
ADAC Laboratoires	26,4
Hogan System	22,9
Fortune System	22,3
Management Science Amer	20,8
King Radio	20,0
United Technologies	11,1
IBM	5,0
C.G.E.	4,5
General Electric	3,2
Boeing	3,1
Renault	2,6
General Motors	2,6

Source: Revue Française de Gestion, Fortune and Louvain, Danila N., Le management de la recherche-développement, Revue Française de Gestion, no. 56, 1986. Goetschin P., Technologie et management, Revue Economique et Sociale, 44th year, Lausanne, November 1986, pp. 223–6.

enlarged by cooperation between enterprises in different countries when it becomes possible for the joint product to be sold on a very much wider market. Table 4.12 shows R&D spending relative to turnover for some American and European companies.

The additional risks inherent in the fragmented European market (different technical standards, regulations, protection, etc.) are a spur to closer cooperation between European firms.

Need to standardise

Complex systems or high-tech products will yield a profit only if they can be made standard in as many countries as possible and this kind of standardisation can be achieved only by close cooperation between the different national industries at the R&D stage.

There are four types of industrial standards:[26]

- *Information standards*: these lay down terminology and the measurement methods and tests for evaluating and quantifying product characteristics.
- *Compatibility standards*: these specify product characteristics to ensure compatibility with complementary products or systems.
- *Range standards*: these define a certain level of permissible product characteristics, e.g. measurements, etc.
- *Quality standards*: these are developed to ensure acceptable product quality in various aspects.

By way of example we may mention the agreement reached between eight European computer manufacturers (Bull, Nixdorf, Siemens, Philips, Thomson, Olivetti, ICL and STET) with the avowed intent of ensuring that the multiplicity of options which the standards allow should not render it impossible to make compatible equipment. Similarly in the USA, manufacturers such as IBM, Wang, Burroughs, ATT, etc. set up COS (cooperation for open systems) earlier this year and Japanese manufacturers, with MITI encouragement, launched POSI (promotion conference for Osi in Japan) in November 1985.

148 Research and Innovation

Each of these organisations defines a corpus of standards for a well-defined application and the member manufacturers conform.[27]

EEC members have shown determination to strengthen their R&D links because their chances of survival and independence are bound up with the rate of scientific and technological innovations which they can achieve. However, reality has shown that such efforts still need following up, particularly at enterprise level. The European collaborative projects currently in progress[28] could provide a development base for European enterprises and a more general framework for the promotion of closer industrial relations.

Table 4.13 shows how European executives are motivated in the matter of R&D cooperation. The study was carried out by Mariti and Smiley[29] and is based on articles in the European financial press, interviews with European executives and a sample of 70 cooperation agreements concluded in 1980.

Table 4.13 Motivation for R&D cooperation

Motivation	%
Transfer of technologies	29
Technological complementarity	41
Marketing agreements	21
Economies of scale	16
Risk sharing	14

Source: Mariti and Smiley (1983).

4.4.2 Forms of R&D cooperation

Though it has been practised in Europe for some years there are few empirical studies of inter-enterprise cooperation and its characteristics and effects, and even less literature on R&D cooperation alone.

Cooperation between enterprises may take different forms, e.g. informal agreements, medium- or long-term contracts, licences, consortia or joint ventures. The mode adopted will depend on the strategies of the particular enterprise and the degree of aggressiveness of its attitude to the other partner (see chapter 3).

The principal forms of cooperation which enterprises adopt are as follows.

Horizontal cooperation

Here the cooperating enterprises are more or less identical, have the same specialisation and manufacture the same products; they sell them in identical or different markets and are thus competitors.

The situation can present certain difficulties as R&D constitutes a major competitive weapon. The obligation to pool results reduces the incentive to increase the effort because each partner is aware that any additional R&D may benefit his competitor.

The advantages of this form of cooperation derive from the increased financial resources available for R&D and the economies of scale for development work. A further benefit is the fact of 'dynamic' economies: a joint learning curve can speed up the process of invention and innovation.

Vertical cooperation

Here the cooperating enterprises have consecutive activities in the final product production chain. Conduct of the arrangement is much easier because each enterprise carries out the specific part of the project best suited to its capacities. Task allocation is easier when the enterprises have different equipment and objectives.

Radial cooperation

This is the most complex form because it combines the complementary capabilities of two or more different enterprises in a diversified project. One enterprise usually assumes the role of main contractor and in this capacity is responsible for overall coordination, the others acting as subcontractors. It is the trickiest type of cooperation to set up and stability is often under threat. Its internal stability is always vulnerable to behaviour based on participation in the agreement with an eye to seizing as much information and knowledge as possible for minimum contribution in order to strengthen its own position and become aggressive at the earliest opportunity. Its external stability is vulnerable to third-party strategies designed to thwart the partners' strategies and provoke conflicts of interest.

In a more general way, coordination within this type of technological agreement is a priori both cumbersome and expensive, for, in reality, the collaborating firms may have very different objectives, strategies, planning horizons and appetites for risk.

Between 1975 and 1984, 70% of R&D cooperation agreements were of the horizontal type.

Jacquemin's work[30] on 212 technical cooperation agreements between European enterprises found the following:

- 2 participants 70%
  more than 2 participants 30%

- same nationality 30%
  different nationalities 70%

- within EEC 26%
  outside EEC 74%

- agreement 77%
  joint company 23%

- horizontal 70%
  vertical 30%

- process 33%
  product 67%

- final product 59%
  component 41%

It is interesting to note that horizontal agreements (between competitors) were easily the most common and that there were so few radial agreements that they have been lumped in with vertical agreements.

4.4.3 Radial cooperation

As we saw, this type of cooperation agreement is difficult to set up and manage. Nevertheless it is one of the more valuable strategies for controlling major new technological generations. Biotechnology provides a good illustration.[31] Control of future biochemical technologies largely depends on the combinatory nature of the R&D and one winning strategy is to increase joint working between the new chemistry and the new biology.

- Based on a very advanced chemicals industry, Europe has developed skills in enzyme and fermentation engineering. If it succeeded in mastering vegetable and animal cell culture it would establish decisive synergy between the two. Europe is very strong in agriculture and could thus use this as a means to cross the boundary (see figure 4.3).

Both sides are dragging their feet: chemicals enterprises, as we know, are reluctant to throw themselves wholeheartedly into biotechnology and CAP maintains fermentation material prices at levels which are a disincentive to innovation – yet this is a chance to transform European agriculture into a trump card for a future technological generation.

Base technology   Biotechnology meets new chemical technology   Base technology

Biology	Cell engineering	Genetic engineering	Protein engineering	Chemistry
	Vegetable and animal cell culture	Fermentation engineering	Enzyme engineering	

Figure 4.3 Synergy between two major technologies
Source: Nizet (1987).

- There has been much American development of cell and genetic engineering. Once the Americans master protein engineering, synergy will be established between these two major fields.

- Japanese agriculture is not highly advanced and there is no powerful chemicals industry. Japan has therefore made for the heart of the matter and developed a strong base in genetic and fermentation engineering. From this they can radiate outwards and try to link the two fields. We thus see that radial cooperation is important and even essential for this kind of strategy.
- Bionics is a similar case. This new field demands mastery of three different technologies:

  - Information technology
  - Biotechnology
  - New materials technology

There are signs that Italian enterprises may be embarking on this road: the coming together of Ferruzi (Bio), Olivetti (Information) and Montedison (new materials) could represent the beginnings of a winning European strategy at world level.

4.4.4 Unequal cooperation

In an unequal situation the strategic management of the alliance is of prime importance (see chapter 3).

Doz studied unequal cooperation in the area of technological agreements.[32] Based on a pilot study he makes the following points:

- Convergent objectives: even where the partners complement each other to a significant degree it is difficult to achieve convergent objectives. There is always a competitive element in a relationship of this kind and strategies designed to seize or safeguard specific technologies can distort the situation or make it dangerous.
- Consistency of roles and positions in the larger organisation: internal coalitions and struggles for power may be targeted on the alliance and may develop strategies which the weaker partner cannot cope with easily.
- The interface between the partners often lies at an operational level remote from general management. The executives here may have very different ways of managing an ambiguous position in which each partner is also the other's competitor.

The extent to which both partners benefit from cooperation will depend on their skill in managing this ambiguity.

4.5 MANAGEMENT OF R&D AND INNOVATION

If a policy of R&D cooperation is to be developed there must be proper management. European cooperation between badly managed activities can only lead to second-rate results. We have seen that the mastery of technical progress is a decisive competitive tool provided that the R&D is part of a strategy designed to guide and make best use of it.[33]

4.5.1 Exploiting the technological environment

Work at Louvain shows the most effective enterprises do not confine innovation to 'house' R&D but conduct an external policy which systematically exploits the technological environment.

- That environment plays a major part in the enterprise's innovative capability. The quality of its relations with external technical agents is a vital factor of its progress-strategy. A significant proportion of ideas and sources leading to progress come from outside rather than from house R&D alone.
- Innovative enterprises have developed their perception of the technological environment systematically and exploit a range of outside sources. The ability to innovate is associated with openness to the outside and such enterprises are run as 'open systems' with continuous involvement in transactions with their environment.
- Perception and exploitation of the technological environment depend on central organisational characteristics. The structures of an enterprise whose practice this is are livelier, more receptive to question and change and more organic than bureaucratic. They often have frontier units to provide a continuous enterprise/environment interface which are distinguished by their ability to pick up and pass on relevant information for a number of highly specific problems.

154 Research and Innovation

This suggests that efficient enterprises will have a positive attitude to cooperation.

A preferred form of exploitation of the technological environment is cooperation with the universities. The Japanese have adopted this as a systematic international strategy, notably in the form of bilateral national cooperation agreements in the field of science and technology. The list of the main agreements (see appendix 26) shows that the majority were concluded over the last ten years and cover the technologies of the future. Then there are the contracts concluded between the undertakings and the universities. A recent survey[34] shows that:

> almost all American universities involved in research worthy of the name receive financing from individual Japanese companies for the conduct either of specific research or of research associated with the outcome of existing university research. The total amounts involved range from 150 million to 200 million dollars ... The American university system professes complete freedom of information and action in this area. It refuses to accept any control by the Pentagon.[35]

Lastly, the research contracts concluded between a large corporation and the new technological SMEs represent an interesting source of progress.

When Japanese companies commission research by American or European SMEs:

> their aim is to acquire the entire knowhow of these teams. They send large numbers of engineers to monitor the work on the spot, with a view to anticipating the results in order to secure product type-approval, to conduct marketing tests and to launch production as soon as possible. The American research serves as a basis for the Japanese companies to pursue the development of numerous applications. These Japanese companies frequently have access to the world market, and they are not interested in selling, or even exchanging, their knowhow once they are in a position to do otherwise.

Research and Innovation   155

These Japanese companies are sufficiently dynamic to capitalize in their own right on the expansion of technology, whereas the American corporations often release highly competent individuals who create on their account what they should have created on their employer's account.[36]

4.5.2   Close relation between R&D and marketing

In efficient enterprises cooperation between the commercial and R&D departments is well organised. There is on-going confrontation between the two sets of logic and there are more differences of opinion but more skill in managing them. This is brought out by most of the relevant studies and one, Essex University's Sappho project,[37] was particularly concerned with this area. By comparing successful and failed innovations the writers make the following points with regard to the successes:

- Potential customers' expectations and desiderata are better understood and are included in the reckoning at the time of design and development.
- The innovation is not launched on the market until it is known that the response and quality are both satisfactory.
- The innovation is marketed in a far more developed way; the enterprise realises that every innovation has to be 'sold' and needs specific promotion.

Organisation theory places great emphasis on the integration of the different departments in a firm.[38] It assumes specific mechanisms plus skills in conflict management and communication.

4.5.3   Management of research staff

Research workers are experts and cannot be treated like managerial staff. The risk to the enterprise is that the experts will lose sight of the strategy and pursue scientific projects bearing no relation to the market or the competition.

Molitor[39] shows that the ability of enterprises here is low. His work made it possible to type research workers on the basis of two criteria which are important to the enterprise:

- *The researcher's involvement in the corporate strategy*: does he see himself as an element of his company's competitiveness or does he pursue purely scientific projects which are divorced from market/production applications?
- *The researcher's career objectives*: does he see research as his career or is he, rather, hoping to leave it for management?

Using these criteria, Molitor shows that there are four types of research worker:

- The 'expert' who regards himself as an active agent of strategy and looks to a career in research. This category is the most useful to corporate competitiveness.
- The 'scientist' who also looks to a career in research but has no interest in strategy. This category is, of course, less useful to corporate competitiveness.
- The 'manager' who is interested in strategy and aims to leave research as soon as he can to go in for management. The enterprise soon loses him from its research staff.
- The 'careerist' who has no interest in the strategy and no longer does research but is gambling on an ambiguous situation in which his outside chances are enhanced by belonging to the enterprise and his internal chances are enhanced by his outside contacts (see figure 4.4).

Career \ Strategy	Main interest	No interest
Research	Expert	Scientist
Management	Manager	Careerist

Figure 4.4 Typology of R&D people

Only the first category is of genuine use in the creation of competitive advantages. Molitor's work shows European performance to be poor in this respect and his sample breaks down as follows:

experts	15.5%
scientists	32.5%
managers	33.2%
careerists	18.8%

He recommends the institution of a specific expert career with a separate salary structure and status within the traditional hierarchy; this would associate research staff more closely with strategic thinking and integrate research more effectively into the enterprise's other functions: production, marketing, finance, etc.

4.5.4 R&D decentralisation and integration

- It is interesting to note that efficient enterprises such as IBM or GE integrate technology at the SBU (strategic base unit) level. An EIRMA study[10] shows that this is not so in Europe where R&D is still very often located at the corporate or divisional planning level. This implies a top-down view in which R&D management takes no active part in practical decisions.

  According to certain writers, this greatly reduces the integration of R&D into the enterprise's strategic manoeuvring and thus its effect on the enterprise's competitiveness.

- It is worth emphasising here that the studies show small units to be more innovative and creative than large. This applies to laboratories and enterprises alike. As we have shown, America's lead in technology rests notably on scientific SMEs which can provide continually updated technical progress and the point is well illustrated by Highway 128 and Silicon Valley. The difference in creativity is explained by:

  - More rigorous research staff selection.
  - More precise research and innovation objectives.
  - Greater researcher awareness of costs and time limits.

158   Research and Innovation

- Closer relations with production and marketing.
- A resultant strengthening of strategic motivation.[41]

4.5.5   Innovation as an entrepreneurial process

- Innovation requires flexible structures, good failure-tolerance, an open attitude to the market and competition. It also requires the presence of entrepreneurs or 'intrapreneurs' making their own specific contributions: a vision of potential progress, sufficient appetite for risk to go ahead and a personal authority which inspires loyalty and team spirit. This is not the place to summarise the many relevant studies[42] but they all come back to structures and management style. In order to keep its 'intrapreneurs' a large efficient enterprise will create space within the organisation allowing much greater freedom and room for initiative than hitherto. The company background, climate and management style are, of course, involved. Traditional European enterprises lag behind in this field to a disturbing extent.[43]
- In a high-performance enterprise which sees innovation as a process which can develop only in a climate of initiative, freedom and participation the whole organisation tends to be innovative. A recent survey carried out by Arthur D. Little[44] shows that the type of participatory climate found in Japan tends to increase corporate creativity from every point of view (see figure 4.5).

4.5.6   Management of technological resources

Several recent studies show that high-performance enterprises manage their technological resources more systematically and professionally. In a recent book, Jacques Morin[45] adopts an approach which shows clearly that mastery of technical progress will depend on appropriate professional capacity, as regards both strategic choices and management. Under the heading 'Management of technical resources' (MTR) he catalogues the growing importance of methods of:

Research and Innovation

We at Arthur D. Little see innovation occurring in *at least* the following areas.

Question 14:
To what degree do you see innovation needing to occur in each area in your organisation or core business?

Response: A Great Deal

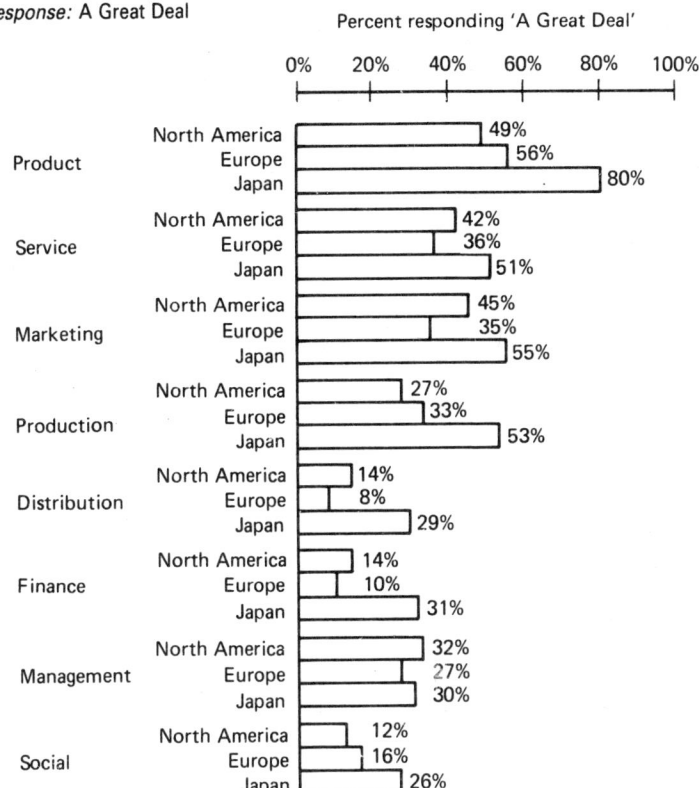

Figure 4.5 Participatory climate increases Japanese corporate creativity
Source: Little (1985).

- Optimising
- Enriching
- Safeguarding
- Recording
- Valuing
- Monitoring

an enterprise's technological assets. Several other approaches indicate a similar trend.[46]

160 Research and Innovation

4.5.7 Role of top management

Innovation and R&D will only be integrated fully enough into a firm's global strategy if management is sufficiently aware and convinced.[47] Arthur D. Little's investigation reveals fairly marked differences between European top management and its Japanese and American competitors (figure 4.6).[48]

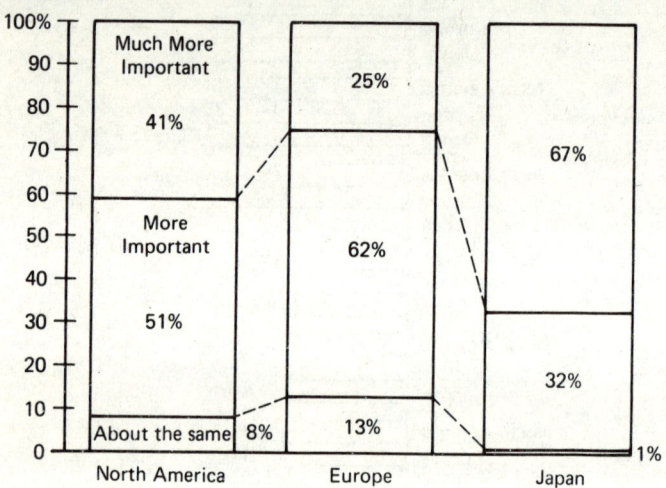

Question 4:
How is the need for innovation changing in your organisation? Is it becoming:

Figure 4.6 Need for innovation: USA, Europe and Japan
Source: Little (1985).

NOTES

1. This chapter owes much to Arenas (1986).
2. Five indicators are used for the comparison:
   - R&D spending
   - Patent registrations in the USA
   - Technological balance of payments
   - High-tech product output and market share
   - High-tech product imports and exports
3. de Woot et al. (1971); Heyvaert (1972); de Woot and Desclee (1984).
4. Altshuler et al. (1984); Abernathy (1978); Clark (1979).

5　Ergas (1984).
6　The USA represented 38% of the OECD GDP for 1981, the EEC 32% and Japan 15% (Ergas 1984).
7　Hager, W., Noelke, M. and Taylor, R. 1982: *EEC Protectionism: Present Practice and Future Trends*, European Research Associates, Brussels.
8　Jacquemin, A. and Spinoit, B. 1986: *Economic and Legal Aspects of Cooperative Research: A European View*, New York.
9　Télésis, excerpts 1981–5, Paris 1986.
10　Ergas (1984).
11　Ergas (1984).
12　Ergas (1984).
13　Ergas (1984).
14　*Economist*, 6 December 1986.
15　Dunning and Pearce (1981).
16　Ergas quotes illuminating figures on this. In a population of American SMEs, 46% of first-year sales were to the federal government. In 1981 federal contracts with high-tech SMEs accounted for $2.5 billion.
17　Little (1971); Larsens and Rodgers (1985); de Kerorguen and Merlant (1985).
18　*Le Monde*, 27 September 1979.
19　Sciberas et al. (1978).
20　Le Foll (1985); Durand and Feuillee (1986).
21　See appendix 25.
22　CPE Bulletin no. 20, October 1985, p. 81.
23　EIRMA (1972).
24　EUREKA (1986).
25　*Aviation Week and Space Technology*, May 1983.
26　Ergas (1984).
27　*Trends/Tendencies*, 11th year, November 1986; *International Herald Tribune*, 19 February 1985.
28　Particularly EUREKA, ESPRIT, BRITE, RACE, EUROTRA and in biotechnology materials and raw materials (see appendix 25).
29　Marita and Smiley (1983).
30　Jacquemin et al. (1985).
31　Nizet (1987).
32　Doz (1986); Petrella (1986).
33　de Woot et al. (1971); Goetschin (1986); Ketteringham and White (1984); Harris, Shaw and Somers (1984); Arenas (1986); Heyvart (1972); Keith (1983).

34 Japan is buying its way into US university labs, *Business Week*, 24 September 1984.
35 CPE Bulletin no. 31, October 1986, p. 45.
36 Bayen, M., CPE Bulletin no. 31, October 1986, p. 47.
37 Sappho Project, *Success and Failure in Industrial Innovation*, University of Sussex and Centre for the Study of Industrial Innovation, London 1973. Confederation of British Industry (1979); Petrella (1983).
38 Lawrence and Lorsch (1982).
39 Molitor (1971).
40 EIRMA (1986).
41 Confederation of British Industry (1979).
42 Pinchot (1985); Drucker (1985); Kanter (1983); Survey on the new entrepreneurs, *Economist*, 24 December 1983; The coming entrepreneurial revolution, *Economist*, 25 December 1976.
43 de Woot and Desclee (1984).
44 Little (1985).
45 Morin (1985).
46 Little (1981).
47 de Woot and Desclee (1984).
48 Little (1981).

Final comments

SENSE OF URGENCY

European integration is taking place more slowly than the globalisation of competition. In high-tech sectors many of our enterprises are forced to internationalise in unfavourable conditions. Global industrial strategies are developing very fast and unless we react even faster we may lose tomorrow's battles. Our American and Japanese competitors are not waiting for the common market to become a reality before they move ahead and create global competitive advantages. As we have seen, our enterprises are caught up in a fragmented European model which tends to destroy competitiveness. Forced to internationalise, they mostly do so from a national rather than a European base and can thus find themselves in an inferior position to their competitors. The consequences can be disastrous for Europe, particularly if we consider the following:

- Few enterprises are capable of internationalising independently. In fact, their strategic capability is not global and does not allow them to acquire sufficient world competitive advantages. In this situation they can fall behind, decline and lose the capacity to seize future opportunities.
- Many enterprises then opt for cooperation with American or Japanese partners who, because their national base is wider and their model creates competitiveness, are often more powerful, more advanced and more dynamic. In this situation European firms are in danger of occupying only a marginal place in alliance networks and being dominated by their foreign partners.

Final Comments

- We could thus lose leadership of emerging systems because the national bases are too small and the position of our enterprises in alliance networks too often subsidiary. The best would then specialise in niches but would not be able to give Europe control of those new technologies. Lacking adequate strategic capability, Europe would become a second-rate economy and would find it increasingly difficult to catch up in industry and technology.

Our analysis of corporate strategy makes this a perfectly credible picture unless we speed up the construction of a more integrated industrial and technological Europe. Many others have sounded the alarm before us.

A number of measures have been taken on the initiative of the Commission and European governments but we shall continue to lose ground until the degree of effort and, particularly, the rate of implementation are enough to carry us over the thresholds of size, complexity and durability required for the development of new competitive strategies.

PRIORITY MECHANISMS OF A GLOBAL APPROACH

In such a complex field the most dangerous temptation is to think that a piecemeal approach or a 'quick fix' will restore the situation.

It is the European model which destroys competitiveness that must be changed. This calls for a global approach.[1] 'Global approach' does not mean that we must become obsessed with detail in a framework of bureaucratic planning which would make the model even more rigid. Global approach means that we must act powerfully and simultaneously on a few mechanisms for change which could be combined to achieve the desired results.

If we turn first to corporate strategy, the European model which destroys competitiveness helps us to identify the priority mechanisms and reach the following hypothesis: if, in the high-tech sectors we could create a European demand which widened the prospects and opportunities open to our enterprises,

Final Comments

firms would soon develop more powerful strategic capability and acquire international competitive advantages; because this would improve their profitability, they would then be able to face greater technological and commercial risks and we should have the beginnings of a European spiral of progress; the model would then create competitiveness.

Mechanisms which could increase our enterprises' competitiveness include:

- A few large-scale European projects
- More cooperation
- Opening up public orders and doing away with the national champion policy
- Unified standards
- Improved supply of technology.

This with an eye to achieving fast an integrated market sufficiently competitive for the mechanisms of progress to have a dynamic effect.

Large-scale European projects

The principal value of large joint projects is the creation of sufficient demand for high tech to encourage enterprises to raise their sights and widen their strategic perspective. We have seen the success of Airbus and Ariane and there are other high-tech areas where joint projects would play a decisive role: telecommunications (ISDN), defence, artificial intelligence, etc. The objections are only too familiar: state control, bureaucracy, protection of national champions, etc. What we must remember is that in advanced technology the two great competing economic models depend largely on government spending.

Even if we add all the European budgets together, we do not match up. Another point to remember is that Japan and the USA manage to combine large public aid with genuine competition. The development of a European 'strategic view' is essential to guide the choice of large joint projects. This vision results from a concerted approach by enterprises, social forces and public authorities, but it needs a catalyst; in Japan this is the

MITI, in the USA the Defense Department and Space Agency.

Here it is up to the Commission, guided in particular by FAST analyses and scenarios; the role fits well into its mission as guardian of the treaties and organ of initiative and proposal.

Only if it increases its influence over the choice of long-term industrial strategies shall we ever create the European base our enterprises need. There is no other way. The truth of this is such that the Commission's role is beginning to be recognised even in the field of political cooperation.

> Originally resisted and restricted, the presence and role of the Commission in the structures of political cooperation has ultimately been universally accepted and the London report marks the end of this process in its statement that the Ten attach importance to the fact of the Commission of the European Communities being fully associated with every level of political cooperation.[2]

What holds good for the high-tech sectors may also hold good for the development of the Third World. This could be a source of a new kind of large-scale project which in its own way would also relate to the emerging technological systems. If Europe were thus to broaden its policy we could expect our enterprises to look to creative leaderships in non-triad markets and to seek involvement in a development process which is well-known to have great potential.

More cooperation

Industrial/technical cooperation is a priority mechanism for developing the strategic capability of our enterprises.

- Though it represents the 'second best' compared with independent growth, we know that for the major technologies of the future it is by now the only option left. Industrial cooperation is bound up with the existence of big projects; these are an incentive to cooperation which, in turn, makes it possible to carry out more ambitious projects. Thus the two mechanisms will have a convergent effect.
- R&D cooperation is the feature of the policy which is most accessible to enterprises and the Commission. Esprit's suc-

cess established both the urgent need felt by our enterprises and the speed of their response. It is thus a priority route which should be pursued and enlarged, particularly the radial form which is well-suited to exploit the potential for combining technologies. However, cooperation alone is not enough to create a European industrial base. Without the support of specific industrial projects our enterprises will continue to carry out R&D which is not sufficiently converted into international competitive advantage.

- Given the ambivalence of cooperation strategies where competition between the partners does not necessarily come to an end, it seems important to promote mastery of methods of managing alliances and consortia and a degree of balance between partners.

Public contracts

To major enterprises and SMEs alike public contracts play a decisive part in high tech. In the USA it is quite common for the first five years of a high-tech SME's life to depend entirely on public orders. Not only does Europe fail to match the USA and (in certain areas) Japan in this respect, but the contracts themselves are fragmented and mostly restricted to national champions. This is one of the most destructive practices observed in the European model of competitiveness; it rules out specialisation, aggravates task duplication and over-capacity and prevents European enterprises from developing their strategic capability to a continental and even less a world scale.

If our enterprises are to strengthen their strategic capability it is a major priority to open public procurement to European competition and make them a tool for European integration. This is, of course, bound up with the existence of big joint projects and the two mechanisms could have a cumulative convergent effect.

Unified technical standards

This is a very precise, very complex issue which has been the subject of many studies. It is decisive for European corporate competitiveness. Countless technical obstacles block the European path: telecommunications, defence, TGV, etc., and as a result we are forced to submit to standards laid down by large foreign multi-nationals which use them as a weapon of strategic dominance. Every step towards European or universal standards will increase the number of outlets available to our enterprises and thus serve to strengthen their strategic capability.

The real efforts already being made in this area, particularly for OSI, must be speeded up.

Improved supply of technology

The more conducive an industrial framework to creativity, innovation and the regeneration of scientific and technical skills, the more vigorous it is. Three key areas are relevant:

- *Improving our advanced technology training*: we have seen how far Europe is behind in the training of engineers; this is not only a matter of quantity. Relations between industry and universities should also be improved: science parks, agreement on programmes, research funding, etc.
- *Strengthening the business schools*: The strategic capability of our enterprises depends greatly on the quality of their management resources: methods, attitudes, internationalisation, etc. The quality of management will also determine the quality of R&D, the quality of technical cooperation agreements and the ability to convert innovation into competitive advantage.
- *Regeneration of the industrial fabric*: the industrial set-up should be more open so as to promote competition by innovation and a priority target here is a proliferation of highly technical SMEs for we know the major role played by scientific SMEs in American control of high tech. Many other factors will help to vitalise the European industrial scene, particularly its tolerance of the creative destruction process; as we have seen, competitive models tend to favour creation rather than prevent destruction. It is not easy to strike a balance and ultimately this is a political question

outside the scope of this report; in any case, it has been discussed in detail elsewhere.[3]

Development of corporate strategic and societal capability

As we saw, efficient enterprises see their strategic capability as a matter of continuous systematic creation not only of information, know-how and networks but also of human resources; the creation of a climate of initiative and responsibility at every level becomes a competitive factor. Development of the human potential in terms of productivity and creativity is a most effective competitive weapon. The structures of too many European enterprises are still autocratic or bureaucratic and their evolution towards more participative management must be accelerated. At societal level the effective enterprise seeks to increase the part it plays in joint projects or more general policies and to help deal with social problems brought about by economic and technical change.

In this field the systematic development of a capacity for dialogue and socio-political cooperation at European level would be an important competitive mechanism.

CONCLUDING THOUGHTS

Has Europe already been left behind? Would not an internationally oriented enterprise do better to turn to the Triad instead of Europe? These questions lie at the roots of our work.

The answer is unequivocal: many enterprises have already made the choice and may now be in an inferior position because there is no adequate European base. For the sectors of tomorrow where the die has not yet been cast we must create a sufficiently strong European base for our enterprises to internationalise with a strategic capability at least equal to that of their major American and Japanese competitors.

Demosthenes was right when he harangued the Athenians faced with the growing menace of Philip of Macedon:

For you know well, Athenians, that what has most contributed to Philip's success is that he has always been there before us,

170 Final Comments

ready to act. Master of an army ever under his control and knowing in advance what he intends to do ... Whilst we, we prepare ourselves only in disorder and confusion after tidings of the event. What is the result? We arrive when the battle is over. Thus are all our resources wasted in total loss.

NOTES

1 Davignon (1977; 1981a; 1981b).
2 de Schoutheete (1986).
3 Albert and Ball (1983).

Appendices

1	Evolution of research and development (R&D)	172
2	Emergence of the Triad	180
3	Performance in computer business	181
4	Respective weights of aircraft manufacturers	182
5	Generic strategies	182
6	Main characteristics of successful firms	183
7	The strategic capacity	184
8	The value chain	184
9	Alliances in the telecommunications and semi-conductor industries	185
10	Origin of biotechnology patents	188
11	Sophistication of the environment	189
12.1	Europe's technology gap	190
12.2	Evaluation of European technologies by Japanese industrialists	191
13	Japanese take-off in new technologies	192
14	Some samples of experience curves	193
15	Marginal efficiency of investment	196
16	Share of public expenditure in national income	198
17	IBM's strategic adaptations	199
18	Expansion of telecommunications service 1847–2000	204
19	Top UK take-over bids of 1986	205
20	Changes in the pattern of foreign direct investment, 1980–1985	206
21	Principal cooperation agreements in semiconductors	209
22	Organisational models for cooperation	211
23	Olivetti's strategic partnerships, 1985	212
24	Ranking of computer manufacturers before and after the partnership between Bull, HIS, NEC	213
25	Major European technological projects	214
26	Japan's bilateral agreements in R&D	217

APPENDIX 1 EVOLUTION OF RESEARCH AND DEVELOPMENT (R&D)

Table A1.1 Development in gross internal R&D expenditure

	1981 Million U$	%	1983 Million U$	Real growth 81–83
USA	73,678	46.4	88,329	3.8
Japan	25,574	16.1	33,493	8.2
EEC	47,536[a]	30.4	52,346[b]	2.5

[a] 10 countries.
[b] 5 countries.
Source: OCDE, Indicateurs de la Science et de la Technologie RD, invention et compétitivité, Paris, 1986.

Table A1.2 Number of researchers

	1981 Full-time	%	Real growth 79–81
USA	683,700	41.8	5.5
Japan	392,625	24.0	3.9
EEC[a]	414,640	25.5	3.5

[a] 10 countries.
Source: OCDE, Indicateurs de la Science et de la Technologie RD, invention et compétitivité, Paris, 1986.

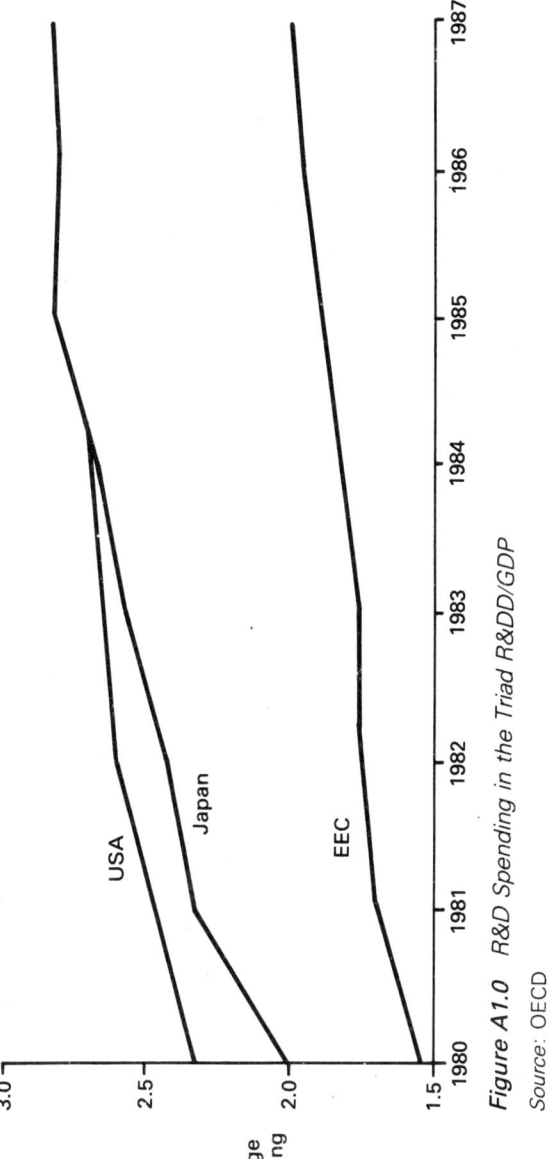

Figure A1.0 R&D Spending in the Triad R&DD/GDP

Source: OECD

174 Appendices

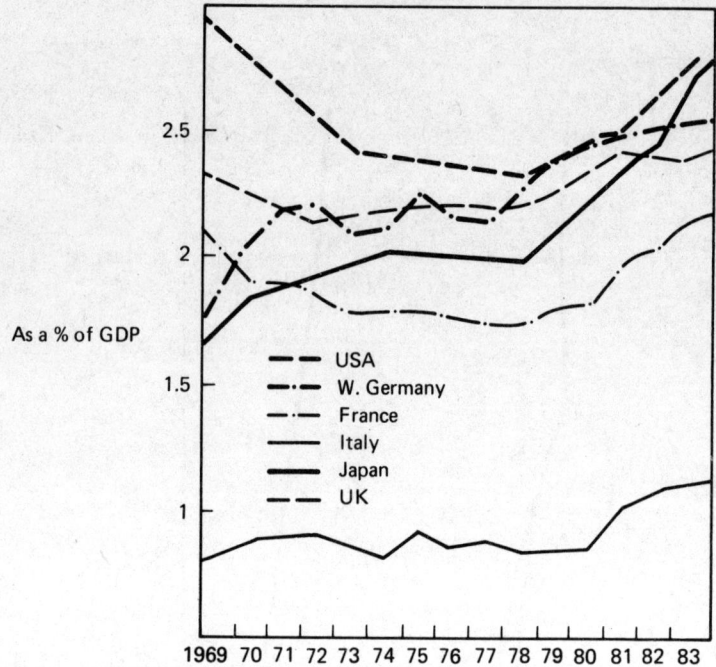

Figure A1.1 Total R&D spending
Source: IFRI (1986).

Appendices 175

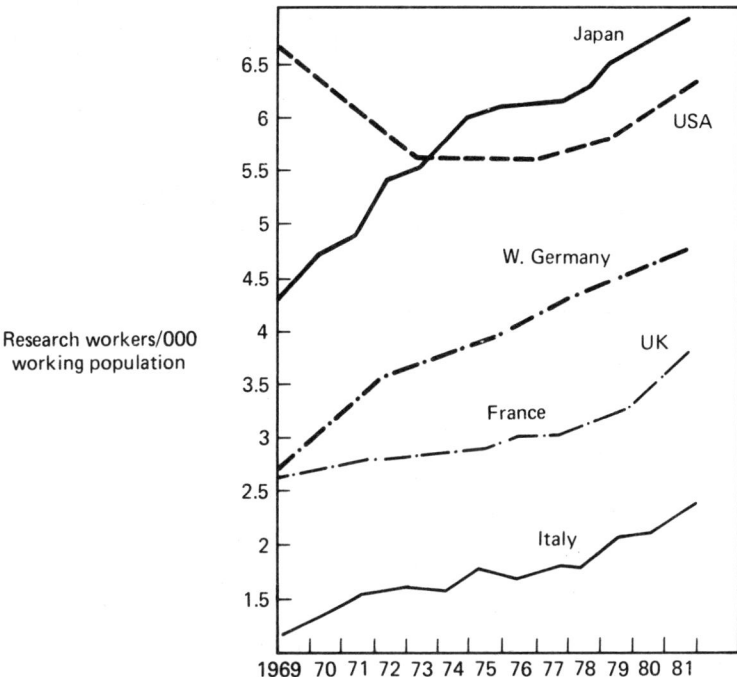

Figure A1.2 No. of research workers per head of population
Source: IFRI (1986).

176 Appendices

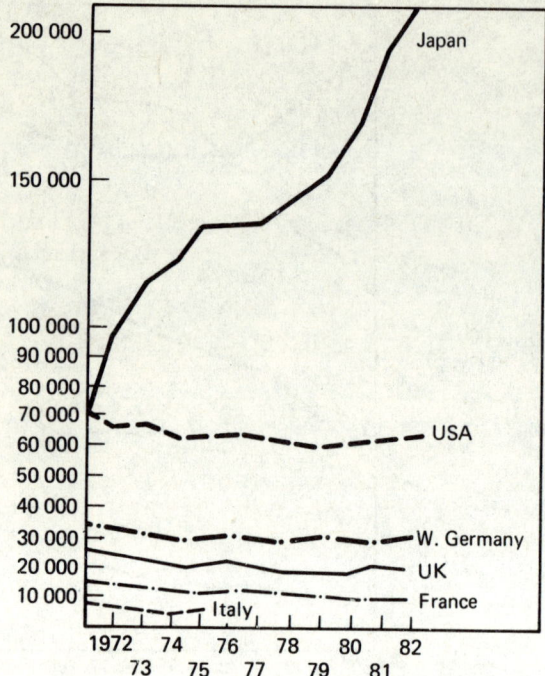

Figure A1.3 Patent applications in the advanced countries
Source: IFRI (1986).

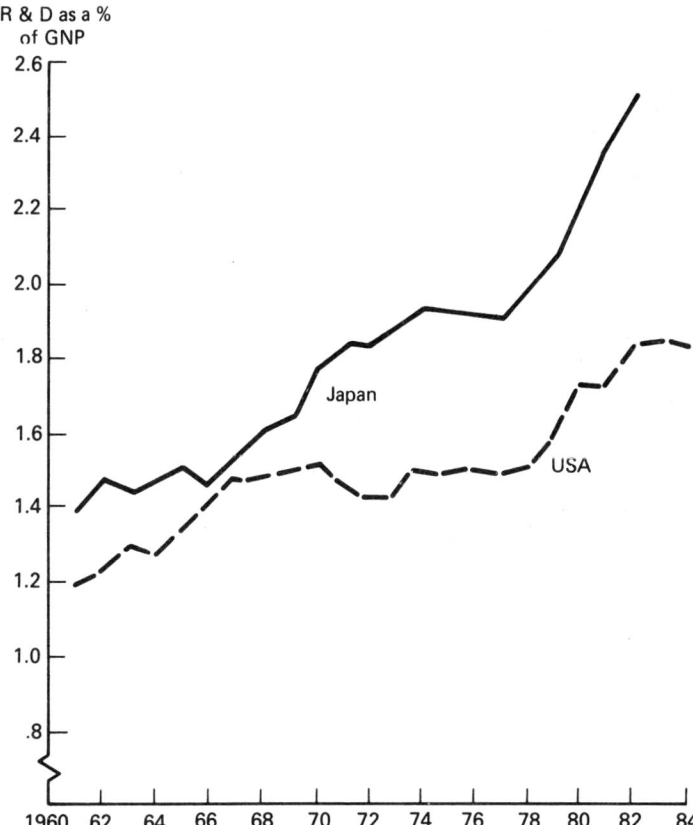

Figure A1.4 Trends in civil R&D expenditure by the US and Japanese governments

Source: CPE Bulletin no. 20, October 1985, p. 66.

Research and development expenditure by US companies on a sector-by-sector basis during 1984 was as follows:

Table A1.3 Research and development expenditure by US companies

Sector	Sales (10^6 $)	Profits (10^6 $)	R&D expenditure 10^6 $	profits	per employee
Aerospace	61,823	2,825	2,937	77	4,335
Semiconductors	12,008	871	989	75	4,842
Instrumentation	15,773	795	942	75	4,061
Telecommunications	74,451	2,695	2,792	64	4,577
Automated office equipment	16,799	962	920	60	4,334
Electronics	48,084	2,296	2,060	58	2,962
Computer-integrated manufacturing	14,988	534	456	53.4	2,275
Software	3,958	371	309	46	5,386
Pharmaceuticals	53,604	5,255	3,826	45.7	6,499
Data processing Computers	91,691	9,072	6,825	45	6,773
Rubber	24,595	769	569	44	1,965
Motor vehicles	169,200	9,058	5,681	43	4,301
Chemistry	119,340	5,527	3,643	34.5	4,249
Electricity	53,092	3,800	1,637	28	2,442
Textiles	10,052	227	81	21	570
Domestic electrical appliances	9,384	410	129	18	1,230
Preservative materials	13,470	599	184	17	1,559
Iron and steel	29,776	224	148	16	739
Paper	31,943	1,551	314	13	1,261
Food	76,803	3,306	671	11	1,014
Oil	366,858	17,545	2,385	6.4	3,109

Source: CPE, Bulletin no. 20, October 1985, pp. 5 and 16.

R&D EXPENDITURE BY US UNDERTAKINGS[1]

Research and development expenditure by the 100 largest US undertakings rose to $36,000 million in 1984 (as against $32,000 million in 1983). According to the forecasts, this expenditure would reach $40,000 million in 1985.

On average, R&D expenditure amounts to 5% of the undertakings' sales i.e., about $5,000 per employee. The companies that invested most in R&D are the following:

	$000 M
● IBM	: 3.1
● General Motors	: 3.08
● ATT	: 2.7
● General Electric	: 1.0
● United Technology	: 1.0
● ITT	: 0.97
● Eastman Kodak	: 0.83

Table A1.4 Financing of R&D by American industry

	% of turnover (1984)	Annual growth (average 79–84)
Information technology	7	+20%
Pharmaceuticals	6.5	+18%
Aeronautical	4.6	+18%
Automobile	3.5	+5%
Mechanical engineering	3.1	+7%
Chemical	3	+17%
Petroleum products	0.6	

Source: Batelle Institute, Geneva.

SUPPORT FOR R&D BY THE JAPANESE PUBLIC AUTHORITIES

The Japanese Government has given absolute priority to R&D over a long period. From 1964 to 1970 the Japanese R&D budget increased by 129%, and from 1970 to 1979 by 80% (compared with an increase of only 15% in the US R&D budget over the same period). In 1964 the Japanese industrial R&D budget was equivalent, in volume, to only 4% of that of the United States. By 1979 this percentage stood at 25%. The number of research staff and engineers working in Japanese laboratories rose from 172 000 in 1970 to 273 000 in 1979.

A major part of this research effort has been devoted to projects jointly involving public and private laboratories and geared towards medium-term industrial objectives (fifth-generation computers, biotechnologies, new materials, energy).

The results of this concerted action by the Japanese Government and Japanese industry are already apparent in a number of sectors.

APPENDIX 2   EMERGENCE OF THE TRIAD

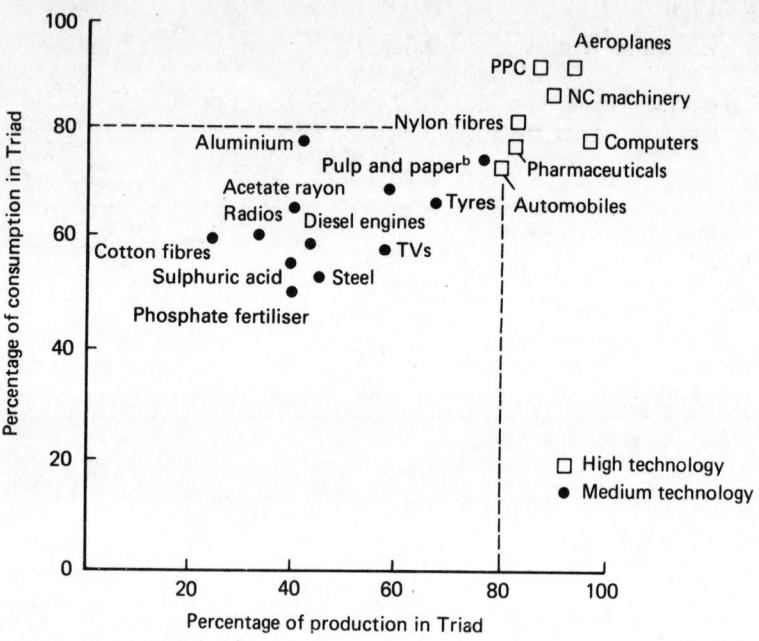

Figure A2.1 *Share of the Triad in the world market: selected segments. Most high-tech products are still produced and consumed in the Triad*[a]

[a] Ohmae (1985).
[b] Including Canada.

Source: Data from McKinsey analysis of US Department of Commerce *Statistical Abstract*, 1981. Nomura Research Institute, Japanese Ministry of Finance, *International Statistical Abstract*, Prime Minister's Office of Japan, 1981.

APPENDIX 3 PERFORMANCE IN COMPUTER BUSINESS

Table A3.1 Performance in computer business, 1985

Company	Sales US$ 000	Net income US$ 000	Employees	% Sales	Net income % Equity	Net surplus (40% Net income)
IBM	50,056	6,555	405,535	13.1	20.5	2,622
Philips	18,079	276	345,600	1.5	4.7	110
Siemens	17,833	490	348,000	2.8	10.4	196
Digital	6,686	444	89,000	6.7	9.8	178
Honeywell	6,624	281	94,022	4.3	11.0	112
HP	6,505	489	84,000	7.5	12.3	196
Fujitsu	6,396	364	74,187	5.7	15.0	146
Sperry	5,687	286	77,716	5.0	9.6	114
Burroughs	5,037	248	60,519	4.9	10.0	99
IBM (RFA)	4,493	289	28,172	6.5	35.4	116
NCR	4,317	315	62,000	7.3	13.6	126
IBM (FR)	4,181	320	22,452	7.7	25.1	128
Canon	4,008	155	34,129	3.9	9.3	62
IBM (UK)	3,942	399	18,798	10.1	37.4	160
IBM (Japan)	3,835	306	16,775	8.0	22.7	122
Control data	3,679	(567)	38,856	—	—	—
Olivetti	3,215	264	48,944	8.2	19.3	106
Wang	2,351	15	31,061	0.7	1.2	6
Rank Xerox	2,271	74	29,651	3.3	6.0	30
Ricoh	2,231	68	25,000	3.1	8.9	27
Apple	1,918	61	4,300	3.2	11.1	24
Bull	1,793	12	26,403	0.7	4.5	5
East Asiatic	1,573	19	15,969	1.2	11.4	8
Nixdorf	1,333	57	23,290	4.3	6.5	23
Esselte	1,187	21	17,177	1.8	10.5	8

Source: UCL and *Fortune*, August 1986.

APPENDIX 4   RESPECTIVE WEIGHTS OF AIRCRAFT MANUFACTURERS

Table A4.1   Comparison between Aérospatiale and the American Steam Roller

Company	Turnover FR 000 million	Payroll 000
United Technologies (United States)	118.7	184
Boeing (United States)	103	104
McDonnell Douglas (United States)	86.7	97
Rockwell (United States)	86.1	123
Hughes (United States)	46.8	80
British Aerospace (Great Britain)	28.7	75.5
Aérospatiale (France)	24.6	35
MBB (FRG)	18.9	35
CASA (Spain)	2.3	9
Aérospatiale+MBB+British Aerospace+CASA	74.5	156

Source: Le Nouvel Economiste, no. 555, 29 August 1986, p. 36.

APPENDIX 5   GENERIC STRATEGIES

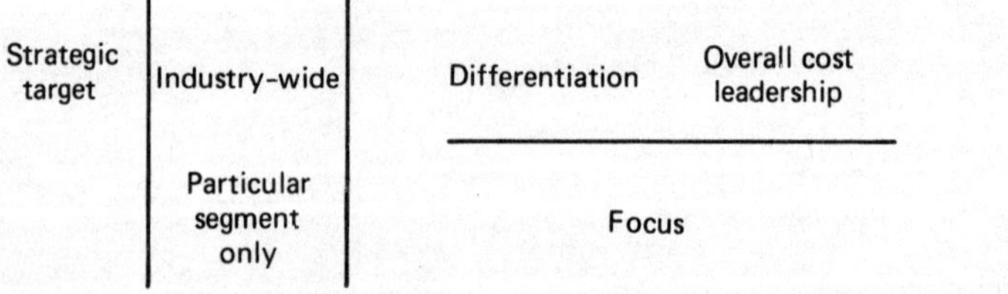

Figure A5.1   Generic strategies

Source: Porter (1980; 1985).

Appendices 183

APPENDIX 6 MAIN CHARACTERISTICS OF SUCCESSFUL FIRMS

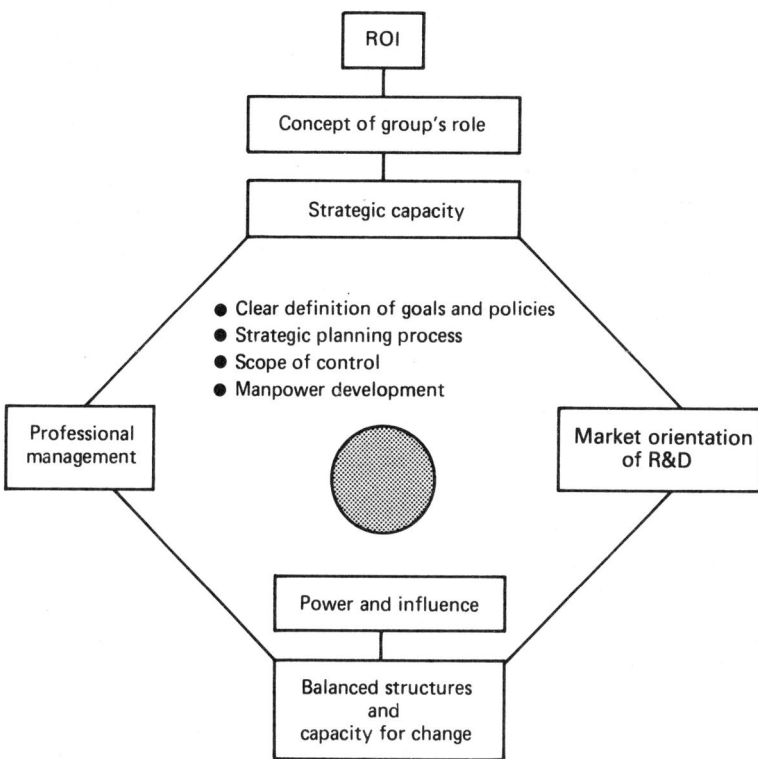

Figure A6.1 Main characteristics of successful firms

Source: CRECIS Research Project on European Groups, Louvain, University of Louvain.

APPENDIX 7 THE STRATEGIC CAPACITY

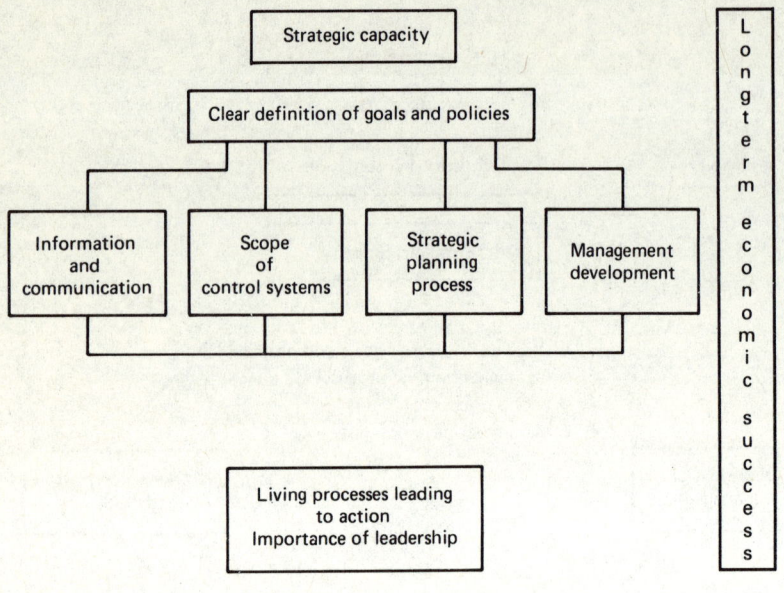

Figure A7.1 *The strategic capacity*
Source: de Woot and Desclee (1984).

APPENDIX 8 THE VALUE CHAIN

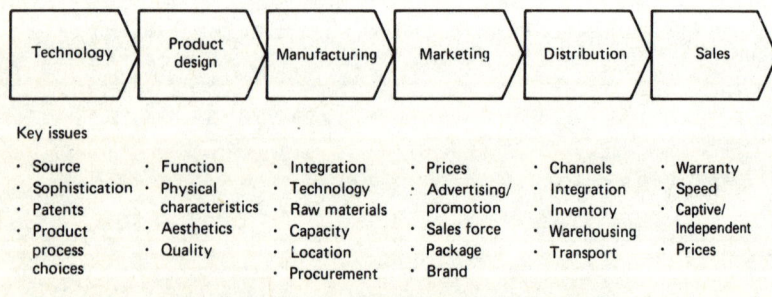

Figure A8.1 *The realities of global competition*
Source: McKinsey in Ohmae (1985).

Appendices 185

APPENDIX 9 ALLIANCES IN THE TELECOMMUNICATIONS AND SEMICONDUCTOR INDUSTRIES

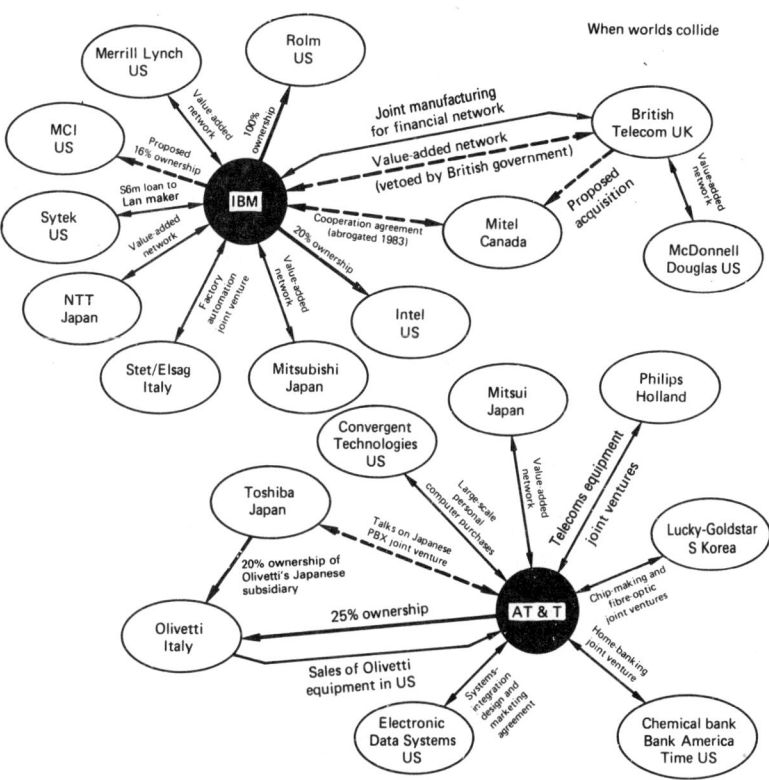

Figure A9.1 Alliances in the telecommunications industry
Source: *Economist*, 23 November 1985, p. 36.

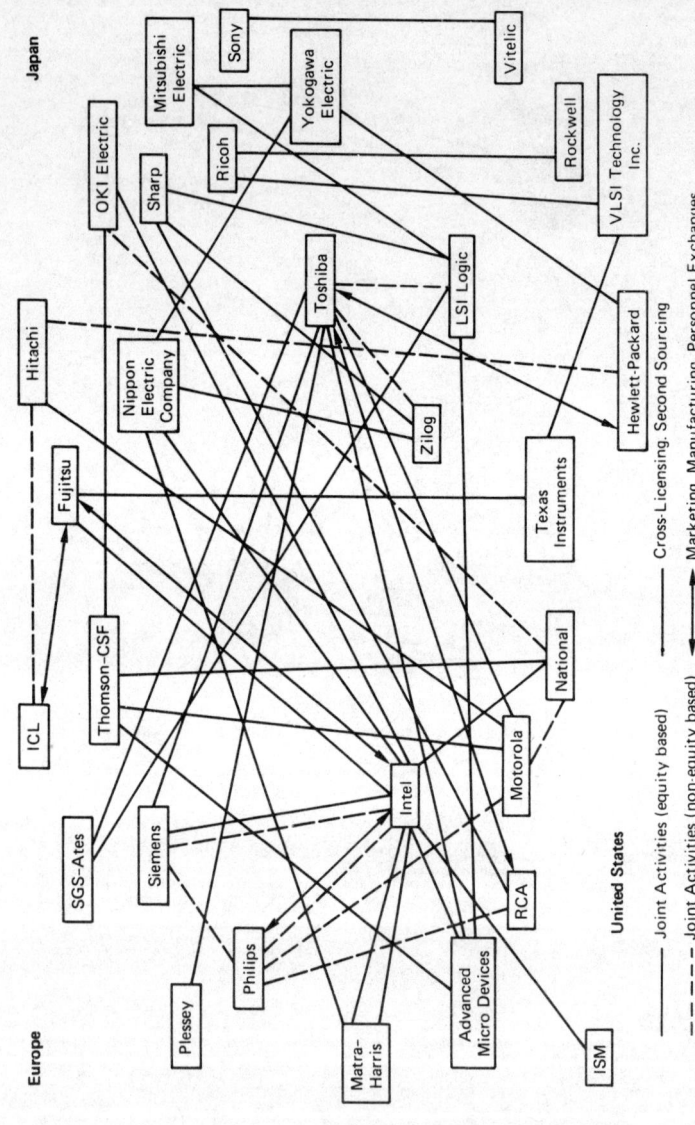

Figure A9.2 Alliances in the semiconductor industry

Source: SRI (1985–6). Report no. 730, Strategic Partnership, Gorbis and Yorke, p. 7.

Appendices 187

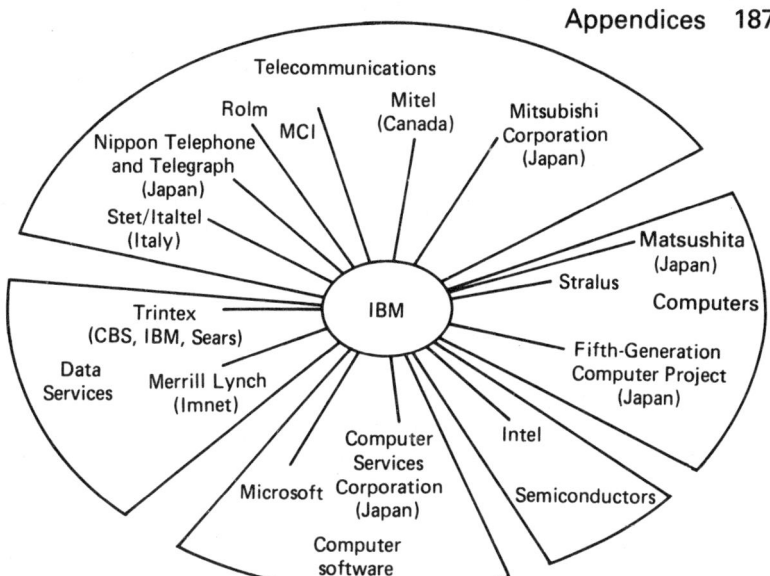

Figure A9.3 *IBM's alliances*

Source: SRI (1985–6). Report no. 730, p. 8.

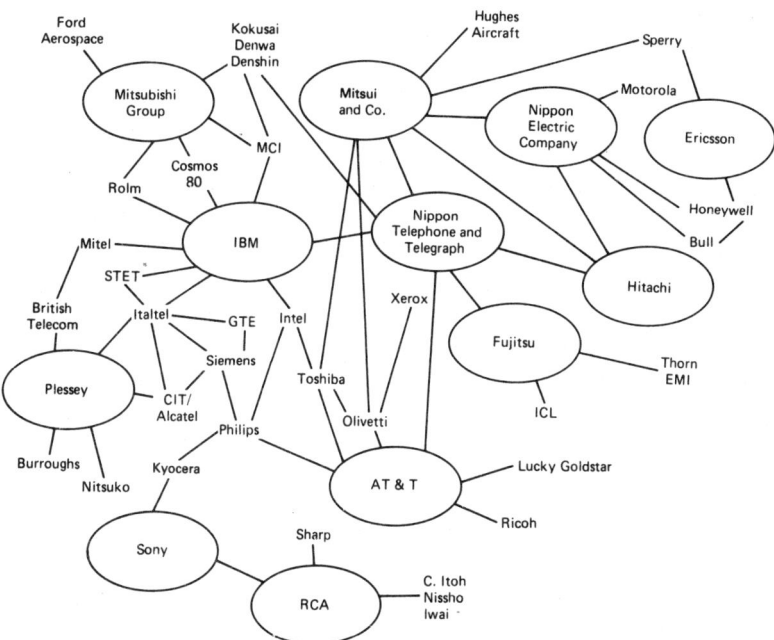

Figure A9.4 *Alliances in telecommunication*

Source: SRI (1985–6). Report no. 730, p. 32.

APPENDIX 10 ORIGIN OF BIOTECHNOLOGY PATENTS

Origin of biotechnology patents[2]

An exhaustive study on US patents in the biotechnologies sector has been published by Bioteknomics Inc. The study, headed by Dr Robert C. Aries, is entitled 'Biotechnology Patents in 1983'.

It deals with the six patent categories defined by the US Patent Office: genetic engineering, enzymes, immobolised enzymes, tissue cultures, starch hydrolysates and amino-acids.

Table A10.1 shows the number of patent applications filed by the USA, Japan and the European countries in 1982–5.

Table A10.1 Biotechnology recent applications filed by the USA, Japan and Europe

Category of patent	USA	Japan	Europe
Genetic engineering	62	13	26
Enzymes	49	19	25
Immobilised enzymes	47	24	23
Tissue culture	32	2	6
Starch hydrolysate	14	4	8
Amino-acids	7	10	5

Another study carried out by the same company shows that 9,000 patent applications in the field of molecular biology and microbiology were filed between 1963 and 1983 and that in 1983, out of 632 patents filed, 337 were of US origin.

Appendices 189

APPENDIX 11 SOPHISTICATION OF THE ENVIRONMENT

Europe lags the U.S. and Japan in most modern infrastructure[a]

Table A11.1 European lag in modern infrastructure, 1980–1

Installed base per 10,000 Hab.	USA	Japan	Europe
Telephones	7,700	4,200	3,500
PABX lines	1,445	483	485
Televisions	6,350	2,450	2,300
Photocopiers	17	20	10
Computers	10	4	3
NC Machine tools	32	42	25
Robots	0.15	0.70	0.10
CT-scanners	0.05	0.01	0.01
Nuclear electr. (kwh)	1,308	735	826

[a] Télésis (1985); excerpts 1981–5.
Source: ATT, NRI, Financial Times, UN Statistics, Jetro, Maptec, Télésis estimates.

Europe is sacrificing its future[a]

Table A11.2 Number of graduates in 1979 (000)

	Engineering sciences	Natural and cognitive sciences
USA	100.4	120.3
Japan	82.5	13.5
UK	18.6	22.3
France (est.)	10.0	15.0
Germany	6.4	7.9

[a] Télésis (1985); excerpts 1981–5.
Source: OECD (unpublished data).

190 Appendices

Table 11.3 Stock Exchange Markets (in $000 million)[a]

	GDP 1984	Market capitalisation at 30.3.84	GDP 1985	Market capitalisation at 31.12.85
USA	3,619.2	1,528.7 (42.2% GDP)	3,871.7	1,975 (51%)
Japan	1,233	638.2 (51.7% GDP)	1,271.4	909 (71.5%)
FRG	612.3	86.1	606	178
France	489.4	41.6	497	89
GB	424.5	235.1	416	328
Italy	348.4	25.2	352.6	65
Switzerland	91.4	48.5	89.9	90
Total of all 5 European countries	1,966	436.5 (22.2%)	1,961	750 (38.2%)

[a] IFRI (1986).
Sources: 1 CISI-Wharton, July 1985. 2 Morgan Stanley Capital International Perspective, Geneva.

APPENDIX 12.1 EUROPE'S TECHNOLOGY GAP

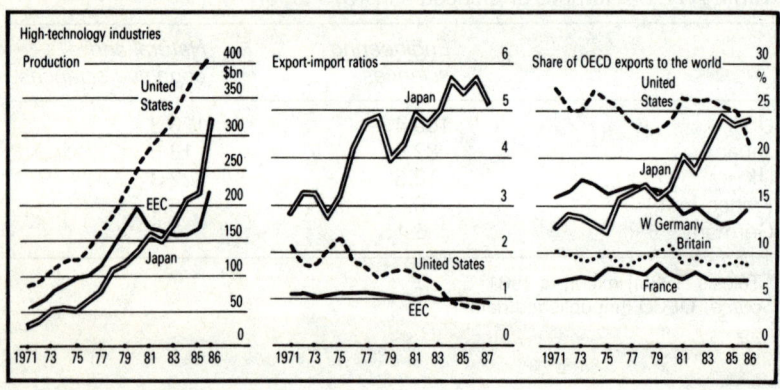

Source: *The Economist*, 4th Feb. 1989.

APPENDIX 12.2 EVALUATION OF EUROPEAN TECHNOLOGIES BY JAPANESE INDUSTRIALISTS

	Japan	USA	Europe
Semiconductors			
– VLSI	very good	good	fair
– Microprocessors	very good	very good	fair
– MFG & test equipment	good	very good	fair
– Next gen. materials	very good	very good	fair
Optoelectronics & telecommunications			
– Optical fibres	very good	good	fair
– Comm. network	good	very good	fair
– S.C. laser	very good	very good	fair
– Digital electronic switching	good	good	very good
Computers			
– 5th generation	very good	good	good
– Supercomputers	very good	very good	fair
– Mainframes	very good	very good	fair
– Minicomputers	good	very good	fair
– Personal computers	good	very good	fair
– Software	fair	very good	very good
Biotechnology			
– Interferon	good	very good	good
– Monoclones	good	very good	good
– Bioreactors	fair	very good	fair
– Seeds, etc.	good	very good	good
New materials			
– Ceramics	good	very good	good
– High performance plastics	fair	very good	good
– Carbon fibre	very good	good	fair
– High perform membranes	good	very good	fair
New metal material			
– Amorphous metal	good	very good	fair
– Hydrogen storage alloy	good	very good	fair
– 'Memorising' alloys	good	very good	fair
– High-conductive metals	good	very good	fair
New energy			
– Amorphous solar battery	very good	good	fair
– Nuclear fuel cycle	fair	very good	good
– Coal liquid and gasification	fair	very good	good
– Oil shales and sands	good	very good	good
– Heavy oil cracking	fair	very good	good
Aircraft, space, defence			
– Aircrafts	fair	very good	good
– Jet engines	fair	very good	good
– Satellites	fair	very good	fair
– Missiles	good	very good	fair
– Ships	good	very good	fair
– Tanks	fair	very good	good

□□□ very good □□ good □ fair

Figure A12.2 *Comparative technological strength: a Japanese perspective*

Source: Télésis (1985).

APPENDIX 13 JAPANESE TAKE-OFF IN NEW TECHNOLOGIES

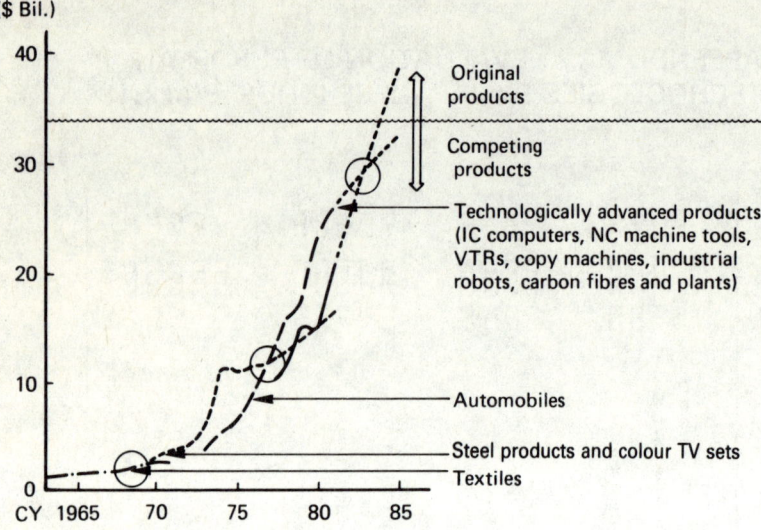

Figure A13.1 Japanese leading export products in each period[a]

[a] Figures after 1981 are estimates.

Source: Nomura Research Institute.

1	The Second Industrial Revolution
2	Communication and Information Systems
3	New Materials
4	Biotechnology

Figure A13.2 Where advanced technologies have taken off

Source: Nomura Research Institute.

APPENDIX 14 SOME SAMPLES OF EXPERIENCE CURVES

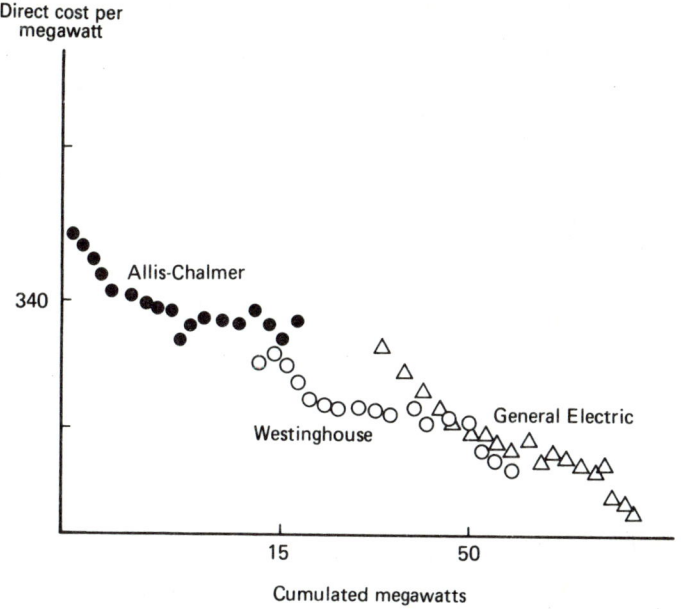

Figure A14.1 Instances of experience curves, steam turbines, 1946–1963

Source: R. G. Sultan (USA). Confidential documents divulged at an antitrust trial.

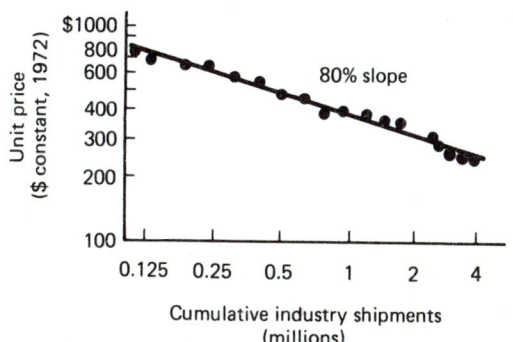

Figure A14.2 Three-ton, split-system air conditioners, 1957–1974

Source: The Boston Consulting Group, *Travaux sur l'industrie pour huitième plan*, Paris, 1979.

194 Appendices

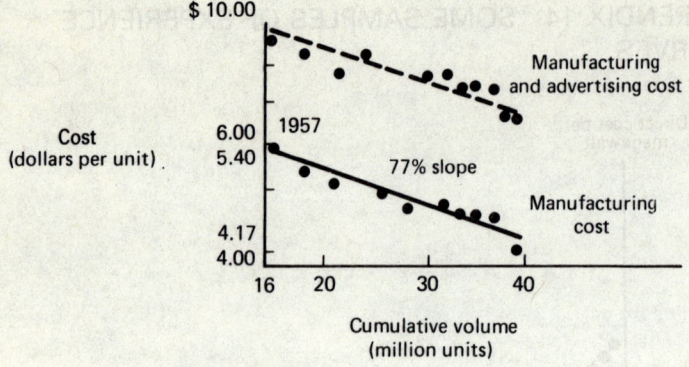

Figure A14.3 Electric shavers

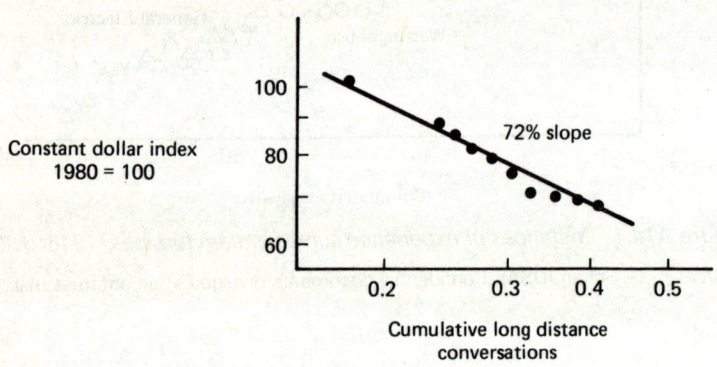

Figure A14.4 Long-distance telephone rates

Appendices 195

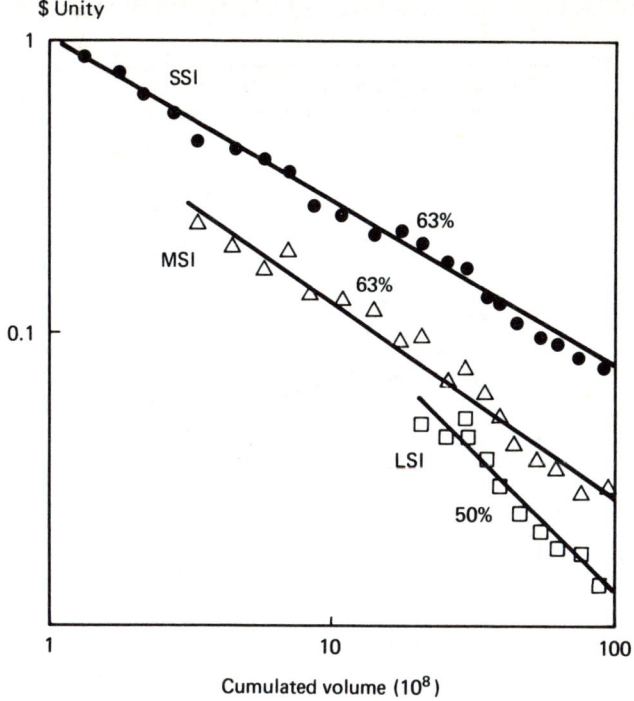

Figure A14.5 Price of integrated circuit logicals (constant $ 1958)

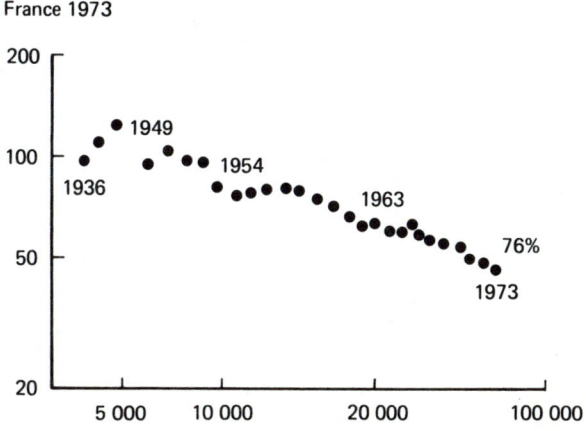

Figure A14.6 Distribution transformers: price of unit power (KVA)

APPENDIX 15 MARGINAL EFFICIENCY OF INVESTMENT

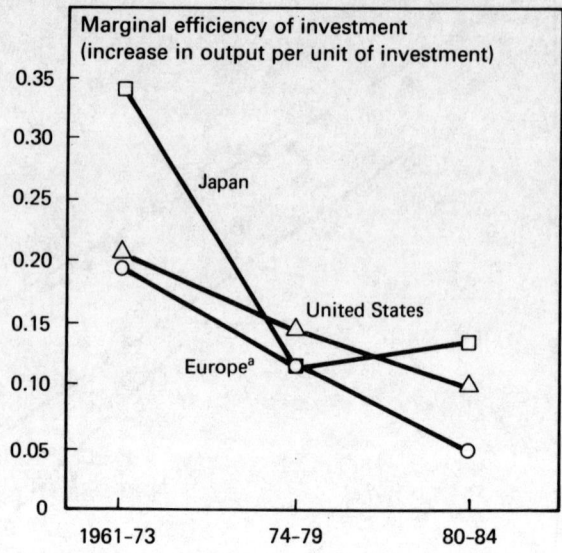

Figure A15.1 *Japan, USA and Europe: 1961–1973 to 1980–1984*

[a] West Germany, France and Britain.
Source: Reconsider Japan, *The Economist*, 26 April 1986.

Appendices 197

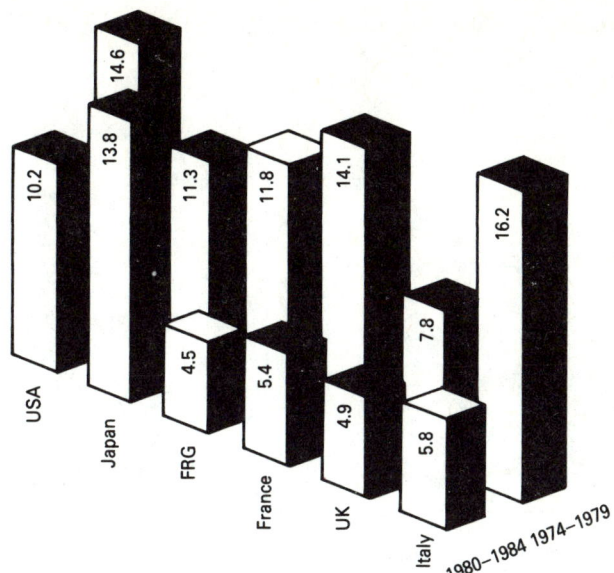

Figure A15.2 Large European countries vis-à-vis Japan and the USA
Source: OECD, *Issues in Science and Technology*, 1986. Quoted by IFRI (1986).

APPENDIX 16 SHARE OF PUBLIC EXPENDITURE IN NATIONAL INCOME

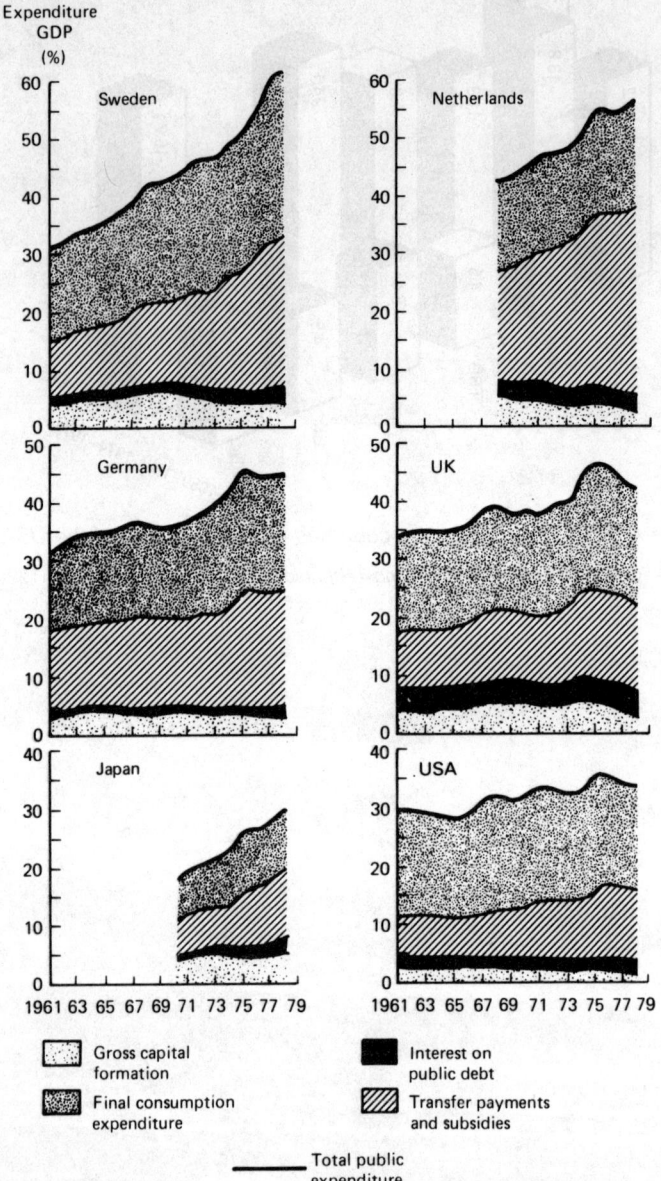

Figure A16.1 *Share of public expenditure in national income*
Source: Télésis (1985).

APPENDIX 17 IBM'S STRATEGIC ADAPTATIONS[3]

1960–70 IBM world no. 1 in computers: >50% of world stock

1970–80 Various attacks and challenges

- Compatible equipment
  - Amdahl selling equipment to IBM standards
  - Compatible manufacturers take 10% of world market
  - Costly price war

- Mini-computers
  - IBM misses the boat
  - Digital Equipment – lion's share – world no. 2 in total sector

- Microcomputers
  - Apple launches first PC in 1979

- Minis and MCPs challenge centralised concept of computers with individual problem-solving scenario

- Multiple proceedings a worry, particularly in communications
- Onset of decline?
  - Declining profits
  - Cash crisis
  - Standstill in telecom
  - No presence in minis or MCPs
  - Outside future transmission standards

'Citadel under siege'

In its most famous business ... IBM will soon cease to be a significant force ... hundreds of new companies are bursting into existence.

200 Appendices

Can anyone explain how established computer manufacturers missed such a large market?

Why was the entire industry left to reckless entrepreneurs, lucky amateurs and newcomers to computer manufacture?

The answer is that this market was too bizarre to fit any predictions made by established means. And over the next 30 years we will see similar scenarios – again and again.

Adam Osborn 'Running Wild' (Silicon Valley)

1978–84 IBM counter-attack

- *Environment*: IBM = US stronghold
  - Proceedings come to an end
  - ATT broken up

- *Strategy*

  1 Extract new capital: $2,000 million loan (1979–80)
  2 Increase competitiveness:
     - ★ $20,000 million investment (1978–82) in modernisation and automation
  3 Regain initiative in traditional markets
     - ★ Thwart compatible manufacturers: new equipment
     - ★ Proceedings and agreements
  4 Launch massive attack on new markets and confirm position as no. 1 in communications
     - ★ PC: 25% → 50% of world = IBM standards
     - ★ Satellite business system
     - ★ New teleinformation network concept
  5 Change commercial structures: customer v product approach
  6 Associate with other enterprises, e.g. Intel
  7 Be involved in environment

1984 IBM wins total communications sector

- Computers
- Micros
- Software
- Office and accounting machines
- Private telephone systems
- Components
- Telecommunications networks
- Robotics

'Such a spectacular turnaround so fast'

- 1982 ROS = 12.8%
  ROE = 22.0%

Association and cooperation

- Intel (16%) integrated circuits

- Rolm (19%) private telephone systems

- Communications and networks:
  - Sears Roebuck – Videotex to the customer
  - CBS – information in the home
  - Merrill Lynch – financial information

- Disquettes: fifth, ATT subsidiary

- Teledyne: assembly of new PC

Appendices

Table A17.1 Electrical and electronic equipment, 1965

Enterprise	Net surplus (40% net profit) (in BFr M)
IBM	9,500
GE	7,100
Philips	2,200
Siemens	900

Table A17.2 Competitive structure, 1975

	World market share %	Costs production %	Self-fin. sales %	Added-value wages %	Rn sales %
IBM	62.0	62.2	21.8	2.44	6.9
Honeywell	9.6	74.2	20.8	2.02	7
ICL	2.4	79.0	17.0	1.58	9.5
Siemens	2.5	87.0	9.9	1.37	–
CII	0.8	90.0	8.2	1.30	7.8

Table A17.2 (cont.) Competitive structure, 1975.

Company	Sales ($ 000.000)	Net income ($ 000.000)	Employees	Net income % Sales	Net income % Equity	Net surplus (40% net income) $ (000.000)	Net surplus B.F. (000.000)
IBM	34,364	4,409	364,000	12.8	22.1	1,760	88,000
Siemens	16,962	279	324,000	2	8	111	5,555
Philips	16,092	162	336,000	1	3	64	3,200
Control Data	4,292	155	56,000	3.6	9	62	3,100
HP	4,254	383	68,000	9	16.3	153	7,600
Burroughs	4,095	117	62,000	2.9	5.8	46	2,300
Digital equipment	3,880	417	67,000	10.7	13.2	208	10,400
IBM (FRG)	3,762	266	27,621	7	45	106	5,300
IBM (F)	3,390	205	20,778	6	28	82	4,100
Olivetti	2,468	75	49,763	3	9	30	1,500
IBM (UK)	2,169	182	15,337	8	23	72	3,600
IBM (J)	1,947	142	13,400	7	16	56	2,800
Ricoh	1,537	48	17,800	3	8	19	960
ICL	1,303	22	28,700	2	11	8	440
CII-HP	1,236	(205)	21,864	–	–	–	–
Apple	583	61	3,391	10.5	23.8	30	1,500

Source: *Fortune*, August 1983.

APPENDIX 18 EXPANSION OF TELECOMMUNICATIONS SERVICE FROM 1847 TO THE YEAR 2000

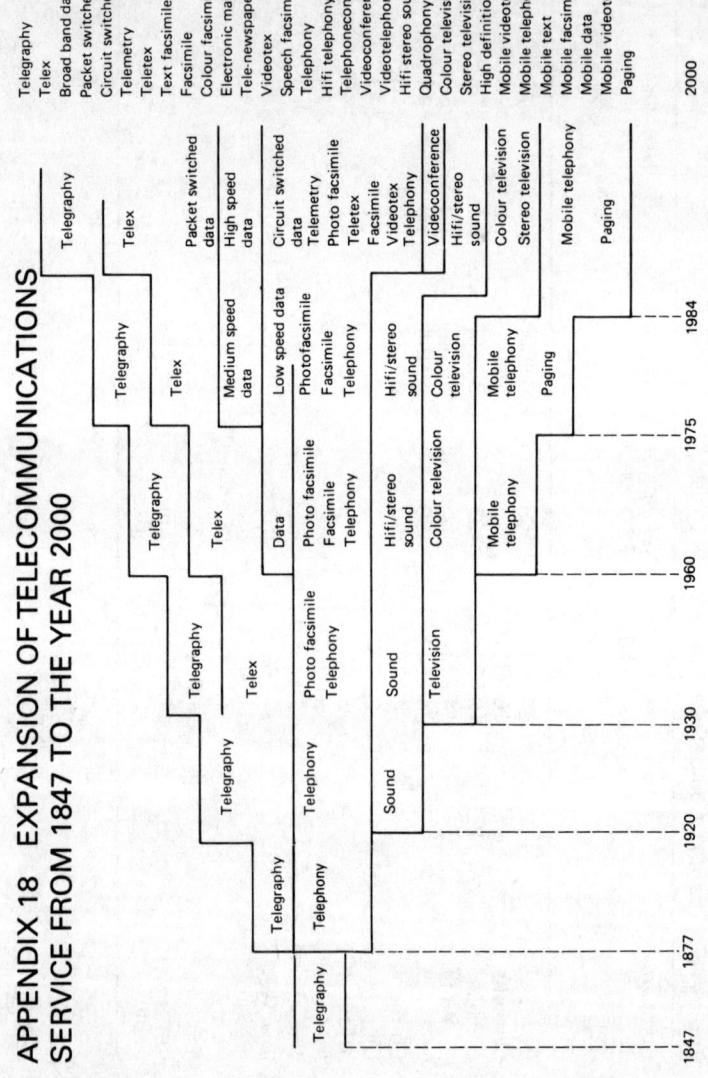

Figure A18.1 Expansion of telecommunications service from 1847 to the year 2000

Source: Excerpt of report: ERT (1986).

Appendices 205

APPENDIX 19 TOP UK TAKE-OVER BIDS OF 1986

Table A19.1 Top takeover bids of 1986

Bidder	Target	Cost	Status
Hanson Trust	Imperial Group	£2.6bn	Successful
United Biscuits	Imperial Group	£2.6bn	Agreed then failed
Guinness	Distillers	£2.5bn	Agreed
Argyll Group	Distillers	£2.5bn	Failed
Uniliver	Chesebrough Pond's (US)	£2.1bn[a] ($3.1bn)	Agreed
Dixons	Woolworth Holdings	£1.8bn	Failed
Elders IXL	Courage (from Hanson Trust)	£1.4bn	Agreed
Lloyds Bank	Standard Chartered Bk	£1.3bn	Failed
BTR	Pilkington Glass	£1.1bn	In progress
Gulf Resources	Imperial Continental Gas	£750m	Referred to Monopolies Commission
Rank Organisation	Granada	£750m	Blocked by IBA
Vantona Viyella	Coats Paton	£690m	Agreed
Dee Corporation	Fine Fare/Shoppers Paradise (from Asscd. Brit. Foods)	£686m	Agreed
British & Commonwealth	Exco	£673m	Agreed
Hanson Trust	SCM (US)	£65m[a] ($930m)	Successful
Prudential	Jackson National Life (US)	£420m) ($608m)	Agreed
Allied-Lyons	Majority stake in Hiram Walker drinks business (Canada)	£420m[a] ($606m)	Agreed
P&O	Stock Conversion	£402m	Agreed
ICI	Glidden (US, from Hanson Trust)	£400m[a] ($580m)	Agreed

[a] Approximate sterling figure only (US dollar price in brackets).
Source: Financial Times, 31 December 1986, p. 13.

APPENDIX 20 CHANGES IN THE PATTERN OF FOREIGN DIRECT INVESTMENT, 1980–1985[4]

Table A20.1 Inflows and outflows of foreign direct investment by major countries and regions, 1980–1985 (billions of SDRs)

Type of flow Region and country	1980	1981	1982	1983	1984	1985
Inflows Developed market economies	31.6	36.0	27.2	31.3	38.7	33.5
of which:						
United States	13.0	21.6	12.6	11.2	24.7	17.7
Western Europe[a]	16.5	14.4	13.5	15.3	10.6	14.3
Japan	0.2	0.2	0.4	0.4	–	0.6
Developing countries and territories	7.0	12.2	13.3	10.6	12.0	12.8
of which:						
Africa	0.1	1.5	1.5	1.6	1.5	1.3
South and South-East Asia	2.0	4.4	4.3	4.5	5.0	5.1
of which:						
China	..	0.2	0.4	0.6	1.2	1.6
West Asia	0.1	–	0.3	0.3	0.6	0.4
Latin America	4.8	6.1	6.8	3.6	3.7	4.4
Total	38.6	48.2	40.5	41.9	50.7	46.3
Outflows Developed market economies	41.0	42.8	21.1	31.7	42.7	49.8
of which:						
United States	14.8	8.1	2.2	2.5[b]	7.6[b]	15.1[b]
Western Europe[a]	20.6	24.3	17.8	20.3	23.6	22.1
Japan	1.8	4.2	4.1	3.4	5.8	6.3
Developing countries and territories	0.8	0.2	0.9	0.9	0.5	0.9
of which:						
South and South-East Asia	0.1	0.1	0.4	0.3	0.2	0.7
West Asia	1.3	–	0.1	0.3	0.1	0.1
Latin America	0.3	0.1	0.4	0.3	0.1	0.1
Total	41.8	43.0	22.0	32.6	43.2	50.7

[a] Excludes Switzerland for 1980–1982.
[b] Excludes transactions between United States parent companies and their financial affiliates in the Netherlands Antilles.
.. Not available.
– Nil or negligible.
Source: United Nations Centre on Transnational Corporations, based on International Monetary Fund, *Balance of Payments Yearbook*, various issues.

Table A20.2 Average annual flows of foreign direct investment into the United States,[a] by home country and by mode of investment, 1980–1981 and 1984–1985

		Inflow	Distribution of investment by mode				
	Years	(Millions of dollars)	Mergers acquisitions, increased equity	Joint ventures	New plants	Real estate	Other
			%				
Canada	1980–1	2,481.0	37.7	0.5	4.1	56.0	1.7
	1984–5	2,622.2	66.7	0.1	1.1	31.0	1.0
France	1980–1	1,793.5	89.3	0.2	1.1	8.7	0.7
	1984–5	284.5	91.2	–	1.0	4.3	3.4
Germany, Federal Republic of	1980–1	1,897.0	45.5	–	36.1	12.7	5.7
	1984–5	1,786.0	74.1	–	9.8	14.1	1.1
Japan	1980–1	2,102.0	15.4	0.9	45.4	11.4	15.1
	1984–5	3,890.0	24.9	12.7	30.4	24.1	6.3
Netherlands	1980–1	7,076.0	41.3	14.2	5.8	21.4	31.5
	1984–5	3,471.0	88.1	–	1.6	3.8	6.4
Switzerland	1980–1	1,012.5	65.2	–	5.5	28.3	0.9
	1984–5	1,788.0	90.5	–	4.3	3.2	0.2
United Kingdom	1980–1	4,394.5	74.2	–	4.2	21.3	0.3
	1984–5	5,807.0	82.3	0.6	1.9	12.8	2.3
Other developed countries	1980–1	1,494.0					
	1984–5	1,685.5					
Eastern European countries	1980–1	34.5					
	1984–5	16.0					
Developing countries	1980–1	724.5					
	1984–5	1,268.0					
All countries	1980–1	23,009.5	55.3	1.7	7.4	31.4	4.3
	1984–5	22,618.0	73.4	2.2	6.2	14.1	3.9

The data on the distribution by mode of investment are based on a sample that may not be representative of the whole population.
[a] Excludes reported flows from the Netherlands Antilles.
.. Not available.
– Nil or negligible.
Source: Annual review of 'Foreign direct investment in the United States'. *Survey of Current Business*, various issues; *Foreign Direct Investment in the United States: Transactions* (Washington, D.C., United States Department of Commerce), various issues.

Table A20.3 Japan: Outflow of foreign direct investment, 1975 and 1980–1985 (Millions of dollars)[a]

Destination	1975	1980	1981	1982	1983	1984	1985
Developed market economies	1,274	2,619	3,766	4,188	3,867	5,602	7,916
of which:							
North America	905	1,603	2,536	2,911	2,701	3,545	5,495
Western Europe	210	577	826	876	989	1,937	1,930
Other countries	159	439	404	401	177	120	491
Developing countries	1,883	2,076	5,164	3,516	4,279	4,555	4,302
of which:							
Western hemisphere	371	582	1,137	1,499	1,878	2,289	2,616
Asia	1,124	1,195	3,358	1,404	1,862	1,667	1,469
Others	388	299	689	613	539	599	217
Total	3,157	4,695	8,930	7,704	8,146	10,157	12,218

The figures in this table differ from those in table A20.1, owing to the fact that they come from different sources.
[a] CTC Reporter, no. 23, spring, 1987. p. 6.
Source: Ministry of International Trade and Industry, Japanese Multinational Facts and Figures, various issues.

APPENDIX 21 PRINCIPAL COOPERATION AGREEMENTS IN SEMICONDUCTORS[5]

1976 Siemens (FRG) – Intel (USA)

technical collaboration in integrated circuits and mcps (agreement amplified in 1983)

1978 Philips (Netherlands) – Signetics (USA)

Philips purchases share in Signetics (Signetics becomes part of Philips in 1984)

1981 Philips (Netherlands) – Motorola (USA)

agreement on joint mcp development

1981 Matra Harris (Fr) – Intel (USA)

company set up in France to make C-mos using Intel technology

1981 Nixdorf (FRG) – Ferranti (UK)

exchange of semiconductor technologies

1982 Thomson (Fr) – Motorola (USA)

cooperation in the development of 2-pole semiconductors, C-mos and 32 bit mcps based on Motorola technology

1982 SGS (It) – Toshiba (J)

transfer of Toshiba high-density C-mos know-how to SGS

1983 Matra (Fr) – NEC (J)

agreement on second source mcp compatibility

1984 Thomson Csf (Fr) – Motorola (USA)

research on new telecommunications components

1984 Thomson Csf (Fr) – AMD (USA)

research on new telecommunications components

1984 Philips (Netherlands) – Motorola (USA)

licence for mcp 68,000

1984 Racal (UK) – General Instruments (USA)

licence for custom C-mos

1984 Matra (Fr) – Harris Semiconductor (USA)

51/49% joint venture

1984 Siemens (FRG) – Fujitsu (J)

various types of agreement including supply of mcps

1984 SGS (It) – Ericsson (Sweden)

joint development of custom integrated circuit production plus Ericsson commitment to buy SGS components

1984 SGS (It) – IBM (USA-It)

IBM commitment, within the wider STET-IBM agreement, to buy predetermined minimum quantities of SGS components.

APPENDIX 22 ORGANISATIONAL MODELS FOR COOPERATION

Table A22.1 Organisational models for cooperation

Organisational model	Advantages	Disadvantages
Cooperative (example: Tornado)	Admits political considerations to the decision making process	Economic inefficiencies often result from interjection of political factors
	Popular with politicians because it allows them to retain control of consortia decisions	As a result of political control, decisions are frequently delayed, or incorporate compromises that are harmful to consortia interests
	Because decisions are made on a basis of consensus, no governments lose prestige vis-à-vis the other participants	No single strong leader
Integrated (example: Airbus)	Decision making by professional managers	Selection of managers may be based upon political factors
	Board of directors structure is flexible enough to allow weighting of participants' managerial influence according to actual contribution, thus avoiding perceived loss of prestige	In practice, single firms and governments may dominate
	Board of directors structure readily accommodates addition of new member firms	Working relationships among firms are subject to change
Pilot-role (example: F-16)	Decision making by professional managers	Many politicians are unwilling to relinquish control of the project
	Economic considerations are given high priority	Loss of opportunity for politicians to pursue political objectives
	Single strong leader makes rapid decisions	Perceived loss of prestige for firms and governments that follow leadership of pilot
		Potential for abuse of power by pilot-role firm and government

Source: Spreen (1986).

APPENDIX 23 OLIVETTI'S STRATEGIC PARTNERSHIPS, 1985

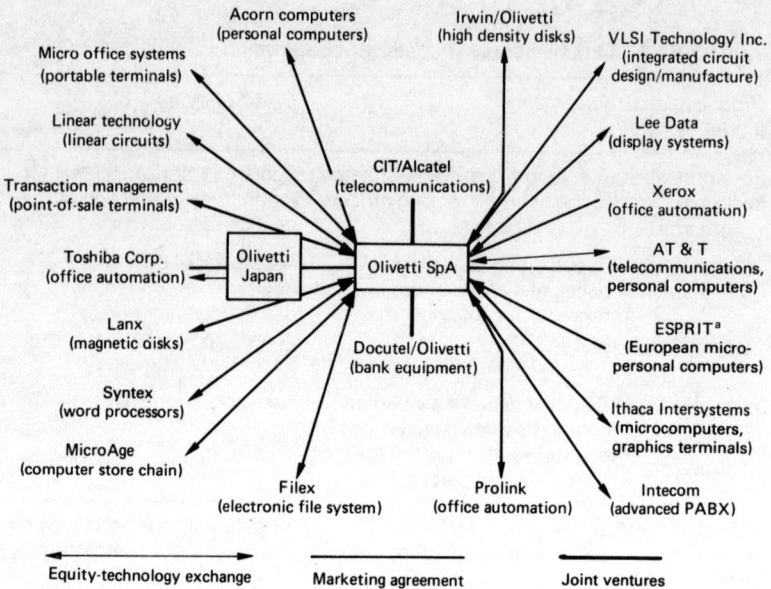

Figure A23.1 *From typewriters to office automation*

[a] European Strategic Programme in Information Technologies.

Source: SRI (1985–6).

Appendices 213

APPENDIX 24 RANKING OF COMPUTER MANUFACTURERS BEFORE AND AFTER THE PARTNERSHIP BETWEEN BULL, HIS, NEC

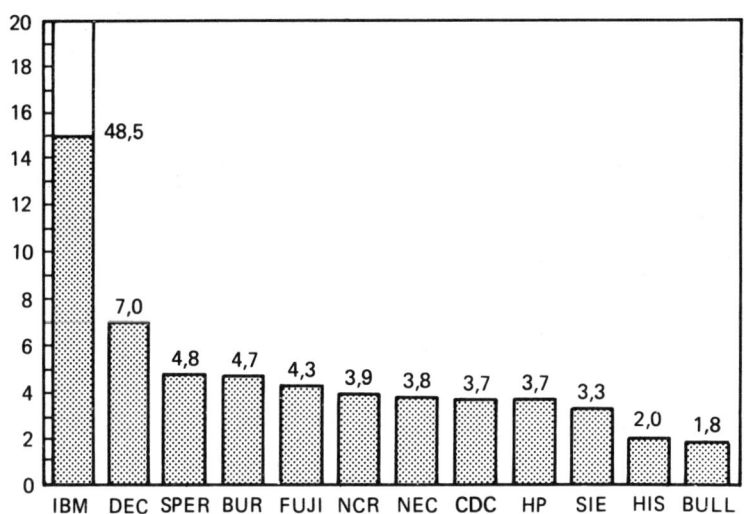

Figure A24.1 EDP revenues, 1985, not taking into account partnership between Bull, HIS, NEC

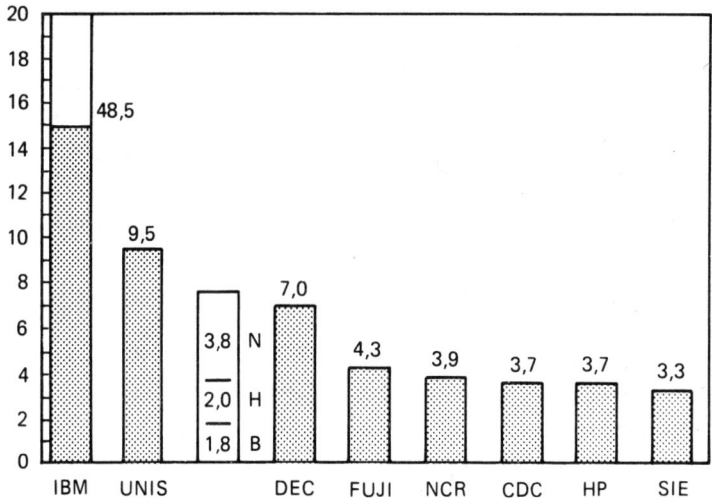

Figure A24.2 EDP revenues, 1985, taking partnership into account

APPENDIX 25 MAJOR EUROPEAN TECHNOLOGICAL PROJECTS[6]

European technological cooperation takes very different forms. Each operation seems to produce a separate legal form, truly a case of Europe à la carte or DIY. For example, there are agreements between governments and business firms (Airbus, military equipment), and projects coming under a specific organisation (Ariane and Hermes under the European Space Agency). Since the mid-1980s, two kinds of initiative have tended to dominate: EEC projects (ESPRIT, RACE, BRITE, EURAM, Energy, COMETT) and the Eureka project.

Projects planned and managed within the EEC

These emerged in the 1984–6 period, inspired by recognition of Europe's increasing lag in certain high-tech sectors. They also aim to avoid the errors of the past (the cumbersome bureaucracy from which Euratom in particular suffered) and to maintain maximum possible flexibility in execution.

- ESPRIT (European Strategic Program for Research and Development in Information Technology). The ESPRIT project (28 February 1984) was both the first and the most ambitious of the Community programmes.

  The project relates to information technology: basic technologies (high-tech micro-electronics, advanced data processing, software technology) and specific applications (automated offices and computer-managed factories). It is a ten-year project (phase 1 (ESPRIT I) will run from 1984 to 1988) and has a 1.5 thousand million ECU budget (a little under Fr 10 thousand million) of which the Community and industry will each bear 750 million.

  The originality of ESPRIT is three-fold: (1) project activity covers the pre-competition areas (it accounts for 25% of European pre-competitive research); (2) its flexibility (two-source financing) ensures decentralised management which rules out the creation of research centres; (3) the formula adopted protects it from GATT criticism.

By the end of 1985 170 cooperation projects had been launched, 448 organisations were taking part and 1,300 people were employed full-time on the venture (2,000 by mid-1986).
- ESPRIT II (1987–93) is to develop advanced robotics projects (man/machine communication).
- RACE (Research and Development in Advanced Communications Technology for Europe) (March 1985). This is a high-tech telecommunications research project: preparation of a European reference model for broad band integrated communications (planning for a new telecom infrastructure), development of basic technologies for the model (integrated circuits, opto-electronics, software components, etc.).

The initial phase will run from mid-1985 to the end of 86 with a 42.9 million ECU budget (a little under Fr 250 million) 22.1 million of which will be provided by the EEC.

RACE was inspired by the anxiety aroused by the proliferation of agreements between European enterprises and American or Japanese companies. Another factor was the low EEC spending on telecommunications per head of population – $32 compared with $80 for the USA and $46 for Japan.

The initial phase will be followed by two further stages (1986–91 and 1991–6).
- BRITE (Basic Research in Industrial Technologies for Europe). The project is designed to encourage an inflow of the new technologies (laser and particle technology; assembly methods) into traditional industries. Its budget will be equally funded by the EEC and industrial companies, each providing 125 million ECU. Several hundred projects are currently being considered.
- EURAM (European Research for Advanced Materials). Like the other projects, EURAM (1986–9) was inspired by anxiety over Europe's situation, this time its 'vulnerability in materials' (and particularly by the fact that 4 out of 5 materials patent applications come from American or Japanese enterprises). The project comprises combined basic

materials research and development engineering upstream from manufacturing industry.
- Energy. In May 1986 the EEC decided to allocate 360 million ECU support (some Fr 2.4 thousand million) for the period 1986–9 to energy-saving and alternative energy projects (by the year 2000 alternative energy sources could meet 5% of EEC energy consumption).
- COMETT (Action Programme of the Community in Education and Training for Technology). This was adopted on 5 December 1985 to strengthen cooperation between the universities and industry to provide training for the new technologies.

  It will be spread over three years (1987–9) and will receive 65 million ECU (some Fr 430 million). 10,000 scholarships will be available.
- Eureka (European Research Coordination Agency). Eureka was the outcome of a French initiative in April 1985. Its first object is to provide a response to SDI (President Reagan's so-called Star Wars speech of 23 March 1983) or, more precisely, to the American Defence Secretary's letter of 26 March 1985 with its firm invitation to America's allies to associate themselves with SDI.

  As France saw it, only a technological Europe 'would allow the requisite cooperation on an equal footing with our major international partners, particularly the USA and Japan. A subcontracting Europe, a Europe working under licence, would not be Europe.' (Extract from the letter of April 1985 from the Foreign Minister to his European colleagues.)

APPENDIX 26 JAPAN'S BILATERAL AGREEMENTS IN R&D

Table A26.1 Japan's bilateral agreements in R&D

Agreement	Date	Duration
1 Scientific and technical cooperation		
Japan – USSR	October 1973	2 years (renewable)
Japan – France	July 1974	,, ,,
Japan – Federal Republic of Germany	October 1974	,, ,,
Japan – Poland	November 1978	,, ,,
Japan – USA	May 1979	10 years (renewable)
Japan – USA (excl. energy sectors)	May 1980	April 1987
Japan – China	May 1980	2 years (renewable)
Japan – Australia	November 1980	November 1987
Japan – Indonesia	January 1981	2 years (renewable)
Japan – Yugoslavia	May 1981	,, ,,
Japan – Brazil	May 1984	,, ,,
Japan – India	November 1985	,, ,,
Japan – Korea	December 1985	,, ,,
2 Exchange of information		
Japan – USSR	October 1973	January 1988
Japan – Romania	April 1975	2 years (renewable)
Japan – Federal Republic of Germany	November 1977	,, ,,
Japan – Bulgaria	March 1978	,, ,,
Japan – Czechoslovakia	November 1978	,, ,,
Japan – Hungary	May 1979	,, ,,
3 Other agreements		
USA – Japan Scientific Cooperation Programme	June 1961	Ikeda – Kennedy agreement
USA – Japan Conference on the use of natural resources	January 1964	Declaration to the 3rd US – Japan – Europe Committee on Trade and Economic Affairs
Japan – Canada consultations in the field of science and technology	March 1972	Joint Declaration
Japan – Korea symposium on science and technology	September 1968	Joint Declaration

Nuclear energy and the development of space not specifically mentioned.
Source: Science and Technology in Japan, June, 1986. CPE (1986).

Table A26.2 Main areas covered by the cooperation agreements

Topics	Countries
Photovoltaic energy	Japan – Italy
Controlled thermonuclear fusion	USA – EEC
Photosynthesis	Japan
Breeder reactor	USA – France
Food technology	France – UK
Aquaculture	Canada
Remote sensing in space	USA
High-speed trains	Fed. Rep. Germany – France
Urban and domestic development in the developing countries	France
Advanced robotics	Japan – France
Impact of new technologies	France – Italy
Biotechnologies	France – UK
Advanced materials	UK – France
New technologies and education/training	Canada – France
Acceptability of new technologies	UK
Biological sciences	EEC
High-energy physics	USA
Solar exploration	USA

Source: CPE (1986).

NOTES

1. CPE (1985: 5, 16).
2. CPE, Paris, Bulletin no. 31, Oct 1986.
3. UCL (Université Catholique de Louvain) CRECIS (Centre de Recherche: Changement, Innovation, Stratégie) 1984.
4. CTC Reporter, no. 23, spring 1987, pp. 3, 5, 6.
5. Source: Database network.
6. IFRI (1986).

References

Abernathy, W.J. 1978: The Productivity Dilemma: Roadblock to Innovation, in *The Automobile Industry*, Baltimore, Johns Hopkins University Press.
Albach, H. 1983: Innovationen für Wirtschaftswachstum und internationale Wettbewerbsfähigkeit, in Rheinisch-Westfälische Akademie der Wissenschaften, Opladen.
Albach, H. 1985: Innovation und Imitation als Produktionsfaktoren, Vortrag gehalten auf dem 15. Wirtschaftswissenschaftlichen Seminar, Innovation, Beschäftigung und Wachstum, in Ottobeuren vom 23, September.
Albert, M. 1983: *Un pari pour l'Europe*, Paris, Seuil.
Albert, M. and Ball, J. 1983: Report to the European Parliament, Strasbourg-Brussels.
Altshuler, A. et al. 1984: *The Future of the Automobile*, Boston, MIT Press.
Ansoff, I. 1979: *Strategic Management*, London, Macmillan.
Archier, G. and Serieyx, H. 1984: *L'entreprise du troisième type*, Paris, Seuil.
Arenas, E. 1986a: Le management strategique de six groupes espagnols, Working Paper, Louvain, University of Louvain.
Arenas, E. 1986b: European dimension of R&D and Innovation, Working Paper, Louvain, University of Louvain.
Argyris, C. 1964: *Integrating the Individual and the Organisation*, New York, Wiley.
Bayen, M. 1984–7: Rapports du Centre de Prospective et d'Evaluation, Paris, CPE.
Bibeault, D.B. 1981: *Corporate Turnaround*, New York, McGraw Hill.
Booz, Allen, Hamilton 1987: Paris, CIM User Survey.
Boston Consulting Group 1984: *Perspectives on Experience*, Boston, BCG.
Buigues, P.A. 1985: *Prospective et competitivité*, Paris, McGraw Hill.

Bylinsky, G., The High-Tech Race, *Fortune*, 13 October 1986.
Centre de Prospective et d'Evaluation, see CPE.
Center for European Policy Studies, Bruxelles, see Ergas et Jacquemin.
Center for the Study of Industrial Innovation 1972: Success and Failure in Industrial Innovation, A Report on Project Sappho by the Science Policy Research Unit, London, University of Sussex.
Center on Transnational Corporations, Reports, New York, UN.
Channon, D. 1978: *The Service Industries*, London, Macmillan.
Clark, R. 1979: *The Japanese Company*, Yale, Yale University Press.
Confederation of British Industry 1979: *Innovation and Competitiveness in Smaller Companies*, London.
CPE (Centre de Prospective et d'Evaluation), Cahiers et études, Ministère de la Technologie et de l'Industrie, Paris, 1984 to 1987.
CPE Bulletin, no. 20, October 1985, Paris.
CPE Bulletin, no. 31, October 1986, Paris.
Crozier, M., and Friedberg, E. 1977: *L'acteur et le système*, Paris, Seuil.
Daems, H. 1977: The Holding Company and Corporate Control, Nijhoff, Leiden.
Danila, N. 1986: Le management de la R&D *Revue Française de Gestion*, no. 56.
Davignon, E. 1977: Trends in European Industrial Policy, address given at Georgetown University.
Davignon, E. 1981a: Bilan et perspectives de la politique industrielle de la CEE, *Courrier européen*, no. 110, Paris.
Davignon, E. 1981b: European Industrial Strategy, in *Future of Business* series, no. 3, Georgetown.
Davignon, E. et al. 1986: Conditions for Partnership in International Economic Management, A Report to the Trilateral Commission, 32.
De Lamarter, R. T. 1986: *Big Blue: IBM's Use and Abuse of Power*, London, Mead.
Delmas, P. 1985: *Le Cow-Boy et le Samourai: Reflections on Japanese-American Competition in High Technology*, Paris, Ministry of Foreign Affairs.
de Schoutheete, P. 1986: *La coopération politique européenne*, Brussels, Labor.
de Woot, 1968: Pour une doctrine de l'entreprise, Paris, Seuil.
de Woot et al. 1971: *Entreprises performantes et stratégie de progrès*, Fondation-Industrie-Université, Brussels.
de Woot, P and Desclee, X. 1984: Le management stratégique des groupes industriels, *Economica*, Paris.
Doz, Y. and Prahalad, C. K. 1987: *The Multinational Mission*, London, Macmillan.

Doz, Y., Hamel, G. and Prahalad, C. K. 1986: Strategic Partnership: Success or Surrender? Working Paper, Insead, London Business School and University of Michigan.

Doz, Y. 1986: Technology Partnership Between Larger and Smaller Firms: Some Critical Issues, Working Paper, Insead, August.

Drucker, P. F. 1985: *Innovation and Entrepreneurship*, New York, Harper & Row.

Dunning, T. H. and Pearce, R. D. 1981: *The World's Largest Industrial Enterprise*.

The Economist, Survey on: Aldershot, Gower.

The Coming Entrepreneurial Revolution, 25 December 1976
Japan, 23 February 1980
The New Entrepreneurs, 24 December 1983
Aircraft Industry, 1 June 1985
Telecommunications, 23 November 1985
High Technology, Japan and the United States, 23 August, 1986
Telecommunications, 17 October 1987

Durand, and Feuillee, P. 1986: Principaux aspects de la diffusion et de la valorisation de la recherche publique en France, Luxembourg, CEE.

EIRMA 1972: Cooperative International Research, Working Group Reports, no. 9, Paris.

EIRMA 1986: Developing R&D Strategies, Working Group Reports, no. 33, Paris.

Ergas, H., 1984: Why Do Some Countries Innovate More Than Others? CEPS Papers, Louvain-la-Neuve, Bruxelles.

EUREKA 1986: Les trésors cachés de l'Europe des sciences, Science et Avenir, special non-series issue no. 58, Paris.

European Foundation for Management Development 1981: Facing Realities: A Report of the European Societal Strategy Project, Brussels.

European Institute for Advanced Studies in Management 1981: *Facing Realities*, Brussels.

European Round Table of Industrialists, ERT 1986: Clearing the Lines, November.

FAST: TET 4, TET 9, SERV 4, SERV 5, SERV 7, COM 1, COM 2, COM 8, ALIM 1, etc.

Fondation Europe et Société 1986–7: Cahiers 1 to 5, Paris.

Gallo, M. A., 1986: The Advisability of a European Base in the Internationalization of Spanish Engineering, Penelope Working Papers, ISE, Barcelona.

Gille, L. 1986: Eléments pour une prospective des réseaux de télécommunications européens, CEE, COM 1, Brussels.

222 References

Godet, M. 1987: *Scenarios and Strategic Management*, London, Butterworths.

Goetschin, P. 1986: Technologie et management, *Revue Economique et Sociale*, 44th year Lausanne, November, pp. 223–6.

Gorbis, M. 1985–6: Strategic Partnership: A New Corporate Response, Report, no. 730, SRI International, Winter.

Goshal, S. 1987: Global Strategy: An Organizing Framework, *Strategic Management Journal*, vol. 8, pp. 425–40.

Grinyer, P. H. 1986: Working Paper, St Andrews, University of St Andrews.

Grinyer, P. H. et al. 1980: Strategy, Structure, the Environment and Financial Performance in 48 UK Companies, *Academy of Management Journal* 23, pp. 193–220.

Hager, W., Noelke, M. and Taylor, R. 1982: *EEO Protectionism: Present Practice and Future Trends*, Brussels, European Research Associates.

Hall, W. K. 1980: Survival Strategies in a Hostile Environment, *Harvard Business Review*, September–October.

Harris, J., Shaw, R. and Somers, W. 1984: *Competitive Strategic Management*, New Jersey, Prentice Hall.

Hedlund, G. and Zander I. 1986: Swedish MNC Strategies for Europe, Penelope Papers, Stockholm School of Economics.

Hedlund, G. 1986: Patterns in Swedish Firm's International Activities, Report for the Penelope Project, Stockholm School of Economics.

Heyvaert, H. 1972: *Stratégie et Innovation*, Louvain, Université de Louvain.

Hope, E. 1985: Innovation in High-Technology Industries, Working Paper, CEPS, Brussels.

IFRI 1986: Institut Français de Relations Internationales, Rapport Ramsès 86–87, Compétitions et affrontements, *Economica*, Paris.

Jacquemin, A. 1984: Coopération entre les entreprises et droit économique, International Association of Economic Law Symposium, Brussels.

Jacquemin, A., Lammerant, M. and Spinoit, B. 1985: Compétition européenne et coopération entre entreprises en matière de R&D, Collection Evolution de la concentrations et de la concurrence, n. 80, Brussels, CEE.

Jacquemin, A. and Spinoit, B. 1986: *Economic and Legal Aspect of Cooperative Research: A European View*, New York, M. Bender.

Jacquemin, A. 1984: *European Industry: Public Policy and Corporate Strategy*, Oxford, Clarendon Press.

Jacquemin, A. and De Yong, W. 1977: European Industrial Organization, London, Macmillan.

References

Jacquier, J. F. 1986: Un géant trop petit, *Le Nouvel Economiste*, no. 555, Paris, 29 August, pp. 32–7.
Jarillo, J. C. 1986: European Strategies for Small and Medium-Sized Companies, Working Paper for Penelope, ISE, Barcelona.
Kanter, R. M. 1983: *The Change Masters*, New York, Simon & Schuster.
Kayser, G. 1986: Working Paper for the Penelope Project, Bonn.
Keith, P. 1983: Les perspectives du développement technologique en Europe face aux nouvelles contraintes internationales, Science Policy Research Unit, University of Sussex.
Kerorguen de and Merlant, Ph. 1985: Technopolis, in *Revue Autrement*, no. 74, November, Paris.
Ketteringham, J. and White, J. 1984: *Making Technology Work for Business*, in *Competitive Strategic Management*, New York, Prentice Hall.
Larsens, J. and Rodgers, E. 1985: La fièvre de la Silicon Valley, Paris, Editions Londreys.
Lambin, J. J. 1986: *Le marketing stratégique*, Paris, McGraw-Hill.
Lawrence, P. R., Lorsch, J. W. 1982: *Organizational Environment*, New York, Irwin.
Le Boucher, E. 1986: Le triangle de l'électronique, *Le Monde*, 29 April.
Le Foll, J. 1985: Les aides publiques à l'industrie; éléments d'évaluation économie et prévision, no. 70.
Little, A. D. 1971: *La route 128 et les nouvelles entreprises technologiques*, Paris, ADL.
Little, A. D. 1981: *Stratégie et technologie*, Paris, ADL.
Little, A. D. 1985: *Management Perspectives on Innovation*, Cambridge, Mass., ADL.
Lorenzoni, G. and Ornati, O. 1987: Constellations of Firms and New Ventures, Working Paper, New York University, January.
Lorenzoni, G. 1986: From Vertical Integration to Vertical Disintegration, Working Paper, Bologna, University of Bologna.
MacKintosh, I. 1986: Sunrise Europe, quoted by The European Round Table of Industrialists, in *Clearing the Lines*.
Mariti, P, and Smiley, R. 1983: Cooperative Agreements and the Organization of Industry, *Journal of Industrial Economics*, June.
Molitor, M. 1971: Chercheurs et organisation, Louvain, UCL.
Morin, J. 1985: L'excellence technologique, Paris, Publi-Union.
Nizet, B. 1987: Offre et demande de personnel hautement qualifié dans le domaine de la biotechnologie, Actions nationales de recherche en soutien à FAST, Contrat FAST no. 26, Working paper, Louvain.
Nora, S., Minc, A. 1978: L'informatisation de la société, Documentation Française, Paris.

OECD 1986: Indicateurs de la science et de la technologie: R&D, invention, compétitivité, Paris.

Ohmae, K. 1985: *The Triad Power*, New York, Free Press.

Oultremont (d'), P. 1986: Les actions de la CEE dans le domaine des télécommunications, *Gestion 2,000*, no. 4, Louvain, pp. 189–201.

Page, J. P., Turcq, D., Bailly, M. and Foldes, G. 1987: La recherche de l'excellence en France, Paris, Dunod.

Peters, T. and Waterman, R. 1983: *In Search of Excellence*, New York, Harper & Row.

Petrella, R. 1983: Changements dans l'environnement externe de la R&D et la dimension européenne, CEE, May, Brussels.

Petrella, R. 1986: R&D and Technology Management: Making Cooperation Work, Conference Transcript, New York, The Conference Board.

Piantoni, C. F. 1986: L'industrialisation de la créativité, Working Paper, Milan, SDA Bocconi.

Pinchot, G. 1985: *Intrapreneuring*, New York, Harper & Row.

Porter, M. 1980: *The Competitive Strategy*, New York, Free Press.

Porter, M. 1985: *The Competitive Advantage*, New York, Free Press.

Ramses 86–7, Compétitions et affrontements, *Economica*, Paris, 1986, p. 324.

Rodgers, B. 1986: The IBM Way, *Business Week*, 20 January.

Rumelt, R. P. 1982: Diversification Strategy and Profitability, *Strategic Management Journal*, vol. 3, pp. 359–69.

Saias, M. A. and Hall, D. J. 1980: Strategy Follows Structure!, *Strategic Management Journal*, vol. 1, pp. 149–63.

Saias, M. A. 1985: *Competitive Strategies*, Working Paper, Aix-Marseilles, University of Aix-Marseilles.

Saias, M. A. and Montebello, M. 1980: Strategic Management in Western Europe, in Glueck, W. F., *Strategic Management and Business Policy*, McGraw Hill.

Sallenave, J. P. 1984: Direction générale et stratégie d'entreprise, Paris, Les Editions d'organisations.

Schumpeter, J. A. 1949: *The Theory of Economic Development*, Cambridge, Mass., Harvard University Press.

Sciberas, E. et al. 1978: Competition, Technical Change and Manpower in Electronic Capital Equipment: A Study of the UK Mini-Computer Industry, Science Policy Research Unit, Brighton.

Serieyx, H. and Archier, G. 1984: L'entreprise du troisième type, Paris, Seuil.

Sicard, C. 1987: Pratique de la stratégie d'entreprise, *Hommes et Techniques*, Paris.

Sinatra, A. 1986: Cooperation Agreements, Working Paper, SDA Bocconi, Milan.

Spreen, W. 1986: International Cooperation in the Aerospace Industry, IAG, Louvain, University of Louvain.

SRI Stanford Research International 1985–6: Report no. 730, Strategic Partnerships: A New Corporate Response, Gorbis M., Yorke K., Winter.

Stopford, J. and Dunning, J. 1982: *Multinationals: Company Performance and Global Trends*, London, Macmillan.

Stopford, J. and Turner, L. 1985: *Britain and the Multinationals*, New York, Wiley.

Télésis 1985: Télésis and Industrial Policy, press cuttings and report excerpts, Paris.

Turcq, D. 1985: Les stratégies d'accords internationaux des entreprises japonaises, Ministère du redéploiement industriel et du commerce extérieur, Paris.

Turcq, D. 1986: La tunique de Nessus, les stratégies d'accords internationaux des entreprises japonaises, Cahier d'études, nos 85–7, ESCP, Paris.

Index

Accor 31
acquisitions, US 82–3
AEG 50
Aérospatiale 108, 110, 113
Agnelli 30
agreement networks 90
agreements, bilateral national cooperation 154
agriculture 151 *see also* EC, Common Agricultural Policy
Airbus 4, 5, 21, 32, 97, 110–15, 131, 165
aircraft, military 32; management models 115–18
aircraft: production 10; manufacturers 182
Albach, Horst x
Alcatel 72, 73
Alfa-Laval 87
alliance portfolio 90
Amdahl 94
American development process 39, 40 Fig.2.2
American model 35–9; cooperation 102–3
Apple 57, 60, 81
Arenas, Eduardo x
Ariane 4, 21, 32, 131, 145, 165
Aron, Raymond xi
artificial intelligence 165
ASEA Robotics 86
'Atlantic' enterprises 13
ATT 4, 37, 50, 59, 65, 69, 70, 71, 72, 73, 74, 85, 90, 102, 118–19
aviation industry 102, 103, 106–18; European, 48, 51–2

BAe 108, 110

Bekaert 81
Benetton 81
Besse 30
bionics 6, 11, 54, 152
biotechnology 6, 11, 32, 77n., 151–2; European 51; Japanese 29; origin of patents 188; R&D budgets of biggest companies 29 Table 2.1
BL 89
Blue Circle 29
Bocconi University 104
Boeing 4, 13, 37, 50, 81, 85, 97, 102, 107, 108, 110, 112
Boston Consulting Group 43
BRITE (Basic Research in Industrial Technologies for Europe) 48, 143, 215
British Oxygen 83
British Telecom 69, 70
Bull 50, 94, 119, 213
business schools ix, 168

Calvet 30
CAM–CAD (Computer Assisted Manufacture–Computer Assisted Design) 11, 44
Canada 70
Carrefour 31
CASA 110
catering, communal 31
cell engineering 151–2
cement industry 29–30
Centre National d'Etudes Spatiales, France 146
CGE 50, 70
"champion" 18
chemicals industry 28–9, 127, 131, 151–2; European 50

226

Index

Cit-Alcatel 72
Club Méditerranée 31
collaboration 18, 60
COMETT (Action Program of the Community in Education and Training for Technology) 216
commercial cooperation 88–9, 105
communications, Japanese 40
communications networks 140; *see also* information technology; telecommunications
compact discs 56
competition: characteristics 2; creative or destructive? 22–6; European 35–53; new forms of 9–13; and strategic capability 8–27
competitive advantages 13–15, 23; European lack 51–3; Japanese 43–4; US 37–9
competitive models, cooperation and 99–106
competitiveness: defined 8–9; mechanisms for global 165–9; process destroying 26 Fig. 1.2; process enhancing 24 Fig. 1.1
components, European sales (1983) 61
components industry 60–4, 95
computer industry 11, 57–60; European compatibility agreement 147; Japanese cooperation agreements 100; performance 181; profitability (1982) 58, (1985) 59; ranking of manufacturers 213; strategic cooperation management 118–21; US 57–60; US compatibility agreements 147
concerted action 21
consumer electronics, Japanese 42, 44, 45, 55–6
consumer goods 11, 38
cooperation 1, 4–5; and competitive models 99–106; as a competitive strategy 88–95, day-to-day management 96–8; future 166–7; international 80–126; management models 115–18, computers 118–21; management of 95–9; organisational models 97–8, 211; R&D 148–53, horizontal 149, radial 149–52, vertical 149; strategic management 98–9; unequal 152–3; and value chain 18–19
cooperation agreements, international 101
cooperative structure 97
corporate responsibilities 20–2
COS (cooperation for open systems), US 147
cost advantages 14, 30
'creative destruction' 5–6, 9, 22–6; 'pro-active policies' 20
creativity 31, 46
cross-subsidisation 43

data banks 17, 137
de Woot, Philippe x
DEC 57, 60
defence 165; US 36, 38, contractors 107, contracts 137–8
defence electronics 32, 143
Demosthenes 169–70
deregulation 12–13, 65, 69
developing countries *see* Third World
Diane Euronet 145
differentiation advantages 14, 30–1
distribution, globalisation of 88–9
dominance 13, 60; and cooperation 90–5
Doz, Yves x, 92, 93–4, 152–3
DRAM market 62
Dunning, T. H. 141

Eagan, 30
EC (European Community): Common Agricultural Policy 48, 151; communications policy 77; cooperation with business 21–2; joint subsidiaries 104; R&D cooperation policy 143–4; role as catalyst 166
economies of scale, world 14
economies of scope 14, 18
EDP (electronic data processing) equipment 10
education 138–40
Edwardes, M. 30
efficiency, components 2
EIRMA 157

Electrolux 87
electronics industry 10, 32; European 51, 53–77; trading surplus and deficit (1984) 55; world market share 53–4; *see also* consumer, electronics; defence electronics; medical electronics
Electronics International Corporation 55
engineering: cooperation in 122–3; Japanese, 42
England 18
environment 19–20; exploiting the technological 153–5; interventionist 19; size of 19; sophistication of 19, 136–7, 189–90
Ergas, H. 130, 135–43
Ericsson 50, 70, 73, 74, 75, 81
Esab 87
ESPRIT (European Strategic Program for Research and Development in Information Technology) 6, 21, 103, 143, 166, 214–15
Esselte 87
Essex University, Sappho project 155
EURAM (European Research for Advanced Materials) 215–16
Eureka (European Research Coordination Agency) 6, 48, 145, 216
Eurogrid 75–6
Europe: fragmentation of market 47, 105, 163; need for global approach 163–70; technological dependence 130
European base, inadequate 4, 169
European enterprises: competitiveness 28–79; direct foreign investment 84–5; overall position 2–3; research agreements 103
European industry, decline of 32 Table 2.2
European model 3, 47–53; cooperation 103–6; and strategic capability 133–5
European non-development process 52 Fig. 2.4

European projects, major 165–6, 214–16
European Round Table of Industrialists 21; report 76–7
European technologies, evaluation by Japanese industrialists 191
experience 14, 43, 70
experience curves 193–5

FAST (Forecasting and Assessing Science and Technology) ix, 166; summary 1–7
fermentation engineering 152
Ferruzi 152
Fiat 30, 31
firms: characteristics of successful 183; US sales compared with European 141
flexibility of structure 17–18, 42
food industry 31
foreign direct investment 80–7; changes in pattern (1980–5) 206–8
fragmentation, European 47, 105, 163
France 47, 131, 143
franchises 122
FRG *see* Germany, West
FTC (Federal Trade Commission), contracts declared to 91
Fujitsu 43, 50, 89, 94

Gallo, Miguel xi, 123
GE 157
GEC 50
Genentech 87
General Dynamics 108
generic strategies 182
genetic engineering 19, 151–2
Germany, West 47, 81, 106, 131, 138–40, 142
Gervais-Danone 31
GFSS 87
Ghidella 30
glass industry 29–30
global industrial strategies 163; mechanisms of 164–9
globalisation of competition 3–4, 6–7, 11–13; reasons for 12–13
GM 31, 77n., 89, 90
Goetschin, Pierre x
Goshal, S. 14–15

government funding for enterprise, European 142–3
government spending 47, 165–6
graduates 140
Grundig 84
GTE 70, 72, 73, 74
Gyllenhammer 30

Hamel, G. 93–4
Hannoun Report 143
Hedlund, Gunnar xi, 85–6
high-tech industries: definition 10; European position 32–3; exports by country 33 Table 2.3
HIS *see* Honeywell
Hitachi 43, 72, 73, 75, 85
Hoechst 83
Hoffman-Laroche 29
Holderbank 29
Honeywell 119, 213
hotels 31
HP 57

IBM 4, 13, 37, 50, 57, 58–60, 63, 81, 85, 90, 94, 102, 157; SNA (system network architecture) and OSI (open standards interconnection) 68–9, 71; strategic adaptations 199–203
ICI 37, 83
ICL 50, 94
incentives 41, 100; to competitive innovation 135–43
industry: relations with universities 5, 36, 41, 49, 102, 140, 154; structure of 17–18, 42, 140–3, 168
information exchange 145
Information Network System, Japan 41, 71
information services, and telecommunications 69–70; US 37
information systems 134, 137; Japanese 40
information technology 6, 11, 17
infrastructure, European lag 136
innovation 1, 5–6, 127–62; capacity for 17–18; competition by 9–11; as entrepreneurial process 158; management 18, 153–60; need for: Europe, Japan, US 160

innovation centres 140
innovative capacity ranking 130–1
instrumentation, European 51
integrated cooperation 97–8, 114
Intel 62
interventionism 19, 47
'intrapreneurship' 18, 158
investment: interchange in Triad 86; marginal efficiency 196–7; planned 41; *see also* foreign direct investment
ISDNs 62, 65, 68, 72, 165
Italy 152; cooperation agreements 104–5; textile industry 122
ITT 62, 65, 70, 72, 73

Jacquemin, A. 88, 93, 150
Jaguar 30
Jaguar aircraft 116
Japan 29, 81, 84, 140, 142, 147; bilateral agreements in R&D 217–18; government R&D support 179–80; new technologies 192
Japanese development process 46 Fig. 2.3
Japanese enterprises, triadic nature of 13
Japanese model 39–46; cooperation 100–2
Jarillo, J. Carlos xi, 121
joint ventures 89, 105; European 103–6
JVC 43, 50

Lafage-Coppée 29
LANS market 64, 69
laws, differing European 106
LDCs *see* Third World
leadership, Japanese 43–4
learning curves 95
Little, Arthur D. 74, 158, 160
Lockheed, 108, 109, 110
Lomé agreements 22
Lorenzoni, Gianni x, 122
Louvain, Catholic University of ix, 15, 115, 131, 133, 135, 153
luxury industries 31

McDonnell Douglas 5, 70
Mackintosh, Ian 75

Index

Magotteaux 81
management, role of top 160
management systems, European 50
management of technical resources (MTR) 158–9
manufacturing industries, market share 129
Mariti, P. 148
market: extended 146–7; and innovation 135–8
market choices 17
market fragmentation, European 47
market pull (technology demand) 5, 135–8
market size 135–6
market sophistication 136–7
marketing, relations with R&D 155
Marks and Spencer 31
mass production, Japanese 56
materials, advanced 11, 32; Japanese 40
Matsushita 4, 72, 75
mature industry 31
mechanical engineering 129
medical electronics, European 51
medium-sized enterprises 49
Mercedes 31
mergers, motor industry 30–1
Messerschmidt-Bolkow-Blöhm MBB 110
'metatechnologies' 10
microelectronics 60–4, 142–3
military spending: Japan 41; US 108, 137–8
Minitelk 32
MITEL 70
MITI 39–42, 71, 100, 147, 166;
  'MITI Vision for the 1960s, 1970s, 1980s' 40
Mitsubishi 69, 72
Mitsui 69, 72
MNCs: and competition 8–27;
  European 50–1; foreign output 82–3; role 1; US 37
models, use of conceptual 1–3; *see also* American model; European model; Japanese model
Molitor, M. 155–7
monopoly 60
Montedison 152

Morin, Jacques 158
motivation: for R&D cooperation 144–8; staff 20–1, 42
motor industry 30, 127, 132–3; mergers 30–1
Motorola 37, 62, 63
multinational companies *see* MNCs
multipolar joint working, *see* agreement networks

national champion policies 3, 5, 25, 142; European 48, 49
National Cooperative Research Act, US (1984) 144
national environmental differences 20
national industrial policies 47
national interests, versus efficiency 4–5
National Science Foundation 140
NEC 43, 70, 72, 73, 75, 85, 94, 119, 213
Neckerman 31
Nestlé 31, 83
Netherlands 63, 81
new enterprises 142
niche strategies 14, 30; European 53
Nippon TT 69
Nissan 89, 90
Nora, Simon 59
Norris, William 144
Northern Telecom 70, 73, 74, 75
Northrop 108
NTT 71

OEM (Original Equipment Manufacturing) agreements 89–90, 93
office automation, Japanese 40
office equipment 10
Olivetti 37, 50, 58–9, 60, 69, 70, 74, 118–19, 131, 152; strategic partnership (1985) 212
optical electronics 11, 32, 54; European 51; Japanese 40
optical fibres 65
organisation theory 155
output per man, comparative European, Japanese, US 41

Panasonic 43

Index

participation, and innovation, Japanese 158, 159
PBXs 69
Pearce, R. D. 141
PENELOPE Project ix; participants x–xi
performance: European 53; Japanese 44–6; US 37–9
personnel training 44
Peugeot 30
pharmaceuticals 10, 28–9, 87; European 50
Philips 4, 37, 50, 56, 58, 61, 63, 69, 73, 74, 75, 84
Piantoni, Gianfranco x
Pilkington 29
pilot role cooperative structure 97
Plessey 50
political logic, versus economic sense 4–5
Porter, M. 14, 30
POSI (promotion conference for Osi in Japan) 147
Prahalad, C. K. 93–4
price policy, corporate 142
privatisation 65–7
product policy 17, 133
production technology, Japanese 44
profitability 23–4; European 34–5, 53; Japanese 44–6; US 37–9
'progress groups' 18
'Prolog' language 32
Prometheus project 145
prospects and opportunities: European 47–50; Japanese 39–42; US 35–6
public contracts 137–8, 167; Europe 48; US 36
public expenditure, share of national income 19–20, 198
public policy and corporate decisions 20; see also government spending

quality strategy 44

R&D: comparative spending 33–4 Table 2.5; cooperation 143–53, forms 148–53; decentralisation and integration 157–8; European 5–6, 128–35; evolution of 173–80; gross domestic spending on 128; management of 153–60; ratio of expenditure to turnover 10, (1983) 146; shares of industrial 129; typology of staff 156–7
RACE (Research and Development in Advanced Communications Technology for Europe) 21, 48, 143, 215
Renault 30
research 127–62; see also R&D
research agreements, European enterprises 103
research jobs, number of 128
research scientists 139
research staff, management of 155–7
resources: development and management of key 16, 133–4; shared 145–6
responsibilities, corporate and societal 20–2
retailing 31
return on assets (1955–80), comparative international 34 Fig. 2.1
risk pooling 146
risk spreading 146
'Rita' network 32
robotics 11, 32, 131; Japanese 40, 42
Rockwell 108
Romiti 30
Rover 30
Rowntree-Mackintosh 31

Saias, Maurice x
Saint-Gobain 29
satellite networks 65
SBU (strategic base unit) 157
Scandinavia 131
Schmücker 30
Schumpeter, J. 7n., 60
Schweppes 31
science parks 140
SDI (Strategic Defense Initiative) 39
sectoral balance 11
semiconductor industry 145; alliances 185–7; cooperation agreements 209–10
service sector 11, 12, 31
SGS-Ates 61

232 Index

shareholding, in foreign enterprises 89
Shell 84
Showa Denko 89
Siemens 4, 37, 50, 58, 61, 62, 63, 81, 85, 94
Sinatra, Alessandro x
SKF 87
small and medium-sized enterprises *see* SMEs
SMEs 1; cooperation 121–2; development of 168; European 49, 121; relations with industry 41; scientific 157; US 36, 38–9
SMUs, new technological 154
societal responsibilities 20–2, 169
Société Générale de Belgique 73
Sony 43, 50, 72
space industries 10, 103; European 48, 143; US 36, 38
Spain 123
specialisation strategies 14, 47
Sprite 48
Standard Electrik Lorenz 62
standards: American-Japanese technical 103; compatibility 147; information 147; need for industrial 147–8, 167–8; quality 147; range 147; telecommunications 68
Stopford, John xi, 81–2
strategic capability 15–18, 23, 169, 184; European 50–1, 133–5; Japanese 42–3; US 37
strategic objectives, defined 8–9
subcontracting 18, 100–1
subsidiaries 81
subsystems 18
supply of technology 138–40, 168–9
Sweden 70, 81, 84, 85–7, 142
Switzerland 81, 87, 131

takeovers 81; UK 205
task duplication *see* cooperative structure
taxation 19, 41
technical cooperation 105
Technics 43
technological balance of payments 130
technological clusters 10

technological dependence, Europe 130
technological licensing agreements 88
technological opportunities 138–40
technology, evaluation in advanced 33 Table 2.4
technology demand 5; *see also* market
technology lags, Europe 32–5
technology push (supply) 5, 138–40, 168–9
Telecom Network 66 Fig. 2.6
telecommunications 10, 32, 54, 64–77, 95, 102, 131, 143, 165; (1847–2000) 204; alliances, 185–7; European, 51, 64, 72–5; Japanese 41, 64, 71–2; sales of equipment and services (1984) 67; US 65–71
Telefunken 83
Telenet 70
telephone systems, private 67
textile industry, Italy 122
TGV 32
Third World 22, 166
Thomson 50, 61, 106
Thomson Brandt 83
Tornado 116
Toshiba 43, 50, 59, 69, 72, 75, 118–19
tourism 31
Toyota 89
training 138–40, 168
Transall 116, 117
transfers of technology 99
Triad, 12, 180; *see also* Europe; Japan; USA
Turcq, D. 93, 100–2, 104–5
turnaround 15–16, 23
Tymnet, 70

UK 131, 142; franchises 122; higher education 138–40; top takeover bids (1986) 205
'ultra-tech' 37, 39, 54
Unilever 84
United Technologies 37
universities, relations with industry 5, 140, 154; European 49; Japanese 41; US 36, 102
university research, enterprise funding of 140
US, Defense Department 166

US, Space Agency 166
USA: biotechnology companies 29;
  direct foreign investment in 83–4;
  new enterprises 142; R&D
  expenditure 178–9; *see also*
  American model
value chain 91–2, 121, 184; and
  industrial cooperation 18–19
VANs 67–8, 69, 72
VHSIC 63

video 45
'virtuous circle' 24, 44
volume strategies 14
Volvo 30, 31, 87
VW 30

world leaderships 28–31

Xerox 37, 81